MACMILLAN DICTIONAR.
of
ACCOUNTING

MACMILLAN DICTIONARY OF
ACCOUNTING

EDITOR

R.H. PARKER

MACMILLAN PRESS
LONDON

First published in 1984 by
THE MACMILLAN PRESS LTD
London and Basingstoke

Associated companies in Auckland, Delhi, Dublin, Gaborone,
Hamburg, Harare, Hong Kong, Johannesburg, Kuala Lumpur, Lagos,
Manzini, Melbourne, Mexico City, Nairobi, New York, Singapore,
Tokyo.

Paperback first published 1985
Reprinted 1986

British Library Cataloguing in Publication Data

Parker, R.H.
  Macmillan dictionary of accounting.
  1. Accounting – Dictionaries
  I. Title
  657'.031'21   HF5621

ISBN 0-333-36327-2

Printed and bound in Great Britain by
Anchor Brendon Ltd, Tiptree, Essex

Preface

Accounting is the language of business and, in the twentieth century, English is the language of accounting. Unfortunately, accounting English is a language of many dialects. This dictionary concentrates on the two dominant ones: the terminology used by British accountants and the terminology used by American accountants. The two terminologies overlap, of course, but the differences are quite considerable. It is a weakness of all previous dictionaries of accounting that they cover either British terms or American terms but not both. I have also included a few references to accounting in other English-speaking countries. British accounting is increasingly influenced by its continental European neighbours. Entries have therefore been included on some European accounting institutions and legal forms.

The dictionary covers not only the meanings of words but sets out practices and explains and discusses theories. I have tried to write in the first instance for students preparing for academic (university, polytechnic, etc.) and professional examinations in accounting and accounting-related subjects. I have also borne in mind the needs of teachers of accounting and of accountants in practice, commerce, industry or government whose exams are behind them but who need a reliable source of reference on topics outside their immediate area of practical expertise. In short, this is a book which should be on the desk of all students and practitioners of accounting!

It is one of the strengths and weaknesses of accounting that its boundaries are by no means clear. A dictionary-maker must, however, draw the line somewhere. A large part of this dictionary covers terms in the core areas of financial accounting, management accounting and auditing. There is also a substantial coverage of public sector accounting and business finance. Taxation is treated in general terms with no attempt to cover detailed rules. I have been selective in choosing terms from such fields as economics, national accounting, company law, information technology, operational research and statistics. I have deliberately tried to cover both academic and practical terms: for example, the curious reader is provided with information on both LENS MODELS and WALK-THROUGH TESTS. Many entries include cross-references (in SMALL CAPITALS) and readers are encouraged to follow these up.

It has been difficult to decide whether to include any biographies. After much hesitation I decided to include only those whose contributions to accounting *literature*, whether direct or indirect, were outstanding. This has resulted in entries describing the careers and talents of (in alphabetical order) F.R.M. de Paula, L.R. Dicksee, A.A. Fitzgerald, H.R. Hatfield, Th. Limperg, Jr., A.C. Littleton, G.O. May, Luca Pacioli, W.A. Paton and E. Schmalenbach. Many of these were, of course, also very successful in public practice or industry. I shall be happy, if there is a demand, to provide in later editions biographies of leading practitioners (for example, some of the founders of the BIG NINE international accounting firms).

The contents of this book reflect nearly 30 years of practising and teaching accounting; thinking, reading and talking about it; and contributing to its literature. During the writing of the dictionary I have referred to many leading works. I should like in particular to acknowledge my debt to (in alphabetical order): S. Davidson, C.P. Stickney and R.L. Weil, *Intermediate Accounting* (Hinsdale, Ill.: The Dryden Press), C.T. Horngren, *Cost Accounting* (Englewood Cliffs, N.J.: Prentice-Hall, 5th ed., 1982), S.R. James and C.W. Nobes, *The Economics of Taxation* (Deddington: Philip Allan, 2nd ed., 1983), T.A. Lee (ed.), *Developments in Accounting* (Deddington: Philip Allan, 1981), R. Ma and R.

Mathews, *The Accounting Framework* (Melbourne: Longman Cheshire, 1979), M. Sherer and D. Kent, *Auditing and Accountability* (London: Pitman, 1983), G. Whittington, *Inflation Accounting* (Cambridge University Press, 1983) and E. Woolf, *Auditing Today* (London: Prentice-Hall International, 2nd ed. 1982). None of the authors of these excellent books is, of course, in any way responsible for the use I have made of their ideas.

'To make dictionaries' said Dr. Johnson, 'is dull work.' I cannot agree with him. Making dictionaries is interesting but exceedingly hard work. My work has been lightened by the comments on my labours of my friend, and former colleague, Professor Chris Nobes of the University of Strathclyde and by my two long-suffering secretaries Mrs. Hilary Ireland and Mrs. Elvy Ibbotson.

The text of the Dictionary is preceded by a few pages of Abbreviations and Acronyms of which accounting and related subjects have all too many, as suggested by the splendid title of an article by Peter McMonnies in *Accounting and Business Research*, Summer 1977: 'EEC, UEC, ASC, IASC, IASG, AISG, ICCAP-IFAC, Old Uncle Tom Cobbleigh and All'. It is a well-informed accountant who does not need this dictionary in order to distinguish the AISG from the IASG!

It is the fate of dictionaries to be in a continual state of revision and expansion and this one, if it is successful in its aims, will certainly grow in size through the years. Constructive comments of all kinds will be most welcome. I hope I shall not hear of FUNDAMENTAL ERRORS but since the first edition of a book is in the nature of a TRIAL BALANCE, I shall no doubt be informed of purported errors of original entry, omission and commission.

R.H. Parker
Exeter, July 1984

Abbreviations and acronyms

Where the meaning of an abbreviation or acronym is given in **bold**, a fuller explanation of the term will be found in the main body of the dictionary.

AAA	**American Accounting Association**
AAANZ	Accounting Association of Australia and New Zealand
AAC	**African Accounting Council**
AAH	Academy of Accounting Historians
AARF	Australian Accounting Research Foundation
ABR	Accounting and Business Research (*see* **accounting journals**)
ABWA	**Association of Accountancy Bodies in West Africa**
a/c	account
ACA	Associate of the Institute of Chartered Accountants in England and Wales *or* Association of Certified Accountants (*see* **accountancy bodies**)
ACCA	Associate of the Association of Certified Accountants
AccSEC	Accounting Standards Executive Committee (of the AICPA)
ACMA	Associate of the Institute of Cost and Management Accountants (*see* **accountancy bodies**)
ACRS	**accelerated cost recovery system** (USA)
ACT	**advance corporation tax** (UK)
AFA	**ASEAN Federation of Accountants**
AG	**Aktiengesellschaft**
AGI	adjusted gross income (US federal income tax)
AGM	**annual general meeting**
AHJ	Accounting Historians Journal (*see* **accounting journals**)
AIA	American Institute of Accountants (former name of AICPA)
AICPA	American Institute of Certified Public Accountants (*see* **accountancy bodies**)
AISG	**Accountants International Study Group**
AJE	adjusting journal entry
ALGOL	ALGOrithmic Language (computer programming language)
ANOVA	**analysis of variance**
AOS	Accounting, Organizations and Society (*see* **accounting journals**)
APB	**Accounting Principles Board**
APC	**Auditing Practices Committee** (UK)
APL	A Programming Language (computer programming language)
APR	**annual percentage rate**
AR	The Accounting Review (*see* **accounting journals**)
ARB	**Accounting Research Bulletin**
ARIMA	autoregressive integrated moving average
ARR	**accounting rate of return**
ARS	**Accounting Research Study**
ASC	**Accounting Standards Committee** (UK)
ASOBAT	A Statement of Basic Accounting Theory
ASR	**Accounting Series Release**
ASSC	Accounting Standards Steering Committee (UK)
ATM	automated teller machine
AUTA	Association of University Teachers of Accounting (former name of BAA)

BAA	British Accounting Association
BASIC	Beginners All-purpose Symbolic Instruction Code (computer programming language)
BCD	binary coded decimal
b/d	brought down
b/f	brought forward
BV	**besloten venootschap**
CA	chartered accountant; (more narrowly) member of the Institute of Chartered Accountants of Scotland (*see* **accountancy bodies**)
C&AG	**comptroller and auditor general**
CAI	computer assisted instruction
CAP	**Committee on Accounting Procedure**
CAPA	**Confederation of Asian and Pacific Accountants**
CAPM	**capital asset pricing model**
CASB	**Cost Accounting Standards Board** (USA)
CCA	**current cost accounting**
CCAB	**Consultative Committee of Accountancy Bodies** (UK and Ireland)
CCE	**current cash equivalent**
c/d	carried down
CD	certificate of deposit
c/f	carried forward
CFA	**cash flow accounting**
CGT	**capital gains tax**
CICA	Canadian Institute of Chartered Accountants
cif	cost, insurance, freight
CIPFA	Chartered Institute of Public Finance and Accountancy (*see* **accountancy bodies**)
CMA	certified management accountant
CNC	Conseil national de la comptabilité (National Accounting Council, France)
co	company
COB	**Commission des opérations de bourse** (Stock Exchange Commission, France)
COBOL	COmmon Business Oriented Language (computer programming language)
CoCoA	**continuously contemporary accounting**
COD	cash on delivery
CONSOB	Commissione nazionale per le società e la borsa (Stock Exchange Commission, Italy)
COP	**current operating profit**
COSA	**cost of sales adjustment**
coy	company
CPA	certified public accountant
CPI	consumer price index
CPM	**critical path method**
CPP	current purchasing power; constant purchasing power (*see* **current purchasing power (CPP) accounting**)
CPU	central processing unit (of a computer)
cr	credit (*see* **double entry**)
CSI	**Council for the Securities Industry** (UK)
CSO	Central Statistical Office (UK)
CTT	**capital transfer tax**
cum div	with the dividend
CVP	cost-volume-profit

DCF	**discounted cash flow**
DDB	**deep discounted bond**
DISC	domestic international sales corporation (USA)
DOS	disc operating system
dr	debit (*see* **double entry**)
DUS	dollar-unit sampling (*see* **monetary unit sampling**)
EBIT	earnings before interest and tax
ECGD	Export Credits Guarantee Department (UK)
ECU	**European currency unit**
EDP	electronic data processing
EEC	European Economic Community
EFL	**external financing limit**
EFT	**electronic funds transfer**
EFTPOS	electronic funds transfer at the point of sale
EMH	**efficient market hypothesis**
EOQ	economic order quantity
EPS	**earnings per share**
ERISA	Employee Retirement Income Security Act (USA)
EV	**economic value**
EVPI	**expected value of perfect information**
EVSI	expected value of sample information
ex div	without the dividend
FAF	**Financial Accounting Foundation** (USA)
FAS	Financial Accounting Standard (USA)
FASB	**Financial Accounting Standards Board** (USA)
FCA	Fellow of the Institute of Chartered Accountants in England Wales (*see* **accountancy bodies**)
FCCA	Fellow of the Association of Certified Accountants (*see* **accountancy bodies**)
FCI	Finance Corporation for Industry (UK)
FCMA	Fellow of the Institute of Cost and Management Accountants (*see* **accountancy bodies**)
FEI	Financial Executives Institute
FICA	Federal Insurance Contribution Act (USA)
FIFO	**first in, first out**
FII	**franked investment income**
FOB	free on board
FORTRAN	FORmula TRANslation (computer programming language)
GAAP	**generally accepted accounting principles**
GAAS	**generally accepted auditing standards**
GAS	**Government Accounting Service** (UK)
GASB	Government Accounting Standards Board (USA)
GDP	gross domestic product
GIGO	garbage in, garbage out
GmbH	**Gesellschaft mit beschra̋nkter Haftung**
GNP	**gross national product**
GoB	Grundsätze ordnungsmässiger Buchführung (German principles of orderly bookkeeping)
HCA	**historical cost accounting**
HIP	**human information processing**
HP	**hire purchase**
HRA	**human resource accounting**
IAAA	**Inter-American Accounting Association**

IAPC	**International Auditing Practices Committee**
IASC	**International Accounting Standards Committee**
IASG	Inflation Accounting Steering Group (UK)
IBRD	International Bank for Reconstruction and Development
ICAC	International Committee for Accounting Cooperation
ICAEW	Institute of Chartered Accountants in England and Wales (*see* **accountancy bodies**)
ICAI	Institute of Chartered Accountants in Ireland (*see* **accountancy bodies**)
ICAS	Institute of Chartered Accountants of Scotland (*see* **accountancy bodies**)
ICCAP	**International Coordination Committee for the Accounting Profession**
ICFC	Industrial and Commercial Finance Corporation
ICMA	Institute of Cost and Management Accountants (*see* **accountancy bodies**)
IDA	International Development Association
IFAC	**International Federation of Accountants**
ILO	International Labour Office
IMF	International Monetary Fund
IPM	**investment period method**
IRR	**internal rate of return**
IRS	**Internal Revenue Service** (USA)
JAE	Journal of Accounting and Economics (*see* **accounting journals**)
JAR	Journal of Accounting Research (*see* **accounting journals**)
JBFA	Journal of Business Finance and Accounting (*see* **accounting journals**)
LIFFE	London International Financial Futures Exchange
LIFO	**last in first out**
LP	**linear programming**
ltd	limited
MBO	**management by objectives**
MCT	**mainstream corporation tax**
MIS	**management information systems**
MUS	**monetary unit sampling**
MWCA	**monetary working capital adjustment**
NAA	National Association of Accountants (*see* **accountancy bodies**)
NAO	**National Audit Office** (UK)
NASDAQ	National Association of Security Dealers and Quotation Analysts (USA)
NCGA	National Council on Government Accounting (USA)
NCSC	National Companies and Securities Commission (Australia)
NEDC	National Economic Development Council (UK)
NEDO	National Economic Development Office (UK)
NIFO	next in first out
NPV	**net present value**
NRV	**net realizable value**
OECD	Organization for Economic Cooperation and Development
OMB	Office of Management and Budget (USA)
OR	**Official Receiver** (England and Wales)
PAYE	**pay as you earn**
P/E	price/earnings
PER	**price-earnings ratio**
PERT	**programme evaluation and review technique**
PESC	**Public Expenditure Survey Committee** (UK)
PIN	personal identity number
P&L a/c	**profit and loss account**
PLC	public limited company (*see* **public company**)

PPBS	**planning, programming, budgeting system**
PPI	producers' price index (USA)
PPP	**purchasing power parity**
PPS	**probability proportional to size** (sampling)
PRT	**petroleum revenue tax** (UK)
PSBR	public sector borrowing requirement
P/V	profit/volume
PWLB	**Public Works Loan Board** (UK)
RAM	random access memory (of a computer)
RAWP	Resource Allocation Working Party (UK)
RC	**replacement cost**
R&D	research and development (*see* **research and development costs**)
ROCE	return on capital employed
ROE	return on equity
ROI	**return on investment**
ROM	read only memory (of a computer)
RPI	retail price index
RRA	reserve recognition accounting (*see* **oil and gas accounting**)
RSG	**rate support grant** (UK)
SA	**société anonyme**
Sàrl	**société à responsabilité limitée**
SATTA	Statement on Accounting Theory and Theory Acceptance
SDR	special drawing right (of the IMF)
SE	**Societas Europea** (European Company)
SEC	**Securities and Exchange Commission**
SFAC	**Statement of Financial Accounting Concepts** (USA)
SFAS	**Statement of Financial Accounting Standards** (USA)
SIAS	**Statement on Internal Auditing Standards**
SIC	standard industrial classification
SIFT	special increment for teaching (UK)
SMDCF	**standardized measure of discounted future net cash flows**
SORP	**Statement of Recommended Practice** (UK)
SSAP	**Statement of Standard Accounting Practice** (UK)
SVA	statement of value added
SYD	sum of the years digits (*see* **depreciation methods**)
TAM	The Accountant's Magazine (*see* **accounting journals**)
TB	**trial balance**
UCC	Uniform Commercial Code (USA)
UEC	Union Européenne des Experts Comptables Economiques et Financiers
UPA	Uniform Partnership Act (USA)
USM	Unlisted Securities Market (UK)
VAT	**value added tax**
VDU	visual display unit
VFM	value for money (*see* **value for money audit**)
WDV	written down value
ZBB	**zero base budgeting**

A

abacus. A calculating frame, especially one with sliding beads on wires. It has given its name to an academic ACCOUNTING JOURNAL.

abatement. A reduction in or a cancellation of, for example, a tax payment. In EX-ECUTORSHIP ACCOUNTS if there are insufficient funds in an estate to meet LEGACIES of the same standing that do not fail by ADEMP-TION, the funds are distributed pro rata and the legacies are said to abate.

ABC method. *See* INVENTORY CONTROL.

ability to pay. A measure of taxable capacity. Ability to pay is based on attributes of taxpayers such as income (the most common in practice), expenditure or wealth.

abnormal performance index. An index of non-systematic changes in share prices used to study the effects of unexpected changes in accounting earnings.

abnormal spoilage. SPOILAGE which should not arise under efficient operations. Abnormal spoilage is controllable and the accounting system should distinguish it from NORMAL SPOILAGE.

above the line. A rather vague term best interpreted as meaning that part of the profit and loss account (income statement) above the measure of earnings on which EARNINGS PER SHARE (EPS) is based. Thus EXCEPTIONAL ITEMS, but not EXTRAORDINARY ITEMS, are above the line. Items above the line affect EPS; items BELOW THE LINE do not.

absorption costing. A method of costing in which both variable and fixed overhead are treated as PRODUCT COSTS and, to the extent that goods manufactured during the period remain unsold, carried forward as part of the cost of stocks (inventories). Unlike VARIABLE COSTING, absorption costing is ac-cepted for external reporting and tax purposes in the UK and the USA.

All materials, labour and variable overhead variances are identical under both absorption costing and variable costing but there is no fixed factory overhead volume variance in the latter system. If stocks increase during an accounting period, absorption costing will report more income than variable costing; if stocks decrease, absorption costing will report less income than variable costing. This arises because absorption costing treats that part of fixed factory overhead relating to unsold stocks as income, whereas variable costing does not. Under absorption costing, income is a function of both sales and production; under variable costing it is a function of sales only.

There is no reason why an absorption costing system should not distinguish on a routine basis between fixed and variable costs. In practice, however, this is not always done. Absorption costing may be combined with actual costs or standard costs. It is more difficult to use with BREAK-EVEN ANALYSIS than is variable costing, since there may be several combinations of sales and production that produce an income of zero.

academic scribblers. Keynes' expressive term for theorists as contrasting with vested interests. Whittington ('The role of research in setting accounting standards: the case of inflation accounting', in Bromwich & Hopwood, *Accounting Standards Setting – An International Perspective*, 1983) assigns four functions to them: (1) they supply the list of 'excuses' from which the 'practical man' chooses and thus, by failing to supply adequate excuses for all situations, may constrain the ultimate choice of models; (2) by respecting the principles of logical consistency in theory construction they improve the models ultimately adopted; (3) they clarify the assumptions which are necessary for a theory to be logically valid, the assumptions in turn clarifying conflicts of interest because different interest groups will subscribe to different assumptions; and (4) insofar as assumptions are factual, they establish their accuracy by empirical research.

accelerated cost recovery system (ACRS). A method of depreciation introduced in the USA by the Economic Recovery Tax Act 1981, and allowing taxpayers to write off tangible fixed assets at a faster rate for tax purposes.

accelerated depreciation. Depreciation charged at a faster rate than is justified by elapse of economic usefulness, especially in order to gain advantages for taxation as, for example, in the US ACCELERATED COST RECOVERY SYSTEM.

acceptance sampling. In an audit context, a sampling plan designed to control the levels of both ALPHA AND BETA RISK. The auditor must specify a minimum unacceptable error rate together with a predetermined level of beta risk, and a maximum unacceptable rejection rate together with a predetermined level of alpha risk.
See also DISCOVERY SAMPLING.

accepting house. In the UK, a financial institution lending money on the security of BILLS OF EXCHANGE.

Accepting Houses Committee. A committee of the leading London MERCHANT BANKS.

accessions tax. A capital tax basing liability on the total of the gifts made to the donee, rather than, as in the case of CAPITAL TRANSFER TAX, on the wealth of the donor. Such a tax is more in accordance with the principle of HORIZONTAL EQUITY.

account. A record in a LEDGER of the transactions that have taken place with a particular person or thing. Accounts may be classified in a number of ways for example, into PERSONAL ACCOUNTS, those that relate to persons such as debtors and creditors; REAL ACCOUNTS, those that deal with NON-MONETARY ASSETS; and NOMINAL ACCOUNTS, those that deal with revenues and expenses.

In a stock exchange context in the UK, an account is a period, usually of two successive weeks, during which deals are made for settlement on ACCOUNT DAY. In the USA, an account is a broker's record of a customer's transactions.

accountability. The obligation of stewards or agents to provide relevant and reliable information relating to resources over which they have control and which have effects on others (principals). Stewards and agents include such diverse persons as company directors, civil servants, university councils and trustees in bankruptcy. Principals include owners (notably shareholders) but also persons without an ownership stake such as creditors, employees, consumers and taxpayers. The scope of accountability can thus be said to extend to all parties affected by the behaviour of those in control of the resources of an organization. The relevant information may therefore be non-financial as well as financial.

Accountability places two obligations upon stewards or agents: they must provide information (render an account) of their dealings with the resources under their control and they must submit to an AUDIT by or on behalf of the person or body to which they are accountable.

Accountability procedures become more difficult if, as is now typical, the steward is larger and more powerful than the person to whom he accounts; there is doubt as to exactly what is being accounted for and the manner in which the account should be rendered; and the consequences of the steward's decisions and actions are delayed and cannot be understood immediately. For these reasons the process of accountability is often subject to REGULATION by law. *See also* AGENCY COSTS.

accountancy. Often used merely as a synonym for ACCOUNTING, but some writers distinguish between accounting and the PROFESSION of accountancy. Unlike accounting, the word accountancy was not used until the second half of the 19th century.

accountancy bodies. Formal organizations of accountants who have acquired theoretical and practical knowledge in the subject. In the UK and the USA such bodies have grown up largely independently of governments. The major UK and Irish bodies (which work together as the CONSULTATIVE COMMITTEE OF ACCOUNTANCY BODIES) are, in order of size with date of earliest predecessor body in brackets:

The Institute of Chartered Accountants in England and Wales (ICAEW) (1870)
The Association of Certified Accountants (ACA) (1891)
The Institute of Cost and Management Accountants (ICMA) (1919)
The Institute of Chartered Accountants of Scotland (ICAS) (1854)
The Chartered Institute of Public Finance and Accountancy (CIPFA) (1885)
The Institute of Chartered Accountants in Ireland (ICAI) (1888)

There is no legislation in the UK and Ireland regulating who may practise as an accountant, but only chartered (i.e., members of the ICAEW, ICAS or ICAI) and certified accountants (i.e., members of the ACA) may act as auditors of companies registered under the Companies Acts. Many members of the British and Irish accountancy bodies practise overseas. Aspiring certified accountants can also qualify for membership overseas.

In the USA, the major bodies are:

American Institute of Certified Public Accountants (AICPA) (1887)
National Association of Accountants (NAA) (1919)

Whereas in the British Isles a 'chartered accountant' must be a member of one of three chartered institutes, in the USA the title of 'certified public accountant' is conferred by an agency of a state or other political subdivision. The Uniform CPA Examination is administered by the AICPA but there is no requirement for CPAs to become members of that body.

Other accountancy bodies are the Institute of Internal Auditors (1941) (international but strongest in the USA) and bodies representing academic interests such as the American Accounting Association (AAA), the British Accounting Association (BAA) and the European Accounting Association (EAA).

Accountancy bodies have been established in most countries of the world; many of them have members entitled to be called chartered, certified or certified public accountants.

accountancy profession. *See* ACCOUNTANCY BODIES, PROFESSION.

Accountants' International Study Group (AISG). An organization formed in 1966 and comprising members from professional accountancy bodies in Canada, the UK and Ireland, and the USA. Its purpose was to study and report on comparative accounting practices. Twenty studies were issued before the AISG was wound up in 1977.

account current. A statement in debit and credit form setting out in chronological order the transactions that have taken place between two persons or organizations. Interest is sometimes calculated at agreed rates on the balances outstanding from time to time. 'Paul Smith in account current with John MacNab' means that MacNab is rendering an account to Smith from his (MacNab's) point of view, debiting Smith with goods sold, or money paid, to him or on his account, and crediting him with goods bought, or money received, from him or on his account.

account day. The day on which all deals for a stock exchange ACCOUNT are settled. In the UK, it is also referred to as settlement day.

accounting. In broad terms, the preparation and communication to users of financial and economic information. The information ideally possesses certain QUALITATIVE CHARACTERISTICS. Accounting involves the measurement, usually in monetary terms, of TRANSACTIONS and other EVENTS pertaining to accounting entities. Accounting information is used for stewardship, control and decision-making.

Accounting and ACCOUNTANCY are often used as synonyms but it is more usual to refer to the accountancy PROFESSION rather than the accounting profession. The distinction between BOOKKEEPING and accounting is to some extent arbitrary but the latter involves analysis and interpretation as well as recording.

accounting assumptions, axioms, concepts, conventions, postulates and principles. Near synonymous terms (see ASSUMPTION, AXIOM, CONCEPT, CONVENTION, POSTULATE, PRINCIPLE) representing attempts by accountants to determine the assumptions, etc., on which the practice of accounting either is based or ought to be based. Numerous lists have been prepared, more particularly in the USA, the most important of which are: the 11 'postulates' of PATON's *Accounting Theory* (1922); the 25 'principles' of Sanders, HATFIELD and Moore's *A Statement of Accounting Principles* (American Institute of Accountants, 1938); the four 'doctrines' and seven 'conventions' of Gilman's *Accounting Concepts of Profit* (1939); the six 'basic concepts' or 'assumptions' of PATON and LITTLETON's *An Introduction to Corporate Accounting Standards* (American Accounting Association, 1940); the 14 'postulates' and eight 'principles' of Moonitz and Sprouse & Moonitz (ACCOUNTING RESEARCH STUDIES Nos. 1 and 3, AICPA, 1961 and 1962); the ten 'concepts' of Grady (Accounting Research Study No. 7, 1965); the four 'basic accounting standards' and five 'guidelines' of ASOBAT (1966); the three 'axioms' and three 'valuation rules' of Ijiri's *The Foundations of Accounting Measurement* (1967); the four 'FUNDAMENTAL ACCOUNTING CONCEPTS' or 'working assumptions' of the ACCOUNTING STANDARDS COMMITTEE's SSAP 2 (1971); and the three 'fundamental accounting assumptions' and three 'considerations' of the INTERNATIONAL ACCOUNTING STANDARDS COMMITTEE's IAS 1 (1975). Still in progress are the STATEMENTS OF FINANCIAL ACCOUNTING CONCEPTS issued as part of the CONCEPTUAL FRAMEWORK project of the FINANCIAL ACCOUNTING STANDARDS BOARD.

accounting bases. In the terminology of UK accounting standards, methods which have been developed for applying FUNDAMENTAL ACCOUNTING CONCEPTS to financial transactions and to items in financial statements.

accounting beta. See BETA.

accounting dictionaries, glossaries, encyclopaedias and terminologies. The first attempt at a glossary of accounting in English is to be found in Stephen Monteage, *Debtor and Creditor Made Easie . . .* (London, 1675). His 'Explanation of Hard words' extends, however, to 15 words only and they are not even listed in alphabetical order. Much better is Roger North's 'A Short and Easy Vocabulary of Certain Words, that in the Language of Accompting take a Particular Meaning' in *The Gentleman Accomptant* (London, 1714). This covers 26 pages and upwards of 100 entries. Still worth consulting for more than historical reasons are George Lisle (ed.), *Encyclopaedia of Accounting* (Edinburgh, 8 vols., 1903-1907), some entries from which are reprinted in Richard P. Brief (ed.), *Selections from Encyclopaedia of Accounting, 1903* (New York, 1978); R.J. Porters, *Pitman's Dictionary of Bookkeeping* (London, 1913); and F.W. Pixley (ed.), *The Accountant's Dictionary* (London, 2 vols., 1922).

Cost accountants have been especially active in this area. The earliest important work on the subject, E. Garcke and J.M. Fells' *Factory Accounts* (London, 1st ed., 1887) contains a useful glossary of terms. R.J.H. Ryall's *Dictionary of Costing* (London: Pitman, 1st ed., 1926) reached a third edition in 1952. Both the UK Institute of Cost and Management Accountants and the US National Association of Accountants have published terminologies.

Of other accountancy bodies, the Canadian Institute of Chartered Accountants publishes both a *Terminology for Accountants* (Toronto, 3rd ed., 1983) and a *Dictionnaire de la comptabilité et des disciplines connexes* (Toronto, 2nd ed., 1982). The UEC publishes a *Lexique UEC* (Düsseldorf, 2nd ed., 1974) and *International Accounting Lexicon. Special edition . . . group accounts* (Düsseldorf, 1980).

In the USA there are dictionaries for accountants and of accounting by, for example, E. Kohler (1st ed., 1952, 6th ed. by W.W. Cooper and Y. Ijiri, 1983) and R. Estes (1981). Neither make any attempt to cover UK terms where they differ from US ones. This problem is, however, tackled in the ACCOUNTANTS INTERNATIONAL STUDY GROUP's *Comparative Glossary of*

Accounting Terms in Canada, the United Kingdom and the United States (1975).

accounting equation. *See* ACCOUNTING IDENTITY.

Accounting Hall of Fame. A hall of fame at the Ohio State University honouring eminent American accountants. Biographies of 36 members of the Hall, including HATFIELD, LITTLETON, MAY and PATON are given in Thomas J. Burns and Edward N. Coffman (ed.), *The Accounting Hall of Fame: Profiles of Thirty-Six Members* published by the University in 1976.

accounting history. The study of the evolution of accounting thought, practices and institutions in response to changes in the environment and the needs of society, and of the effect of this evolution on the environment. International congresses of accounting historians have been held in Brussels (1970), Atlanta (1976), London (1980) and Pisa (1984). *The Accounting Historians Journal* has been published in the USA since 1974.

accounting identity (or equation). The relationship which holds among ASSETS, LIABILITIES and CAPITAL, i.e., assets equals liabilities plus capital or assets minus liabilities equals capital. The former expresses an ENTITY VIEW of a business's operations (the assets are financed both by owners and outside creditors); the latter expresses a PROPRIETARY VIEW (the owners' stake in the business is measured by the excess of their investment in the assets over the liabilities incurred).

The distinction between the two points of view is fundamental and results in radically different suggested solutions in many areas of accounting, e.g., INFLATION ACCOUNTING and CONSOLIDATED FINANCIAL STATEMENTS.

Each item in the identity may be further subdivided and many variants are possible but all BALANCE SHEETS conform to the identity.

accounting journals. Journals aimed at professional or academic accountants or both. In chronological order of first publication, the most important such journals in English and their present publishers are:

1874 *The Accountant* (Tolley, London)
1889 *Accountancy* (Institute of Chartered Accountants in England and Wales, London)
1896 *Public Finance and Accountancy* (Chartered Institute of Public Finance and Accountancy, London)
1897 *The Accountant's Magazine* (Institute of Chartered Accountants of Scotland, Edinburgh)
1905 *Journal of Accountancy* (American Institute of Certified Public Accountants, New York)
1905 *Certified Accountant* (Association of Certified Accountants, London)
1911 *CA Magazine* (Canadian Institute of Chartered Accountants, Toronto)
1919 *Management Accounting* (National Association of Accountants, New York)
1921 *Management Accounting* (Institute of Cost and Management Accountants, London)
1922 *Accountants' Journal* (New Zealand Society of Accountants, Wellington)
1926 *The Accounting Review* (American Accounting Association)
1926 *Cost and Management* (Society of Management Accountants of Canada, Hamilton, Ontario)
1930 *The CPA Journal* (New York State Society of Certified Public Accountants)
1930 *Chartered Accountant in Australia* (Institute of Chartered Accountants in Australia, Sydney)
1932 *Financial Executive* (Financial Executives Institute, New York)
1936 *The Australian Accountant* (Australian Society of Accountants, Melbourne)

1944 *Internal Auditor* (Institute of Internal Auditors, USA)
1945 *Financial Analysts Journal* (Financial Analysts Federation, New York)
1946 *Journal of Finance* (American Finance Association)
1948 *Accounting Research* (Society of Incorporated Accountants, London), publication discontinued in 1958; revived as *Accounting and Business Research* in 1970
1961 *Investment Analyst* (Society of Investment Analysts, UK)
1963 *Journal of Accounting Research* (University of Chicago)
1965 *Abacus* (Sydney University Press)
1965 *International Journal of Accounting Education and Research* (University of Illinois at Urbana-Champaign, Center for International Education and Research in Accounting)
1969 *Accountancy Ireland* (Institute of Chartered Accountants in Ireland)
1969 *Journal of Business Finance and Accounting* (Basil Blackwell, Oxford, UK)
1970 *Accounting and Business Research* (Institute of Chartered Accountants in England and Wales, London)
1974 *The Accounting Historians Journal* (Academy of Accounting Historians, USA)
1976 *Accounting, Organizations and Society* (Pergamon Press, Oxford, UK)
1977 *Journal of Accounting Auditing and Finance* (New York University)
1979 *Journal of Accounting and Economics* (University of Rochester, USA)
1979 *Accounting and Finance* (Accounting Association of Australia and New Zealand)
1981 *Auditing* (Auditing Section of the American Accounting Association)
1982 *Journal of Accounting and Public Policy* (Elsevier Science Publishing Co., New York)
1983 *Journal of Accounting Education* (James Madison University)
1984 *British Accounting Review* (UK)
1984 *Contemporary Accounting Research* (Canadian Academic Accounting Association, Calgary)

N.B. The titles given are those currently in use, which are not necessarily those at the date of first publication. Some journals had predecessors which have been omitted from the list.

accounting machine. A machine designed for the operation of a particular accounting function such as, for example, sales ledger accounting. Accounting machines form a link between manual accounting systems and computerized accounting systems.

accounting period. The period between two successive balance sheets and that for which profit and loss accounts (income statements) and funds statements are prepared. For managers it may be any period of convenient length (e.g., a month) but for shareholders and tax authorities it is usually a year. In the UK, corporation tax is assessed on the basis of a company's accounting period rather than for the FISCAL YEAR.

accounting plan. In countries such as France, a detailed accounting guide (*plan comptable général*) containing not only a CHART OF ACCOUNTS but also definitions of accounting terms, valuation and measurement rules and model financial statements.

The first full French plan was issued in 1947, a revised version came into force in 1959 and a new plan revised to comply with the EEC FOURTH DIRECTIVE came into force on 1 January 1984. The plan is all-pervasive in French accounting: text books are based upon it, as are the requirements for the annual tax return; it is used for national and local government accounting and for the production of detailed national statistics. The plan is administered by a government-appointed National Accounting Council

whose members include accountants, in-
dustrialists and civil servants.

accounting policies. Those specific AC-
COUNTING BASES selected and consistently
followed by a business enterprise as being,
in the opinion of management, appropriate
to its circumstances and best suited to present fairly its results and financial position.
Lists of accounting policies are published in
the annual reports of British and American
companies

accounting principles. In UK company law
the principles according to which the
amounts of all items in a company's accounts
are to be determined. The principles (which
were referred to as 'valuation rules' in the
EEC FOURTH DIRECTIVE) may be summarized as: GOING CONCERN, CONSISTENCY,
PRUDENCE, ACCRUALS, the separated determination of individual items in determining
aggregate amounts, and no set-offs. The first
four are derived from the FUNDAMENTAL AC-
COUNTING CONCEPTS of SSAP 2. *See also*
GENERALLY ACCEPTED ACCOUNTING PRINCIPLES
and PRINCIPLE.

Accounting Principles Board (APB). A
board established by the American Institute
of Certified Public Accountants in 1959 and
responsible for the publication, between
1961 and 1973, of 15 ACCOUNTING RESEARCH
STUDIES (ARSs), 31 Opinions and 4
Statements. The Board was assisted by a
semi-autonomous Accounting Research
Division. Its Opinions were originally intended to be based on prior ARSs but this
approach was effectively abandoned in the
mid-1960s. Those which have not been
superseded still form part of US generally
accepted accounting principles (GAAP).

accounting rate of return. A method of
CAPITAL INVESTMENT APPRAISAL which
measures the average net profit of a project
as a percentage of the average book value.
The project with the highest such return is
assumed to be the best. This method uses
some data (e.g. depreciation) which are not
cash flows and ignores the TIME VALUE OF
MONEY but it remains a popular method of

investment appraisal in practice. It can be
shown that over the lifetime of a project, the
accounting rate of return is a weighted
average of the INTERNAL RATE OF RETURN (IRR),
i.e. over long periods average ARR may be
a good approximation to IRR.

accounting records. LEDGERS, JOURNALS
and supporting documents. In the UK, every
company is required by law to keep accounting records sufficient to show and explain
the company's TRANSACTIONS. They must be
such as to enable financial statements to be
prepared that show a TRUE AND FAIR VIEW and
must disclose, with reasonable accuracy at
any time, the financial position of the company at that time. Accounting records must
also contain a record of assets and liabilities, daily entries of money receipts and
payments, and statements of stock held at
the end of each financial year. Private companies must preserve accounting records for
three years and public companies for six
years.

accounting reference period. In the UK,
a company's ACCOUNTING PERIOD as notified
to the REGISTRAR OF COMPANIES. Unless
notification of another date is given, a company's accounting reference period is deemed
to end on 31 March in each year. Accounts
must be laid before a general meeting of the
company and filed with the Registrar of
Companies within ten months from the end
of the accounting reference period in the
case of private companies and seven months
in the case of other companies. A three
months' extension of these periods may be
claimed if a company carries on business or
has interests outside the UK.

Accounting Research Bulletins. Pronouncements issued between 1939 and 1959
by the Committee on Accounting Procedure
of the American Institute of Certified Public
Accountants. ARBs issued prior to 1953
were published in a restated and revised
form (as ARB No. 43) in that year. The
authority of the bulletins rested upon their
general acceptability. Those that have not
been superseded form part of US GENERAL-
LY ACCEPTED ACCOUNTING PRINCIPLES (GAAP).

Accounting Research Studies (ARS). Fifteen studies, written by both academics and practitioners, and published by the US ACCOUNTING PRINCIPLES BOARD (APB). As originally conceived each APB Opinion was to be preceded by an ARS but this did not in fact happen, although some of the studies were very influential.

Accounting Series Releases. Official policy pronouncements of the SECURITIES AND EXCHANGE COMMISSION on accounting and auditing matters.

accounting standards. Accounting rules and procedures relating to measurement, valuation and disclosure prepared by such bodies as the ACCOUNTING STANDARDS COMMITTEE (ASC) in the UK, the FINANCIAL ACCOUNTING STANDARDS BOARD (FASB) in the USA and the INTERNATIONAL ACCOUNTING STANDARDS COMMITTEE (IASC).

Advocates of accounting standards put forward the following arguments in their favour: accounting information is of the nature of a PUBLIC GOOD, so the forces of demand and supply will not operate effectively; accounting information is of more use if it is published on a comparable basis and COMPARABILITY is not possible without standards; standards provide a generally accepted language for financial statements that renders them more comprehensible to users; standards give financial statements credibility in the eyes of non-accountants.

Standards may be set either in the public sector or in the private sector (*see* REGULATION OF CORPORATE FINANCIAL REPORTING). A number of approaches are possible: the determination and codification of current majority practice; a common law approach, i.e., case by case as a distillation of experience; and the use of an implicit or explicit CONCEPTUAL FRAMEWORK.

See also STANDARD SETTING.

Accounting Standards Committee (ASC). In the UK, the committee responsible for the preparation of STATEMENTS OF STANDARD ACCOUNTING PRACTICE (SSAPs) and the issue of STATEMENTS OF RECOMMENDED PRACTICE (SORPs). It was set up by the Institute of Chartered Accountants in England and Wales in 1970 as the result of serious criticism of the UK accountancy profession during the 1960s. Originally called the Accounting Standards Steering Committee, it later became a joint committee of the Consultative Committee of Accountancy Bodies (CCAB). Appointments to the ASC are made by the presidents of these bodies. Membership of the ASC is part-time and unpaid and has varied since 1971. In 1984 the ASC had 20 members, five of whom were 'users' of accounts. Users need not be accountants.

Although the ASC is responsible for the preparation of SSAPs, they are issued and enforced by the six CCAB bodies. Unlike the FASB, the ASC does not issue interpretations of standards.

accounting system. A set of records and procedures designed so as to handle in routine fashion the TRANSACTIONS (especially those concerning cash, sales and purchases) and other EVENTS affecting an enterprise's operations, performance and financial position.

accounts. In general, all the ACCOUNTING RECORDS of an enterprise. In the UK the term is also used to mean the FINANCIAL STATEMENTS prepared from these records.

account sales. A document showing the gross and net proceeds of a consignment of goods sold by one person for the account and risk of another, and giving details of the expenses and charges in connection with the sale.

accounts payable. Amounts owing by an enterprise, distinguished from ACCRUED EXPENSES and other CURRENT LIABILITIES not arising out of trading transactions. This US term is seldom used in the UK. See CREDITORS.

accounts receivable. Amounts owing to an enterprise, distinguished from PREPAID EXPENSES and other CURRENT ASSETS not arising out of trading transactions. This US term is seldom used in the UK. See DEBTORS.

accrual accounting. An accounting system which, unlike CASH FLOW ACCOUNTING, recognizes revenues and expenses as they are earned or incurred, not as cash is received or paid. So far as possible, expenses are matched against the revenues for the generation of which they have been incurred.
See ACCRUALS.

accruals. One of the accounting principles included in the EEC FOURTH DIRECTIVE and the British Companies Act 1981. The Act requires that all income and charges relating to a financial year shall be taken into account, without regard to date of receipt or payment.

Accruals is one of the four FUNDAMENTAL ACCOUNTING CONCEPTS of Statement of Standard Accounting Practice No. 2 in the UK and one of the three FUNDAMENTAL ACCOUNTING ASSUMPTIONS of International Accounting Standard No. 1. According to SSAP2, where there is a conflict between PRUDENCE and accruals, the former should prevail.

accrued expenses. Expenses (e.g. wages) which have been incurred but not yet paid at balance sheet date. In accordance with the ACCRUALS convention the charge to profit and loss account is increased accordingly and a CURRENT LIABILITY established (in the UK BALANCE SHEET FORMATS it is also permissible to show accruals or accrued expenses as a separate item). *See also* PREPAYMENTS.

accumulated depreciation. The cumulative amount of DEPRECIATION written off a FIXED ASSET as at a balance sheet date. A credit balance, it represents a CONTRA ACCOUNT which is deducted from the historical cost (or revalued amount) of a fixed asset in the balance sheet. It is also referred to as provision for depreciation.

acid test ratio. See QUICK RATIO.

acquired surplus. A US term with a number of meanings, viz. the surplus of an enterprise existing at the date at which another enterprise acquires control; the initial surplus (retained earnings) of a successor enterprise where there has been a pooling of interests and no full capitalization of prior retained earnings; the excess over the cost of acquisition of dividends received by a parent company from a subsidiary's pre-acquisition earnings.

acquisition accounting. The preparation of CONSOLIDATED FINANCIAL STATEMENTS on the assumption that one company has acquired another rather than merged with another. In the UK, acquisition accounting is the norm but MERGER ACCOUNTING is permitted in certain circumstances. In the USA the terms used are respectively purchase accounting and pooling of interests. The latter is more common in the USA than in the UK.

Acquisition accounting differs from merger accounting in that shares issued as purchase consideration are valued at market price not par (and thus give rise to a SHARE PREMIUM ACCOUNT in the books of the acquiring company); assets of the acquiree are adjusted to fair value at the date of acquisition; a goodwill figure (positive or negative) arises on consolidation; and pre-acquisition profits are eliminated from the distributable profits of the group. It follows from the above that not only will the consolidated financial statements differ depending on whether acquisition or merger accounting is used but so also will the financial statements of the acquiring company.

acts of bankruptcy. Statutory tests of INSOLVENCY. In England and Wales a debtor commits an act of BANKRUPTCY in each of the following cases:
(1) If in England or elsewhere he makes a conveyance or assignment of his property to a trustee or trustees for the benefit of his creditors generally.
(2) If in England or elsewhere he makes a fraudulent conveyance, gift, delivery or transfer of his property, or of any part thereof.
(3) If in England or elsewhere he makes any conveyance or transfer of his property, or and part thereof, he creates any charge thereon, which would be void as a fraudulent preference if he were adjudged bankrupt.

(4) If with intent to defeat or delay his creditors he departs out of England, or being out of England remains out of England, or departs from his dwelling-house, or otherwise absents himself, or begins to keep house.

(5) If execution against him has been levied by seizure of his goods under process in an action in any court, or in any civil proceeding in the High Court, and the goods have been either sold or held by the sheriff for 21 days.

(6) If he files in the court a declaration of his inability to pay his debts or presents a bankruptcy petition against himself.

(7) If he fails to comply with a bankruptcy notice, i.e., a notice served upon him by a creditor who has obtained a final judgment against him, calling upon him to pay the debt within seven days, or to secure it to the satisfaction of the creditor or the court.

(8) If he gives notice to any of his creditors that he has suspended, or that he is about to suspend, payment of his debts.

Certain proceedings in relation to judgment debtors in a county court are also treated as acts of bankruptcy. In practice, failure to comply with a bankruptcy notice (No. 7 above) is more common than all the other acts of bankruptcy combined.

actual cost. A cost determined on the basis of historical costs incurred as distinct from budgeted or standard costs.

adaptive capacity. The ability of an enterprise to adapt to a changing environment. Proponents of CONTINUOUSLY CONTEMPORARY ACCOUNTING (CoCoA) argue that adaptation involves the disposal of assets no longer appropriate and the acquisition of new assets that will serve the enterprise better and that therefore adaptive capacity should be measured in terms of CURRENT CASH EQUIVALENTS.

additional paid-in capital. The approximate US equivalent of a SHARE PREMIUM in the UK. Formerly known as 'capital surplus'.

additivity. Conformity with the rules of arithmetic. The necessary conditions for additivity are (1) that the properties of the objects being measured are identical in all respects and (2) that the measurement standard is uniform for all measurements. In times of changing prices the second condition is not met by historical cost accounting and historical cost figures are therefore not additive. More controversially it can be argued that even if general price levels are stable, financial statements which are not drawn up wholly in, say, net realizable values or wholly in current replacement costs are not additive.

ademption. The disposing by a testator of the subject matter of a specific LEGACY during the testator's lifetime. As a result of ademption a legatee loses his legacy altogether.

adjusted R^2. The COEFFICIENT OF DETERMINATION adjusted for DEGREES OF FREEDOM.

adjusting entries. Entries made at balance sheet date in an ACCRUAL ACCOUNTING system in order to take account of such items as depreciation, closing stock (if a PERPETUAL INVENTORY is not in operation), prepaid expenses, accrued expenses, provisions for doubtful debts and accrued interest receivable.

adjusting events. See POST BALANCE SHEET EVENTS.

administrative expenses. In the UK, an expenditure heading required by two of the four PROFIT AND LOSS ACCOUNT FORMATS. Administrative expenses are distinguished from DISTRIBUTION COSTS but no definitions are provided.

administrator. A person appointed by the court to administer the estate of a person who has died intestate, i.e., without leaving a will.

ad valorem. A Latin phrase meaning according to the value.

ad valorem tax. A tax based on the value of goods being taxed, e.g., value added tax and some excise duties.

advance corporation tax (ACT). Under the UK imputation system of corporation tax, the tax payable in advance when a company pays a dividend. The amount payable is tied to the basic rate of income tax. It is deductible from the total corporation tax liability, the balance being known as MAINSTREAM CORPORATION TAX (MCT). ACT helps to maintain the government's cash flow and also ensures that TAX CREDITS passed on to shareholders are always paid for even if for example a company has no taxable income. This is so because ACT is not recoverable if the total corporation tax liability is insufficiently large. Unrelieved ACT may, however, be carried forward indefinitely and back for a number of years. In a company's balance sheet, ACT payable is a creditor due within one year, but ACT recoverable is a deferred rather than a current asset because it is not recoverable until the following accounting period. It is usually deducted from deferred taxation account (under the heading provisions for liabilities and charges) where one exists. Where ACT is irrecoverable it is written off to profit and loss account.

advancement. A payment by a parent, during his or her lifetime, to a child of what the child would receive, as heir or beneficiary, at the death of the parent.

adverse opinion. *See* AUDIT OPINION.

advowson. The right of presentment to a church or to an ecclesiastical office.

African Accounting Council (AAC). A body formed by 27 African governments in 1979 with the objectives of assisting in the establishment of bodies entrusted with accounting standardization in African countries and promoting and carrying out studies in the field of accounting standardization.

age analysis. A periodic listing of debtors accounts (accounts receivable) analyzed by the age of the debt. Age analysis is an essential part of CREDIT MANAGEMENT and control.

agency costs. Costs that arise out of agency relationships. An agency relationship is a contract under which one or more persons (the principals) engage another person (the agent) to perform some service on their behalf that involves delegating some decision making authority to the agent. Agency costs arise because the agent may not always act in the best interests of the principal. The principal is likely to incur monitoring costs in order to limit the aberrant activities of the agent. Monitoring involves not only measuring or observing the behaviour of the agent but also efforts on the part of the principal to control the behaviour of the agent. The agent may incur bonding costs in his efforts to guarantee that he will not take certain actions that would harm the principal or that if this happened the principal would be compensated. Apart from monitoring and bonding costs, further costs may arise from the fact that the agent may take decisions different from those which would maximize the welfare of the principal. These are termed the residual loss. Agency costs are thus the sum of monitoring costs, bonding costs and residual loss.

The concepts of agency theory have been employed in business finance, management accounting, financial accounting and auditing. Using the last two of these as an illustration, it has been argued, for example, that the desire to minimize agency costs explains why, even in an unregulated economy, financial statements may be provided voluntarily by managers to creditors and shareholders and independent auditors engaged to testify to the truth and fairness of such statements. Creditors will prefer a covenant by the shareholders restricting the payment of dividends (since otherwise the managers and shareholders might 'steal' the assets); shareholders may wish to tie management wealth to shareholder wealth by, for example, managerial bonuses based on profits. Disputes relating to such covenants (clauses in articles of association) gave rise to many well-known legal cases in Britain from the 1880s onwards. Such disputes can, it is argued, be avoided by management supplying to creditors and shareholders financial statements that have been examined by an independent third party. It is cheaper for the management than the creditors or the shareholders to produce such statements since the data may already have been collected for internal use, but an outside audit is necessary to give the statements credibility. Originally such audits were typically performed by shareholders but professional auditors were later regarded as both more competent and more independent.

Aktiengesellschaft (AG). The approximate German equivalent of a UK public company.

algorithm. A rule or set of rules for solving a mathematical problem systematically in a finite number of steps.

all-inclusive concept. The inclusion in the profit and loss account (income statement) of all items of profit or loss including EXTRAORDINARY ITEMS and PRIOR YEAR ADJUSTMENTS. It is claimed to leave less to management discretion than the CURRENT OPERATING PERFORMANCE CONCEPT and underlies SSAP 6 in the UK and APB Opinion No. 30 in the USA.

allocation problem. The problem of how to allocate cost of services purchased, when only part of the services are used up in one accounting period. The allocation is between costs to be charged against the revenue of the period and costs accrued as an asset to be used in future periods. The problem is all-pervasive in accounting but arises in particular in the case of the DEPRECIATION of fixed assets. In two monographs published by the American Accounting Association in 1969 and 1974, A.L. Thomas has criticized allocations on the grounds that they are 'incorrigible', i.e. that there is no obviously correct way to allocate costs because no allocation method can be proved to be superior to another (consider, for example, the various DEPRECIATION METHODS).

allotment. The allocation of shares by the directors of a company following applications for them by intending shareholders.

Monies received on application and allotment are debited to an application and allotment account.

alpha risk and beta risk. In an audit sampling context, the risks that an auditor will reject a population when he should have accepted it (alpha risk) and that an auditor will accept a population when he should have rejected it (beta risk). The relative importance of alpha and beta risk depends upon the opportunity cost of getting the decision wrong. For an external auditor beta risk is more important than alpha risk since it includes the possibility of the auditor being sued for negligence, whereas alpha risk includes only the cost of overauditing (which may be borne in whole or part by the client). Alpha risk is associated with a TYPE I ERROR, beta risk with a TYPE II ERROR.

alternative accounting rules. The rules set out in the British Companies Act 1981 allowing the application to company financial statements of accounting procedures based on current cost. Companies must follow either these rules or the HISTORICAL COST ACCOUNTING RULES.

amalgamation. The absorption by one company of the business and net assets of another company, the latter company being dissolved or both companies being dissolved and a new company formed to take over both businesses.

American Accounting Association (AAA). An association of accountants established in 1916 as the American Association of University Instructors in Accounting. The name was changed in 1936. Most of its members are American academic accountants but membership is not limited to Americans or to academics. It has published *The Accounting Review* since 1926 and numerous books, monographs and research studies, notably *An Introduction to Corporate Accounting Standards* (1940) by W.A. PATON and A.C. LITTLETON, *A Statement of Basic Accounting Theory* (1966) and *Statement on Accounting Theory and Theory Acceptance* (1977).

amortization. The redemption of a loan by means of payments into a SINKING FUND; also used as a synonym for DEPRECIATION, especially where the asset being depreciated, e.g., a lease, has a fixed life or is an IN-TANGIBLE ASSET.

analysis of variance (ANOVA). In statistics, the analysis of the total variation in a dependent variable into the proportions accounted for by the explanatory variables and the unexplained or residual variation.

analytical review. The process of examining and comparing figures, financial and non-financial, with internal and external data, in order to help an auditor to form a judgment on their correctness, and on the truth and fairness of the financial statements. It forms part of an auditor's SUBSTANTIVE TESTS. Analytical review involves the use of comparisons (with, e.g., external economic conditions, other companies, other parts of a business, budgets, past data), ratios, graphs and statistical techniques such as regression analysis and time series analysis.

Anglo-Saxon accounting. Accounting and financial reporting as practised in English-speaking countries such as the UK, USA and Australia. Accounting in these countries is based mainly on a common philosophy of presenting a fair view to investors but there are many differences of detail. Compared with Continental European accounting, Anglo-Saxon financial reporting is not much influenced by creditors and tax authorities.

annual equivalent cost. A variant of the NET PRESENT VALUE (NPV) method of CAPITAL INVESTMENT APPRAISAL. The NPV is converted into an annual equivalent cost in which the NPVs are divided by the annuity factor. The annual equivalent cost method is particularly appropriate for choosing between projects with differing lengths of life where continual replacement can be assumed.

annual general meeting (AGM). The annual general meeting of an organization and in particular, in the UK, a meeting of the members (i.e. the shareholders) of a company held at intervals of not more than fifteen months. The first AGM must be held within eighteen months of formation of the company. Most AGMs are formal and brief. The usual business transacted includes reception and consideration of the directors' report and accounts and the auditors' report, declaration of a dividend, election of directors and the appointment of and fixing the remuneration of the auditors.

Apart from annual general meetings the law makes provision for extraordinary general meetings and separate meetings of classes of shareholders.

annual percentage rate (APR). An EFFECTIVE ANNUAL RATE required to be disclosed by UK consumer credit regulations in order to prevent consumers being misled by FLAT RATES.

annual report. Any report prepared at yearly intervals and in particular the report required by law or other regulation to be made annually by the directors of a company to its shareholders. In the UK its contents are largely determined by company law and statements of standard accounting practice and will always include a balance sheet, a profit and loss account, a source and application of funds statement (except for companies with a turnover of less than £25,000 p.a.), and the notes thereto; a directors' report; and an auditors' report. A UK annual report may also include supplementary current cost financial statements; some of the statements recommended in THE CORPORATE REPORT, especially a value added statement; a highlights page; a review by the chairman; and information about shareholdings.

In the USA, annual reports to stockholders, as distinct from reports filed with the Securities and Exchange Commission, are subject to few constraints but where annual reports are combined with proxy solicitations the SEC requires that they contain audited financial statements with comparative figures; a five-year summary of earnings and a management analysis thereof; a brief description of the business; a five-year line of business or product-line report; details of directors and executive officers; identification of the principal market in which the company's securities are traded; and the range of market prices and dividends for each quarter of the two most recent fiscal years. Companies must also state that a free copy of the 10-K REPORT will be supplied to stockholders on request.

In both the UK and USA copies of the annual reports of listed companies are often supplied voluntarily to all who ask for them.

annual return. In the UK, a document which must be completed by a company within 42 days of the ANNUAL GENERAL MEETING and forwarded forthwith to the REGISTRAR OF COMPANIES. Its main contents are:

1. address of registered office;
2. addresses where registers of members and debenture-holders are kept;
3. summary of share capital and debentures, giving number of issued shares of each class, the consideration for them, details of shares not fully paid-up, etc;
4. particulars of mortgages and charges;
5. list of names and addresses of past and present shareholders giving number of shares held and particulars of transfers;
6. names, addresses and occupations of directors and secretaries (and nationality of directors).

Copies of the financial statements, directors' report and auditors' report must be annexed to the return. (UNLIMITED COMPANIES are exempt from filing financial statements; DORMANT COMPANIES are in some cases not audited.)

annuity. A series of equal periodic payments occurring at equal intervals of time. An ordinary or immediate annuity is one in which the payments are made at the end of each period; an annuity due is one in which the payments are made at the beginning of each period (e.g., the premium payments on a life assurance policy). Calculations are usually made in terms of ordinary annuities, an annuity due being regarded as an ordinary annuity payable one period in advance.

The accumulated or terminal value of an ordinary annuity is the sum of the accumulated values at the time of the final payment in the series. Assuming the frequency of payments coincides with the frequency of compounding, this value is denoted $S\overline{n}|i$ and is the sum of the GEOMETRIC PROGRESSION

$$1+(1+i)+(1+i)^2+\ldots+(1+i)^{n-1},$$

i.e.
$$S\overline{n}|i = \frac{(1+i)^n-1}{i}.$$

If continuous compounding is used,

$$S\overline{n}|j = \frac{e^{jn}-1}{j}.$$

The present value of an ordinary annuity is the sum of the present values of each payment in the series. Assuming the frequency of payments coincides with the frequency of compounding, this value is denoted $A\overline{n}|i$ and is the sum of the series

$$(1+i)^{-1}+(1+i)^{-2}+\ldots+(1+i)^{-n},$$

i.e.
$$A\overline{n}|i = 1-\frac{(1+i)^{-n}}{i}.$$

Alternatively, this formula can be derived by multiplying $S\overline{n}|i$ by $(1+i)^{-n}$. If continuous compounding is used,

$$A\overline{n}|j = \frac{1-e^{-jn}}{j}.$$

Where the payments of an annuity are to continue for ever it is called a PERPETUITY. The present value of a perpetuity of £1 is simply $1/i$, since as n tends to infinity, $(1+i)^{-n}$ tends to zero. No meaning can be attached to the accumulated value of a perpetuity.

In HIRE PURCHASE and SINKING FUND problems respectively, it is necessary to use the reciprocals of $S\overline{n}|i$ and $A\overline{n}|i$. It can be shown that

$$1/S\overline{n}|i+i = 1/A\overline{n}|i$$

annuity method. See DEPRECIATION METHODS.

application money. In the UK, the amount per share or unit of stock payable on application for a new issue of shares or debentures.

apportionments. In executorship accounts in England and Wales, apportionments between LIFE TENANT and REMAINDERMAN of the receipts and payments of the estate of a deceased person. Statutory apportionments are made in accordance with the Apportionment Act, 1870; equitable apportionments in accordance with the rules laid down in decided cases.

appropriation account. 1. In the UK an account prepared at the end of the financial year of the spending by central government departments of monies voted by Parliament. It compares the Supply Estimate and any Supplementary Estimates with actual payments made and receipts brought to account, and explains any substantial differences. An Appropriation Account is prepared for each individual Supply Estimate (called a Vote).
2. Another name for a PROFIT AND LOSS APPROPRIATION ACCOUNT.

a priori theories of accounting. The development and rationalization of systems of accounting valuation and measurement by means of deductive reasoning. A priori theories proceed from cause to effect making use of assumed axioms rather than of experience. The production of a priori theories of accounting reached a peak in the 1960s.

arbitrage. Simultaneous purchases of a security, currency, or other asset in markets in which there are differences in price. In aiming to profit from the price difference, the arbitrageur helps to eliminate it.

ARIMA. An acronym for the 'autoregressive integrated moving average' TIME SERIES process.

arithmetic mean. A measure of the central tendency of a group of numerical data obtained by dividing the sum of the quantities by the number of items.

arithmetic progression. A series of numbers in which each number increases or decreases by a constant amount. The sum of an arithmetic progression is given by the expression

$$\frac{n(a+l)}{2}$$

where a is the first term, l the last term and n the number of terms.

articles of association. In the UK, the internal regulations of a company, usually covering such matters as rights of various classes of shares; calls on shares; transfer, transmission and forfeiture of shares; alteration of share capital; general meetings (notice, proceedings); votes and proxies; directors (powers, duties, disqualification, rotation, proceedings); dividends and reserves; accounts; capitalization of profits; audit; winding up; and similar matters. Table A is a model set of articles appended to the Companies Acts which can be adopted by a company in full or in modified form.

The approximate US equivalent is the articles of incorporation.

articulated accounts. Accounts in which the profit and loss account (income statement) and the balance sheet form part of the same DOUBLE ENTRY system, so that the residual balance on the former matches the changes in owner's equity in the latter. Articulation is usually regarded as one of the strengths of double entry accounting but it can sometimes give rise to problems, as in the use of LAST IN FIRST OUT (LIFO) for stocks (inventories), in which a more current cost of goods sold figure is gained only at the expense of an out-of-date balance sheet valuation.

ASEAN Federation of Accountants (AFA). A regional accountancy group formed in Bangkok in 1977 and comprising the professional accountancy bodies of the ASEAN countries (Brunei, Indonesia, Malaysia, Philippines, Singapore and Thailand).

A shares. In the UK, a term often used for non-voting ORDINARY SHARES.

ASOBAT. Acronym for *A Statement of Basic Accounting Theory* published by the AMERICAN ACCOUNTING ASSOCIATION in 1966. The statement was user-oriented and emphasized relevance, verifiability, freedom from bias and quantifiability.

aspiration level. A person's expectations about his or her performance. Knowledge of aspiration levels is relevant to STANDARD COSTING and BUDGETARY CONTROL. Research suggests that a constant achievement of too easily attained goals may adversely affect motivation and performance; as may also a constant failure to achieve goals that have been set so high that they can never be reached. Also, persons tend to have higher expectations and work harder to achieve them when they have been directly involved in setting goals and have developed a personal commitment to their establishment.

asset. Any resource, tangible or intangible, from which future benefits are expected and the rights to which have been acquired as the result of a past or present transaction. This definition (derived from Moonitz and Sprouse, *Accounting Research Study 3*) emphasizes the economic (future benefits), legal (rights) and accounting (transactions) aspects of assets. To be recognized as the asset of an enterprise, a resource other than cash must have four characteristics: it must, either singly or in combination with other resources, contribute directly or indirectly to future cash inflows (or to obviating future cash outflows); the enterprise must be able to obtain the benefit from the resource and control the access of others to it; the transaction giving rise to the claim to or control of the benefit must already have occurred; and the future benefit must be quantifiable or measurable in money units.

It is clear from the above that ownership is not necessary for a resource to be an asset (*see* EXECUTORY CONTRACTS, HIRE PURCHASE AND INSTALMENT SALE ACCOUNTING, LEASE ACCOUNTING). Difficult problems arise in the case of INTANGIBLE ASSETS and HUMAN ASSETS.

asset classification. Assets are traditionally classified as either fixed or current, as required by company legislation in the UK (*see* BALANCE SHEET FORMATS), but for some purposes, e.g., inflation accounting and foreign exchange translation, a monetary/ non-monetary or a historical/current classification may be more appropriate. Tangible assets may be distinguished from intangible assets. No classification is suitable for all purposes.

asset stripping. Identifying and selling off the easily separable assets of a company that has been the object of a successful TAKE-OVER BID. The assets sold have usually been shown in the balance sheet at less than their net realizable value.

asset valuation. Attaching prices to ASSETS and more especially to NON-MONETARY ASSETS. The prices can be past, current, or predicted and also be either exit prices realized or realizable on a sale or entry prices paid or payable on a purchase. Thus a non-monetary asset could be valued for accounting purposes at historical cost (a past entry price), at current replacement cost (a current entry price), at net realizable value (a current exit price) or at net present value (which is based on predicted exit prices).

Each method has its strengths and weaknesses. Historical cost, the most commonly used in practice, is relatively objective, but ignores changes in prices, produces out-of-date balance sheet figures and matches current revenues with past costs. Current replacement cost takes account of changing prices, produces up to date balance sheet figures and matches current revenues with current costs, but is less objective. Net realizable value is of intermediate objectivity and produces up to date balance figures but recognizes unrealized profits and ignores value in use as distinct from value in exchange. Net present value is the least objective measure, and recognizes unrealized profits, but reflects the cash flows that provide an asset with service potential (although these may be difficult, both conceptually and in practice, to attribute to particular assets).

associated company. In UK standard accounting practice (SSAP 1) a company, not being a SUBSIDIARY of the investing group or company, in which either (a) the interest of the investing group or company is effectively that of a partner in a JOINT VENTURE or consortium and the investing group or company is in a position to exercise a significant influence over the company in which the investment is made; or (b) the interest of the investing group or company is for the long term and is substantial and, having regard to the disposition of the other shareholdings,the investing group or company is in a position to exercise a significant influence over the company in which the investment is made. Significant influence in this context involves participation in financial and operating policy decisions (including dividend policy) but not necessarily control of those policies.

In the case of (b) above, where the interest amounts to 20% or more of the equity voting rights, it is presumed that the investing group or company has the ability to exercise significant influence unless it can clearly demonstrate otherwise; and where the interest amounts to less than 20% it is presumed that the investing group or company does not have such an ability unless it can clearly demonstrate otherwise (including normally a statement from the investee company accepting such influence).

Associated companies are usually also RELATED COMPANIES as defined in the Companies Act 1981. Both terms represent UK usage, not US usage.

Associated and related companies are normally incorporated in CONSOLIDATED FINANCIAL STATEMENTS by use of the EQUITY METHOD.

Association of Accountancy Bodies in West Africa (ABWA). An association founded in 1983 as a sub-regional organization of the INTERNATIONAL FEDERATION OF ACCOUNTANTS (IFAC). The founder bodies were the Institute of Chartered Accountants (Ghana) and the Institute of Chartered Accountants of Nigeria.

assumption. A statement accepted without proof as a basis for a line of reasoning. *See* ACCOUNTING ASSUMPTIONS, AXIOMS, CONCEPTS, CONVENTIONS, POSTULATES AND PRINCIPLES.

attributes sampling. In an audit or quality control context, sampling based on the qualitative rather than the monetary characteristics of sampling units. Contrast VARIABLES SAMPLING.

audit. In general, the mechanism within the process of ACCOUNTABILITY whereby the performance of those in control of the resources of an organization is checked or monitored by or on behalf of interested parties. The STATUTORY AUDIT of limited companies is the commonest example, but *see also* DISTRICT AUDITOR, INTERNAL AUDIT, MANAGEMENT AUDIT, SOCIAL AUDIT, VALUE FOR MONEY (VFM) AUDIT.

Audit Commission. In England and Wales a body established by the Local Government Finance Act 1982 and responsible for all local authority audit work including the appointment of both DISTRICT AUDITORS and private sector auditors. The equivalent Scottish body is the Commission for Local Authority Accounts in Scotland.

audit committee. A committee appointed by a company as a liaison between the board of directors and the external auditors. The committee normally has a majority of non-executive directors and is expected to view the company's affairs in a detached and dispassionate manner. Such a committee is required as a condition of listing by the New York Stock Exchange. Audit committees are becoming more common in the UK.

audit evidence. Information obtained by an auditor in arriving at the conclusions on which he bases his opinion on financial statements. The auditor requires evidence both for COMPLIANCE TESTS and for SUBSTANTIVE TESTS. Audit evidence can be classified as follows:
(a) evidence created by processes largely under the control of the auditor and thus with a high degree of reliability, e.g.,
  (i) physical inspection or observation;
  (ii) recomputation of the client's calculations.
(b) evidence created by processes largely under the control of management and thus with a lower degree of reliability, e.g.,
  (i) the books of account which form the foundation of the financial statements;

    (ii) responses to INTERNAL CONTROL QUESTIONNAIRES;

    (iii) explanations received from the client's staff.

(c) evidence created by processes largely under the control of third parties and thus of intermediate reliability, e.g.,

    (i) that part of the accounting records of the client prepared by third parties in the normal course of business (e.g., invoices received);

    (ii) documentation issued by third parties for the benefit of outsiders (e.g., price lists);

    (iii) specific assertions made by third parties at the instigation of the auditor (e.g., circularization of debtors).

Evidence may also be provided by events subsequent to the date of the balance sheet but before the date of completion of the audit.

Auditing Practices Committee (APC). The committee of the CONSULTATIVE COMMITTEE OF ACCOUNTANCY BODIES responsible for the issue of AUDITING STANDARDS in the UK and Ireland. The bodies represented on the APC are the English, Scottish and Irish Chartered Institutes and the Association of Certified Accountants.

auditing standards. Standards designed to give credibility to the independence, objectivity and technical skill of auditors. Auditing standards are issued, for example, by the Auditing Practices Committee in the UK and the Auditing Standards Board in the USA. *See also* GENERALLY ACCEPTED AUDITING STANDARDS.

Auditing Standards Board. A body established by the American Institute of Certified Public Accountants which is responsible for the issue of STATEMENTS OF AUDITING STANDARDS. The predecessor of the board was the Auditing Standards Executive Committee.

audit opinion. The opinion expressed by an auditor upon financial statements. In the UK, if an AUDIT REPORT is unqualified the auditor reports an opinion that the ACCOUNTS show a TRUE AND FAIR VIEW and comply with the Companies Acts. The UK AUDITING STANDARD on qualifications in audit reports classifies qualifications according to whether uncertainty or disagreement is being expressed and according to whether the qualification is fundamental, or material but not fundamental. There are thus four types of qualifications: a 'disclaimer of opinion' in which the auditor states that he is unable to form an opinion as to whether the financial statements give a true and fair view; an 'adverse opinion' in which the auditor states that in his opinion the financial statements do not give a true and fair view; a 'subject to' opinion in which the auditor effectively disclaims an opinion on a particular matter which is not considered fundamental; and an 'except' opinion in which the auditor expresses an adverse opinion on a particular matter which is not considered fundamental.

In the USA an 'adverse opinion' is one in which it is stated that the statements do not present fairly the financial position, results of operations or changes in financial position in conformity with generally accepted accounting principles. A 'disclaimer of opinion' is a statement indicating the inability of the auditor to form an opinion on the fairness of presentation of the financial statements taken as a whole. An 'except for' or 'with the exception of' opinion is used in cases where the probable effects of a matter are reasonably determinable at the time of expressing an opinion on the financial statements but no recognition has been made of this in the statements. A 'subject to' opinion is used where the probable effects of a matter are not reasonably determinable and the final outcome is dependent upon the decision of parties other than management.

audit programme. A description of the work to be done in an audit, serving both as a planning document and as a control on procedures carried out. Although standardized audit programmes are essential for large audits, they have a number of dangers, e.g., they may not be wholly applicable to particular clients; they may discourage originality and spontaneity; they may give opportunities to a client's staff to circumvent the audit.

audit report. A report made by an auditor upon financial statements. A typical report made by a UK auditor in 1984 on a listed company with subsidiaries reads as follows:

'We have audited the accounts on pages . . . to . . . in accordance with approved Auditing Standards.

In our opinion the accounts on pages . . . to . . ., which have been prepared under the historical cost convention as modified by the revaluation of certain tangible fixed assets, give a true and fair view of the state of affairs of the company and the group at . . . and of the profit and source and application of funds of the group for the year then ended and comply with the Companies Acts 1948 to 1981.

In our opinion the supplementary current cost accounts on pages . . . to . . . have been properly prepared, in accordance with the policies and methods described in notes . . . to . . ., to give the information required by Statement of Standard Accounting Practice No. 16.'

A UK audit report is addressed, as required by company law, to the 'members' of a company, i.e. to its shareholders. Auditors do not provide a certificate or a guarantee; instead, they report their opinion as to whether or not the financial statements, i.e. the PROFIT AND LOSS ACCOUNT, the BALANCE SHEETS (that of the holding company and that of the group) and the NOTES TO THE ACCOUNTS, as required by law, and also the Statement of Source and Application of Funds is required by SSAP 10, show a TRUE AND FAIR VIEW. The auditor also reports whether or not all the relevant requirements of the Companies Acts have been complied with. The other contents of a UK annual report are not audited (with the possible exception of supplementary cost accounting statements) but the auditor must by law review the DIRECTORS' REPORT to check that no statement in it is inconsistent with the audited financial statements and in practice will usually extend this scrutiny to other contents of the annual report.

UK audit reports state whether the financial statements have been prepared under the historical cost (HC) convention, the HC convention as modified by, for example, the revaluation of fixed assets, or some other convention under the ALTERNATIVE ACCOUNTING RULES allowed by UK company law. The first paragraph of the report states that the audit has been made in accordance with approved AUDITING STANDARDS.

The audit report attached to MODIFIED ACCOUNTS filed with the Registrar of Companies by SMALL AND MEDIUM COMPANIES is on the following lines:

'The accounts set out on pages . . . to . . . have been prepared on the basis of the modifications available to small companies under section 6 of the Companies Act 1981.

In our opinion, for the year ended . . ., the company is entitled to the modifications available to a small company and the accounts have been properly prepared in accordance with section 6 of the Companies Act 1981.

We reproduce below our audit report to the members of the company on the full accounts (not appended hereto) for the year ended . . .'

(Here follows a normal audit report.)

A typical US auditors' report reads as follows:

'We have examined the statement of financial position of . . . and consolidated subsidiaries as of . . . and . . . and related statements of current and retained earnings and changes in financial position for the years then ended. Our examination was made in accordance with generally accepted auditing standards and accordingly included such tests of the accounting records and such other auditing procedures as we considered necessary in the circumstances.

In our opinion, the aforementioned financial statements present fairly the financial position of . . . and consolidated subsidiaries at . . . and . . ., and the results of their operations and the changes in their financial position for the years then ended, in conformity with generally accepted accounting principles applied on a consistent basis.'

The US report has many similarities to the UK report but there are significant differences also: the report refers to both the current year and the preceding year; the reference to auditing standards is more detailed; the words 'present fairly' are used rather than true and fair view; there is a reference to GENERALLY ACCEPTED ACCOUNT-ING PRINCIPLES rather than to, say, the historical cost convention; there is no reference to compliance with any legal requirements; and there is no reference to any form of inflation accounting (the data required by FAS 33 is not required to be audited).

SHAREHOLDER SURVEYS suggest that audit reports are not widely read — perhaps because of the formality of their wording. It may also be doubted whether many users understand the meanings of the technical terms used. They may also be uncertain as to whether the wording of the report implies that the report covers the detection of fraud and error. *See also* AUDIT OPINION.

audit sample. A check of part only of the accounting records under the scrutiny of an auditor. An audit sample should, if possible, not only be statistically representative of the total accounting population but also be protective, in that it allows the auditor to sample high value items more intensively than low value items; preventive, in that it is drawn in such a way that it is difficult for the organization being audited to predict the items which will be drawn; and corrective in that it increases the chance of identifying and correcting errors. Non-statistical sampling satisfies the corrective and protective objectives; statistical sampling the representative, preventive and protective objectives.

Other desirable characteristics of an audit sample are consistency, simplicity of operation and economic efficiency.

Sampling is used by auditors in both their COMPLIANCE TESTS and their SUBSTANTIVE TESTS.

audit software. Computer packages used by an auditor in the audit of computer operations.

audit trail. The impact of a transaction through all the relevant stages of an accounting system. In a manual system the audit trail comprises a series of written documents but in a computerized system not all the links in the chain will necessarily be produced as hard copy and the audit trail may thereby be broken and harder to trace.

audit working papers. *See* WORKING PAPERS.

authorized minimum share capital. In the UK, the minimum share capital permitted for a public company. The minimum is £50,000 or such other amount as is specified by statutory instrument. There is no authorized minimum for a private company.

authorized share capital. In the UK, the maximum amount of SHARE CAPITAL which a COMPANY LIMITED BY SHARES has authority to issue. Every such company must have an authorized capital which must be stated in the MEMORANDUM OF ASSOCIATION. There is an authorized minimum for public companies (currently £50,000) but not for private companies. There is no authorized maximum. The amount of the authorized share capital is disclosed either on the face of the balance sheet as a memorandum figure or in the notes to the accounts.

average collection period. The speed at which a company collects its debts. It can be calculated as average

$$\frac{\text{debtors} \times 365 \text{ days}}{\text{credit sales}}.$$

Average debtors are usually defined as the mean of opening and closing debtors. Average collection periods differ from industry to industry and from country to country.

average cost. Total cost divided by a measure of activity, such as units of product, hours of service, or number of persons. It is usually necessary to distinguish between average variable cost and average fixed cost.

average deviation. A measure of DISPERSION obtained by calculating the ARITHMETIC

MEAN of the differences (added without regard to sign) between each item of a group of numerical data and their arithmetic mean or other selected point.

average due date. The date on which a single amount can be paid in lieu of several payments on different dates.

average rate of tax. The amount paid in tax as a percentage of income received during a given period. It is below the MARGINAL RATE OF TAX for a PROGRESSIVE TAX; equal to the marginal rate for a PROPORTIONAL TAX; and above the marginal rate for a REGRESSIVE TAX.

avoidable costs. Costs that may be saved by not adopting a given alternative.

axiom. A synonym for ASSUMPTION.

B

backlog depreciation. The under-provision that arises when the amount of accumulated depreciation recorded for a fixed tangible asset is inadequate to cover the cost of its replacement. Backlog depreciation can be subdivided into between-year and within-year. The former arises when current cost depreciation provided in a prior year is less than that provided in the current year because prices have continued to rise. The latter arises if depreciation is charged on, say, a mid-year basis, in order to base it on average costs, and the asset is revalued on an end-of-year basis.

Backlog depreciation can be charged either to income or to capital. The latter is the more commonly advocated (as in SSAP 16 in the UK) and practised, on the grounds that depreciation is merely an allocation of cost (albeit current cost, in this instance). A charge to income is only appropriate if depreciation is regarded as a fund for the replacement of a specific asset.

backwardation. On the London Stock Exchange, the amount paid by a seller of stock in order to delay delivery. *See also* CONTANGO.

bad debt. An amount owing which is not expected to be received and is therefore written off either to a bad debts account or to a previously established provision for bad (or doubtful) debts. *See also* DOUBTFUL DEBTS.

balance. The difference between two sides of an ACCOUNT. It is entered on the lesser side to make both sides equal and then brought down to the opposite side. A debit balance results if the total of the debits in an account exceeds the total of the credits; a credit balance if the total of the credits exceeds the total of the debits.

balance of payments. In the context of NATIONAL ACCOUNTING, the balance on the rest of the world account, in which are recorded transactions between a nation and overseas countries. The balance of payments on current account represents the balance on 'visible' trade or trade in goods plus the balance on 'invisibles' or services. Adding investment and other capital transactions to this gives, subject to any balancing items arising from unrecorded transactions and timing discrepancies, the balance for official financing. Details of official financing (e.g., borrowings from the International Monetary Fund or other governments) are then recorded.

balance sheet. A statement of the assets, liabilities and capital of an organization at a particular date. In the UK, the Companies Acts prescribe BALANCE SHEET FORMATS and that every balance sheet shall give a TRUE AND FAIR VIEW of the state of affairs of the company.

balance sheet equation. Synonym for ACCOUNTING IDENTITY.

balance sheet formats. Methods of presenting the items in a BALANCE SHEET. Until recently, in both the UK and USA, few regulations existed on this matter but certain formats had become generally accepted. The formats developed on different lines in the two countries and it has been said that an accountant who crosses the Atlantic will find that 'the balance sheet appears to be presented upside down and back to front and . . . the financial statements . . . written in what seems to be a partially foreign language' (Carsberg & Eastergard in Nobes and Parker, *Comparative International Accounting*, 1981, p. 10).

UK balance sheets were traditionally presented in a horizontal format with the capital and liabilities on the left and the assets on the right hand side. A model balance sheet of this kind was included in TABLE A during the 19th century but never became mandatory for companies in general, although compulsory formats were laid down by statute for railways and public utilities. In more recent years, balance sheets, at least of listed companies, have been usually presented in a vertical format.

As a result of the Companies Act 1981, passed in implementation of the EEC Fourth Directive, British companies must now comply with balance sheet formats based in part on continental European models. The Act provides a choice of two formats, one horizontal, the other vertical, and classifies items under letters, Roman numbers and Arabic numbers. An example is:

C *Current assets*
  I Stocks
    1. Raw materials and consumables
    2. Work in progress
    3. Finished goods and goods for resale
    4. Payments on account

Items preceded by letters and Roman numbers must be shown on the face of the balance sheet but those preceded by Arabic numbers may be shown in the Notes. British companies adopting the vertical format now normally present their balance sheet is shown below.

Balance sheet formats in the USA differ from the above in that the most liquid assets and liabilities are shown first rather than the least liquid and there are many differences of terminology. One effect of the Companies Act 1981 is to prevent British companies moving closer to US practice.

balance sheet identity. Synonym for AC-COUNTING IDENTITY.

balance sheet total. In general, the total of the two halves of a BALANCE SHEET, however drawn up. In UK company law, the total as shown in the BALANCE SHEET FORMATS and used to define small, medium and large companies. It is equal to FIXED ASSETS plus CURRENT ASSETS.

bank confirmation. A request by an auditor to a bank to confirm details of an audit client's bank accounts, assets of the client

Fixed assets			
Intangible assets	x		
Tangible assets	x		
Investments	x		
	———		x
Current assets			
Stocks	x		
Debtors	x		
Investments	x		
Cash at bank and in hand	x	x	
	———		
Creditors: amounts falling due within one year		x	
		———	
Net currents assets (liabilities)			x
			———
Total assets less current liabilities			xx
			———
Creditors: amounts falling due after more than			
one year			x
Provisions for liabilities and charges			x
Capital and reserves			
Called up share capital	x		
Share premium account	x		
Revaluation reserve	x		
Other reserves	x		
Profit and loss account	x		x
	———		———
			xx
			———

Balance sheet formats

held by the bank, and other financial information.

bank overdraft. An overdrawn balance on cash at bank account (a credit balance in the books of an enterprise, a debit balance in the books of a bank and the statement it issues). Bank overdrafts are a very common form of borrowing in the UK. The bank and the borrower agree upon the maximum size of the overdraft, but interest is only charged to the extent that the overdraft is used.

bank reconciliation statement. A statement reconciling as at a particular date the balance of cash at bank as shown in an enterprise's own records and that indicated on the BANK STATEMENT. In principle the two balances should be equal and opposite but differences may arise for a number of reasons, e.g., cheques drawn but not yet presented to the bank, deposits not yet recorded by the bank, bank fees and charges not notified to the enterprise, and payments made to or by the bank and not recorded by the enterprise. The last two sets of items should be adjusted for before the bank reconciliation statement is prepared.

bankruptcy. The legal status of an individual against whom an adjudication order (i.e., a judicial declaration that a debtor is insolvent) has been made by the court primarily because of his or her inability to meet financial liabilities. The main objects of bankruptcy laws are to secure an equitable distribution of the property of a debtor among the creditors; to enable the debtor to be freed of debts and to make a fresh start; and to protect the interests of the creditors and the public. A bankruptcy petition must be founded upon an ACT OF BANKRUPTCY.

bank statement. The statement rendered, usually monthly, by a bank to a customer. It is an extract of the customer's account from the point of view of the bank and in principle should disclose a balance equal and opposite to that shown in the customer's cash at bank account in his own ledger. See BANK RECONCILIATION STATEMENT.

bar chart. A representation of a statistical series by means of rectangles (bars) of varying heights.

barter. The direct exchange of goods and services without the use of money as either a means of payment or a UNIT OF ACCOUNT. Pure barter suffers from three serious inconveniences: a want of coincidence of needs, a want of a measure of value, and a want of a means of subdivision. A butcher wishing to exchange mutton for rum, for example, has to find an innkeeper who needs mutton and who possesses a quantity of rum that can be agreed to be equivalent to the quantity of mutton on offer. *See also* BOOK-KEEPING BARTER.

base stock. In the context of INVENTORY VALUATION, the calculation of the cost of inventories (stocks and work in progress) on the basis that a fixed unit value is ascribed to a predetermined number of units of stock, any excess over this number being valued by some other method. If the number of units is less than the predetermined minimum the fixed unit value is applied to the number in stock. The base stock method appears to be permitted by company law in the UK but it is not an acceptable method in standard accounting practice (SSAP 9).

Bayes' rule. A formula by which one can determine the revised (posterior) probabilities of various states of nature given the prior probabilities of the states and the results of an experiment. Bayesian techniques provide a way in which subjective impressions may be included in quantitative analysis.

bear. An investor who sells a stock, bond, currency or commodity in the expectation of a decline in its price and the hope of buying it back at a lower price. An uncovered bear (US: shortseller) is one who sells stock, etc., that he does not yet possess. A bear squeeze occurs if action is taken, e.g., by a central bank, to maintain the level of the price. A bear market is one in which prices in general are falling and in which further price falls are expected. A bear raid involves heavy shortselling in the hope of pushing down prices so as to repurchase at lower rates. *See also* BULL, STAG.

bearer securities. Shares, bonds or debentures transferable by simple delivery.

behaviour congruence. Co-ordination of the behaviour of superiors and their subordinates rather than of their goals (as in GOAL CONGRUENCE). An advantage of behaviour congruence is that organizational goals need not be specified.

below the line. A rather vague term best interpreted as meaning that part of the profit and loss account (income statement) below the measure of earnings on which EARNINGS PER SHARE (EPS) is based. Thus, EXTRAORDINARY ITEMS, but not EXCEPTIONAL ITEMS, are below the line. Items below the line, unlike those ABOVE THE LINE, do not affect EPS.

beneficiary. A person who benefits under a will or a trust.

besloten venootschap (BV). The approximate Dutch equivalent of a UK private company.

beta. A measure of the SYSTEMATIC RISK of a company's shares, i.e. the sensitivity of the share price to movements in the market. A share with a beta of 1.0 (a 'neutral' share) will on average move in line with the market. A share with a beta greater than 1.0 (an 'aggressive' share) will on average go up faster in a BULL market and down faster in a BEAR market. A share with a beta of less than 1.0 (a 'defensive' share) will on average fluctuate less than the market as a whole. Betas change over time but most are reasonably stationary. Betas can be measured from market data ('market betas') or from accounting data ('accounting betas'). In the UK, market data are calculated and published by the London Business School Risk Measurement Service. The Esmée Fairbairn Centre at the University of Exeter publishes betas for unit trusts and investment trusts. *See* CAPITAL ASSET PRICING MODEL, CHARACTERISTIC LINE.

beta risk. *See* ALPHA RISK AND BETA RISK.

Big Eight. The eight largest public accountancy firms in the USA, i.e., Arthur Andersen & Co.; Arthur Young & Company; Coopers & Lybrand; Deloitte Haskins & Sells; Ernst & Whinney; Peat, Marwick, Mitchell & Co.; Price Waterhouse; and Touche Ross & Co.

Big Nine. The nine largest public accountancy firms worldwide, i.e., the BIG EIGHT plus Klynveld Main Goerdeler (KMG), represented in the UK by Thomson McLintock & Co. and in the USA by Main Hurdman. All except KMG have their origins in the UK and/or the USA.

bilan social. Literally, a social balance sheet. *See* EMPLOYMENT REPORT.

bill of exchange. An unconditional order in writing addressed by one person to another, signed by the person giving it, requiring the person to whom it is addressed to pay on demand, or at a fixed or determinable future time, a certain sum in money to, or to the order of, a specified person or to the bearer. There are three parties to a bill of exchange: the drawer (the person who writes out the bill); the drawee (the person on whom the bill is drawn and who, after acceptance, becomes the acceptor); and the payee (the person to whom the money is payable: he may be the same person as the drawer). A cheque is a bill of exchange, drawn on a banker and payable on demand. Bills of exchange other than cheques are of much greater importance in international than in domestic trade. Details of them are recorded in bills payable and bills receivable books. Bills of exchange may be discounted, i.e., sold, normally to a bank, for a lesser sum than their face value in order to receive money now rather than at the date of maturity.

bill of lading. A document signed by the master of a ship on behalf of the owners, acknowledging the receipt of goods put on board and setting out the terms and conditions under which the goods will be carried.

bin card. A card recording, for a particular material held in store, receipts and issues and the balance which should be on hand. It is usually kept in quantities only.

Black-Scholes option model. A model developed by F. Black and M. Scholes (*Journal of Political Economy*, May-June 1973) for determining the equilibrium value of an OPTION given certain assumptions. According to the model the value of an option is a function of the short-term interest rate, of the time to expiration, and of the variance of the rate of return on the shares, but is not a function of the expected return on the shares. Specifically

$$V_o = V_s N(d_1) - \frac{E}{e^{rt}} N(d_2)$$

where

V_0 = the current price of one share
E = the price at which the option can be exercised
e = 2.71828 (the exponential constant)
r = the short-term annual interest rate continuously compounded
t = the length of time in years to the expiration of the option
$N(d)$ = the value of the cumulative normal density function.

blue-sky laws. In the USA, state laws governing transactions in securities. The first such law was passed in Kansas in 1911. They are known as blue-sky laws because a judicial decision once characterized some security transactions as 'speculative schemes that have no more basis than so many feet of blue sky.'

bond. In general, a fixed interest security, issued by a central or local government authority or by a company. Bonds are usually redeemable for a fixed amount at a future date. Interest is paid periodically, usually half-yearly or yearly. Bonds may be short-term, medium term or long term. *See also* DEBENTURE.

bond duration. The weighted average period of time which will elapse before the cash flows from a bond are received, the weights used being the present values of the individual cash flows expressed as a fraction of the total present value of the bond. Bond duration is a measure of the sensitivity of bond price to changes in the market rate of interest and is therefore a useful tool for assessing the risk associated with the holding of bonds.

bond immunization. Hedging in such a way that the mean duration of bond investments is set equal to the mean term of the liabilities which the investments are required to satisfy. *See* BOND DURATION.

bonding costs. *See* AGENCY COSTS.

bond table. A table in which are set out the yields to maturity of bonds for which is known the coupon rate, the present market price and the value at maturity.

bonus issue. In the UK, an issue of shares to existing shareholders without further payment on their part. Also referred to as a scrip issue or a capitalization issue. The US term is stock dividend. Bonus issues do not represent a source of funds to a company. In most cases they are created by the conversion of retained earnings or other reserves into share capital. In principle, shareholders are no better off as a result of a bonus issue, since the market price per share might be expected to fall proportionately. In practice the market price may perform differently, partly because unrelated factors may be affecting share prices at the same time and partly because the issue may have drawn favourable attention to the future prospects of the company.

bonus shares. Shares that result from a BONUS ISSUE.

bookkeeping. The systematic recording of financial and economic TRANSACTIONS and other EVENTS. *See* DOUBLE ENTRY BOOKKEEPING, SINGLE ENTRY BOOKKEEPING. Bookkeeping can be distinguished from ACCOUNTING (or ACCOUNTANCY), in that the latter involves analysis and interpretation as well as recording, but the distinction is to some extent an arbitrary one, bookkeeping being regarded as the inferior activity. The word was first used in English in the 17th century.

bookkeeping barter. A system of BARTER in which money is used as a UNIT OF ACCOUNT but not, or only infrequently, as a means of payment. It operated, for example, in colonial New England and in early New South Wales.

book of original entry. *See* JOURNAL.

books of account. A general term for LEDGERS, JOURNALS and other accounting records.

book value. The monetary amount of an asset or a liability as stated in the balance sheet and books of account. In conventional accounting practice it will seldom represent a current market value (replacement cost or net realizable value).

book yield. Synonym for ACCOUNTING RATE OF RETURN.

bottom line. A rather vague term best interpreted as meaning the line that separates ABOVE THE LINE from BELOW THE LINE and constitutes the measure of earnings on which EARNINGS PER SHARE (EPS) is based. Items above the line affect EPS; items below the line do not.

bought ledger. Synonym for CREDITORS LEDGER.

bounded rationality. The reduction by decision takers of their range of review of decisions to be taken in recognition of the limitations both of the information available to them and their ability to handle its complexity.

bourgeois accounting. Soviet name for accounting as practised in capitalist countries.

bourse. French name for a stock exchange or a commodity exchange.

branch accounting. Accounting for geographically separated sections of enterprises. The accounting system adopted depends upon the degree to which the branch is controlled from its head office. A completely non-autonomous branch receives all its merchandise from head office and keeps only memorandum records of cash, debtors, sales, and stocks (inventories) at selling prices, making a periodic return to head office in a prescribed form. Branch managers are encouraged and motivated to maximize sales rather than profit. A rather more autonomous branch will concentrate on gross profit as well as sales and keep a branch trading account. An autonomous branch keeps a complete set of double entry books and prepares financial statements in which the capital section is represented by a head office control account.

Overseas branches have largely been replaced, for legal, taxation and political reasons, by overseas subsidiaries. Both are likely to keep full sets of books and prepare financial statements in a currency different from that of the head office or holding company. Problems of FOREIGN EXCHANGE RISK management and FOREIGN CURRENCY TRANSLATION thus arise.

breakeven chart. A chart on which are plotted total revenue and total cost (divided into fixed and variable) at various levels of activity. Total revenue and total cost are assumed to be linear over the RELEVANT RANGE of production. This is in contrast to the assumption of non-linearity usually made by economists, who do not assume constant unit variable costs or unchanging selling prices. A further assumption is the equality of production and sales. The static nature of break-even charts can be mitigated by the use of SENSITIVITY ANALYSIS, i.e. several charts can be prepared based on differing assumptions about selling prices and levels of costs. Breakeven charts have been described as meat axes rather than scalpels (C.T. Horngren, *Cost Accounting*, 5th ed. 1982, p. 61). They can be used to analyse financial GEARING (LEVERAGE) as well as OPERATING LEVERAGE.

breakeven point. The point at which total revenue equals total cost. It can be expressed either in monetary units or in units of product sold. The latter can be obtained by dividing fixed costs by the CONTRIBUTION MARGIN per unit.

budgetary control. A process that involves the preparation of an initial plan consistent with the goals of a business; its review and adjustment after appropriate discussion; communication of the plan to RESPONSIBILITY CENTRES; comparison of actual performance with planned results; analysis and explanation of deviations (VARIANCES) from the plan; and corrective action if there are significant unfavourable variances.
  See also BUDGET (BUSINESS).

budget (business). A quantitative expression of a plan of action. Budgets serve not only a planning function but also the functions of evaluating, coordinating, communicating, motivating and authorizing. They are thus a major feature of most control systems. Practice varies but most businesses of any size have a MASTER BUDGET subdivided into an OPERATING BUDGET and a FINANCIAL BUDGET. DISCRETIONARY COSTS are more difficult to budget for than ENGINEERED COSTS and NEGOTIATED STATE BUDGETS have to be used. These are usually INCREMENTAL BUDGETS but advantages are claimed for ZERO-BASE BUDGETING.
  Budgets involve much technical accounting. They should, for example, as do FLEXIBLE BUDGETS, allow, where appropriate, for changes in volume over a RELEVANT RANGE of activity. They are also, however, an expression of the human relations within an organization, of MOTIVATION and of MANAGEMENT STYLE. Budgets may be regarded as means of applying pressure and attaching blame. PARTICIPATIVE BUDGETING is an attempt to avoid this but it may lead to ORGANIZATIONAL SLACK and unduly low ASPIRATION LEVELS.

budget committee. A committee assisting

a BUDGET DIRECTOR. It may offer advice, reconcile divergent views and help to co-ordinate budgetary activities.

budget director. The person responsible in relation to a BUDGET for its preparation, and for such matters as establishing procedures, designing forms, collecting and co-ordinating data, verifying information and reporting performance. He or she is usually either the chief accountant (controller) or directly responsible to that official.

budgeted cost. A cost included in a BUDGET. It may also be a STANDARD COST.

budget (governmental). A mechanism for transferring funds to a governmental body and a procedure for controlling that body's activities. It represents both a statement of resources to be made available and a statement of planned future operations. *See also* PLANNING, PROGRAMMING, BUDGETING SYSTEM (PPBS).

budget manual. A written set of instructions serving as rule book and a reference book for a budget programme.

budget period. The period for which a budget is drawn up: typically a year, but longer periods are used for LONG RANGE PLANNING. An annual budget may be broken down into shorter periods.

built-in flexibility. A feature of a tax system resulting in a rise or fall in tax revenue as national income rises or falls. The most important example is a progressive income tax which will cause tax revenue to change more than proportionately with changes in national income. Built-in flexibility is reduced by INDEXATION.

bull. An investor who buys a stock, bond, currency or commodity in the expectation of a rise in its price. A bull market is one in which prices in general are rising and in which further price increases are expected. *See also* BEAR, STAG.

burden. A synonym for OVERHEAD.

business combination. A general term for the bringing together by acquisition (purchase) or merger (pooling of interests) of two or more companies.

business profit. The sum of CURRENT COST OPERATING PROFIT and realizable HOLDING GAINS. In the absence of the introduction of new capital and the payment of dividends, business profit is equal to the current value of a company at the end of an accounting period less the current value at the beginning, both measured in nominal monetary units. It is thus based on a financial CAPITAL MAINTENANCE CONCEPT. It differs from conventional accounting profit and REALIZED PROFIT in that it includes realizable rather than realized holding gains.

It can be argued that business profit reporting is not a form of INFLATION ACCOUNTING since it ignores the effects of changes in the GENERAL PRICE LEVEL. It is possible to make such an adjustment by including only real holding gains. The underlying capital maintenance concept remains a financial one but in terms of constant rather than nominal pounds or dollars.

business risk. RISK related to the industry to which an enterprise belongs and to general economic conditions rather than to GEARING (LEVERAGE). Contrast FINANCIAL RISK.

byproduct. A product with relatively insignificant sales value compared with the major product. The distinction between a byproduct and a JOINT PRODUCT is rather arbitrary. Byproducts may over time become joint products and vice versa. Byproducts may also be difficult to differentiate from SCRAP, but the latter is likely to have relatively less sales value and to be sold outright without further processing.

The accounting treatment of byproducts varies but most methods involve deducting the net realizable value of the byproduct (at the time of sale or at the time of production) from the cost of the main product or products.

C

call. An amount payable on a share subsequent to application and ALLOTMENT. Calls can only be made upon partly-paid shares and are rarely found in the UK in the case of LISTED COMPANIES since The Stock Exchange is not normally prepared to admit to listing shares which remain partly paid.

called-up share capital. In the UK, the amount of the ISSUED SHARE CAPITAL which has been called up, i.e. the amounts the shareholders have been asked to pay to date. Unless there are CALLS in arrear or calls paid in advance, it is equal to the PAID-UP SHARE CAPITAL. Disclosure of the amount of the called-up share capital is required by the BALANCE SHEET FORMATS.

capital. A word used by accountants and economists in many different senses. The primary meaning in accounting is proprietorship interest as represented in a BALANCE SHEET by the contributed and accumulated capital equal in amount to the ASSETS less the LIABILITIES. (*See* CAPITAL ACCOUNT, PARTNERSHIP ACCOUNTS, SOLE TRADER'S ACCOUNTS, SHARE CAPITAL.) The primary meaning in economics, on the other hand, is of capital goods, i.e., the fixed assets and inventories. Both accountants and economists, however, use the word on occasion to refer to both sides of the balance sheet.

capital account. An account recording a proprietorship interest of a fixed rather than a fluctuating account. *See* SOLE TRADER'S ACCOUNTS, PARTNERSHIP ACCOUNTS. In a company limited by shares, accounts are kept for each class of share capital but not for each shareholder, the latter's interest being recorded in a REGISTER OF MEMBERS.

The term 'capital account' had a different meaning in the now defunct DOUBLE ACCOUNT SYSTEM.

capital allowances. In the UK, allowances made to taxpayers in relation to the DEPRECIATION of FIXED ASSETS and in lieu of the depreciation charged in the taxpayer's accounts which is not allowed for tax purposes. The amounts and timing of capital allowances change continually and, because of government attempts to encourage investment in certain fixed assets or in certain locations, have often borne little relation to what has been charged for the purpose of profit measurement, thus creating problems of DEFERRED TAXATION. Unlike many other countries, it is not necessary to record capital allowances in the books of account or the financial statements in order to benefit from them. *See also* FIRST YEAR ALLOWANCE, GOVERNMENT GRANTS, INITIAL ALLOWANCE, WRITING-DOWN ALLOWANCE.

capital asset pricing model (CAPM). A model of the securities market based on PORTFOLIO analysis. According to the CAPM the expected return in equilibrium on any risky asset in a perfect capital market is given by:

$$\overline{R}_j = i + (\overline{R}_m - i)\beta_j$$

where $\overline{R}_j$ is the expected rate of return for security j, $\overline{R}_m$ is the expected rate of return for the MARKET PORTFOLIO, i is the risk-free rate of return and β_j (BETA) is a measure of the SYSTEMATIC RISK of security j. The model rests on the assumption that securities are traded in a PERFECT MARKET in which there are no transaction costs or taxes, all relevant information is freely available to all investors, all investors can borrow or lend any amount in the relevant range without affecting the interest rate and with no risk of insolvency, there is a given uniform investment period for all investors, and investors are risk averse and reach decisions using the MEAN VARIANCE RULE.

The CAPM has proved a fruitful framework for financial research, with important implications for CAPITAL STRUCTURE and measurement of the COST OF CAPITAL.

capital budgeting. The process of identifying, appraising, selecting and monitoring capital investment projects. Capital

31

budgeting is of great importance to a company since not only are large sums of money usually involved but the choice of project may affect the business for many years to come. Capital budgeting procedures include the following: searching for and identifying investment opportunities; deciding which potential investments to consider in detail; estimating the CASH FLOWS associated with them and also their qualitative characteristics; evaluating their economic worth in accordance with the criteria in use in the company; obtaining approval within the company for inclusion of the project in the capital budget; incurring the necessary outlays; continuous checking of actual outlays and receipts against budget estimates; and a POST-COMPLETION AUDIT.

It is sometimes argued that too much attention is paid in the literature to the CAPITAL INVESTMENT APPRAISAL aspect of capital budgeting and too little to finding suitable projects to appraise.

capital consumption. A measure of depreciation used in NATIONAL INCOME AND EXPENDITURE ACCOUNTS and based on current replacement costs.

capital employed. A term normally used in balance sheets to mean the total of shareholders' equity plus long-term debt but sometimes used to refer to the fixed assets plus net current assets. The term is not used in the UK BALANCE SHEET FORMATS but some companies add it voluntarily.

capital expenditure. Expenditure on ASSETS, i.e., on items that are not written off completely against revenue in the accounting period in which the expenditure is made. All other expenditure is REVENUE EXPENDITURE but the dividing line is not always easy to draw. More narrowly, the term capital expenditure is sometimes used (for example, in company law) to refer to expenditure on FIXED ASSETS. In the UK, there must be disclosed, where practicable, in the NOTES TO THE ACCOUNTS the aggregate or estimated amount of contracts for capital expenditure insofar as not provided for, and the aggregate or estimated amount of capital expenditure authorized by the directors but not contracted for.

capital formation. The term used in NATIONAL ACCOUNTING for increases in fixed tangible assets and stocks (inventories).

capital gain. A gain resulting not from operations but from the holding of an asset (see HOLDING GAIN). In practice, the term is usually applied to fixed tangible assets and investments, does not always exclude any inflationary element and for some purposes does not include unrealized gains. Some types of capital gains are really income in disguise. For example, in the UK, the value of national savings certificates is increased during their life in lieu of paying interest.

capital gains tax (CGT). A tax on capital gains as distinct from income. In the UK, CGT applies only when an asset is sold and the gain realized. Owner-occupied houses and motor vehicles are exempt. To avoid the taxation of inflationary gains a very complicated system of INDEXATION was introduced in 1982. Since capital gains both for individuals and for companies (who pay corporation tax on their capital gains) are taxed at lower rates than income there is an incentive, especially for individuals with high marginal tax rates, to attempt to convert income into capital gains.

capital gearing. See GEARING (LEVERAGE) RATIOS.

capital investment. An investment in FIXED ASSETS.

capital investment appraisal. The appraisal of capital investment projects to determine which should be selected. A capital project can be regarded as a set of expected incremental cash flows, i.e. the appraisal involves forecasting those cash flows which are expected to occur in the future only if the project is accepted. Once estimated, the cash flows can be analyzed by use of one or more of four main methods: PAYBACK PERIOD; ACCOUNTING RATE OF RETURN; INTERNAL RATE OF RETURN; and NET PRESENT VALUE.

The two last are DISCOUNTED CASH FLOW methods. Many companies use more than one method and, in spite of general agreement in the literature that discounted cash flow methods are preferable and that net present value is superior to internal rate of return, the most popular method, according to surveys of practice, is the payback period, and the internal rate of return is more popular than net present value.

The payback period method measures the expected length of time over which the undiscounted receipts equal the undiscounted outlays and favours the project with the shortest such period. The accounting rate of return method measures the average book value of the projects, and favours the project with the highest such rate of return. The method is faulty in that it is based on accrual accounting rather than cash flows. Both methods suffer from the fact that they ignore the TIME VALUE OF MONEY.

The discounted cash flow methods avoid these faults. The net present value (NPV) method measures the NPV of a project at the REQUIRED RATE OF RETURN. All INDEPENDENT PROJECTS with a positive NPV are deemed to be acceptable; in the case of MUTUALLY EXCLUSIVE PROJECTS the one with the highest NPV is selected. The internal rate of return (IRR) method measures that rate of interest at which the NPV is zero. An independent project is acceptable if its IRR is greater than the required rate of return; if projects are mutually exclusive the one with the highest IRR is selected.

For independent projects the NPV and IRR methods give the same result, as is shown in the first diagram: the project is acceptable over the range where the NPV is positive, which is the same as that where the required rate of return is less than the IRR.

If two projects are mutually exclusive, however, there is a conflict between the NPV and IRR methods as is shown in the second diagram. The indication of the IRR method is that B is always superior to A since it has the higher rate of return, whereas the NPV method indicates that project A is superior at required rates of return less than C but that project B is to be preferred at required rates of return greater than C. The two methods may be reconciled by varying the internal rate of return method for mutually exclusive projects: the incremental rate of return as between projects is calculated (C in the diagram) and compared with the required rate of return. In certain situations there may be multiple internal rates of return (see INTERNAL RATE OF RETURN).

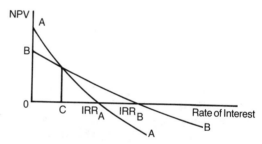

A variant of the NPV is the PROFITABILITY INDEX (also referred to as the present value index). It gives the same indication as the NPV method for independent projects but not for mutually exclusive projects. It is often necessary to choose between machines with differing lengths of life. This can be done by assuming the continual replacement of both machines, and comparing the ANNUAL EQUIVALENT COSTS. Where CAPITAL RATIONING exists, a company attempts to select the optimal combination of capital projects. This may mean the substitution of a project with a lower NPV for one with a higher NPV. MATHEMATICAL PROGRAMMING may be used in this connection.

Capital investment appraisal needs to take account both of taxation and inflation. Cash flows will include those related to tax, including in particular those receipts or diminished payments resulting from government use of the tax system to provide incentives to capital investment such as IN-VESTMENT GRANTS and FIRST YEAR ALLOWANCES in the UK and the INVESTMENT TAX CREDIT in the USA. The required rate of return needs to be calculated on an after-tax basis.

To allow for inflation, cash flows and the required rate of return should either be both in real terms or both in nominal terms. That is, either monetary units of constant purchasing power should be discounted at a real rate of interest, or monetary units in present day values should be discounted at a nominal rate.

There is a number of approaches to the incorporation of risk in capital investment appraisal. These include SENSITIVITY ANALYSIS, the MEAN VARIANCE RULE, SIMULATION, DECISION TREES, and the use of the CAPITAL ASSET PRICING MODEL.

capitalization. A term of several related meanings. It can refer to the composition of a company's long term sources of funds, i.e., its CAPITAL STRUCTURE, or to the total market value of its issued shares (MARKET CAPITALIZATION). The conversion of retained profits and reserves into share capital by means of a BONUS ISSUE is also known as a capitalization. Finally, the term can refer to the process of obtaining a NET PRESENT VALUE by applying an annuity or perpetuity formula to future earnings or cash flows.

capitalization issue. See BONUS ISSUE.

capital lease. US term for FINANCE LEASE. *See* LEASE ACCOUNTING.

capital maintenance concept. A concept in which income results only after capital has been maintained. The problem is thus how to define capital in this context. It can be thought of in either financial or physical terms, the choice depending upon whether a PROPRIETARY VIEW or an ENTITY VIEW is taken. The proprietary view emphasizes the value of the proprietors' investment in an enterprise whether in nominal or constant pounds or dollars. Thus, a financial capital maintenance concept can be based on either nominal monetary units or on units of constant purchasing power. The former

underlies both HISTORICAL COST ACCOUNTING and BUSINESS PROFIT; the latter, CURRENT PURCHASING POWER (CPP) ACCOUNTING.

If an entity view is taken, the emphasis is on the ability of an enterprise to maintain its physical capacity and to continue operating at the same level. Physical capacity is hard to define both conceptually and practically. The physical capital maintenance concept underlies CURRENT COST ACCOUNTING.

Some capital maintenance concepts (e.g., that of SSAP 16 in the UK which includes a GEARING ADJUSTMENT) combine elements of both financial and physical maintenance.
See also CONSUMPTION MAINTENANCE.

capital market. The market for medium and long term finance, e.g. in the case of UK companies, for ordinary shares, preference shares and debentures. *See* MONEY MARKET.

capital market line. A line which expresses graphically all the available combinations of the MARKET PORTFOLIO with riskless borrowing and lending.

capital rationing. A budget constraint on the amount of funds that can be devoted to capital investment in any period. Such a constraint may be applied by a company to its divisions or by governments to, for example, universities (*see* CASH LIMITS).

capital redemption reserve. In the UK, an undistributable reserve arising from the redemption of shares or the purchase by a company of its own shares. The purpose of the capital redemption reserve is to protect creditors by preventing what would otherwise effectively be a reduction in share capital.

capital reserve. In UK company accounting, a RESERVE that is not distributable as a matter of law, prudence or business policy. The term is used in the Companies Act 1948 but not in subsequent Acts. Examples of capital reserves are: SHARE PREMIUM ACCOUNT, CAPITAL REDEMPTION RESERVE (both required by statute) and DEBENTURE REDEMPTION RESERVE.

capital stock. The US equivalent of SHARE CAPITAL in the UK. Unlike the UK, it need not necessarily have a PAR VALUE.

capital structure. The composition of an enterprise's sources of funds, especially long term. It has been shown by Modigliani and Miller that if individuals can borrow or lend at the same market rate of interest as companies, there is no risk of FINANCIAL FAILURE, there are no transaction costs or barriers to the free flow of information, and there are no taxes, the following propositions can be proved: a company cannot increase its value by increasing its GEARING (LEVERAGE); increasing gearing increases both the cost of equity and the cost of debt in such a way that the increases cancel each other out. The processes by which this is achieved include ARBITRAGE and HOMEMADE GEARING (LEVERAGE) which, on the assumptions stated, is a perfect substitute for corporate gearing. If the assumption of no taxes is lifted, the optimum capital structure comprises mainly debt. If the assumption that there is no risk of financial failure is also lifted, the value of a company at first rises as debt is introduced but then falls after a certain point. The degree of gearing thus tends to depend inversely on the amount of the underlying BUSINESS RISK.

In practice capital structure is influenced by such factors as the relative costs of the various sources of capital (*see* COST OF CAPITAL), the amount and stability of earnings, the risk of insolvency, dividend policy, and a desire to retain control.

capital transfer tax. A tax on transfers of wealth, whether or not occurring at the date of death, introduced in the UK in 1975. The tax, unlike an ACCESSIONS TAX, is based on the wealth of the donor but may be paid by either the donor or the donee. There are several exemptions and reliefs and although CTT was introduced in part to reduce the avoidance associated with ESTATE DUTY it is doubtful whether it has in fact done so.

cardinal number. A number expressing 'how many', e.g., 1, 2, 3. See ORDINAL NUMBER.

cash accounting. *See* CASH FLOW ACCOUNTING.

cash book. A book of account containing a record of cash receipts and cash payments. Receipts and payments not made through a bank are normally made through a separate PETTY CASH BOOK. The cash book may be regarded both as a specialized JOURNAL, in that it records one type of transaction in chronological order, and an ACCOUNT (whose balance must be shown in the TRIAL BALANCE) separated from the rest of the LEDGER, in that it records all the transactions relating to a particular asset. In larger businesses it may be divided into a CASH RECEIPTS JOURNAL and a CASH PAYMENTS JOURNAL. The ruling of a cash book depends upon the needs of the business in which it is used.

cash budget. A plan of future cash receipts and payments based on specified assumptions about such items as sales growth, credit terms, issue of new capital and sales and purchases of fixed assets. The purpose of drawing up a cash budget is to ensure that an enterprise neither runs out of cash nor keeps cash idle when it could be profitably invested.

cash cow. A profitable product with a low market growth rate of which a company has a high market share. The cash generated from such products can be used to finance new products (so-called 'stars') that it is hoped will grow at a faster rate and in which the company hopes to obtain a high market share.

cash discount. A discount receivable or allowable on payment of an invoice within an agreed period. In the UK, cash discounts allowed are conventionally treated as an expense and cash discounts received as revenue. If this is done purchases are recorded gross in the first instance. Alternatively, purchases may be recorded net. A merit of this approach is that a cash discount lost account is debited and drawn to management's attention if a cash discount is not taken.

cash flow. The flow of cash into and out of a business. The term is often used loosely to refer to an amount equal to net profit plus depreciation which is the result of movements in WORKING CAPITAL rather than cash.

cash flow accounting (CFA). Measuring and recording the financial activities and performance of an enterprise in cash terms. CFA thus records only cash receipts and cash payments and, unlike ACCRUAL ACCOUNTING, does not record accruals, prepayments, debtors and creditors (accounts receivable and payable) and stocks (inventories). It is argued in favour of CFA that it avoids the arbitrary allocations and subjectivities of accrual accounting and that it is easier to understand. Forecast as well as historical cash flows can be reported and it is claimed that CFA is more closely related than accrual accounting to investors' decision models based on expected cash dividend flows.

CFA may be used as a substitute for or in addition to conventional accounting. If it is used as a substitute and a statement of financial position is required this needs to be stated in terms of NET REALIZABLE VALUES, since these represent potential cash flows. Such a statement would disclose net realized cash assets, readily realizable assets, non-readily realizable assets and non-realizable assets (shown at zero: *see* NON-VENDIBLE DURABLES).

CFA has been criticized for overemphasizing liquidity and for inadequately measuring performance.

cash flow forecast. Synonym for CASH BUDGET.

cash limit system. The system in the UK whereby government spending in specified areas is limited by the amount of cash allocated rather than in real terms. In its application to nationalized industries it is known as an external financing limit system.

cash management. The management of the cash balances of an enterprise in such a fashion as to maximize the availability of cash and of investment income on cash not invested in fixed assets or inventories and also so as to avoid the risk of INSOLVENCY. In Keynes' terminology there are three motives for holding cash: the transactions motive (to meet payments arising in the ordinary course of business); the precautionary motive (to meet unexpected contingencies); and the speculative motive (to take advantage of opportunities as they arise).

The most useful technique of cash management is the CASH BUDGET. An enterprise also needs efficient systems for collecting cash as quickly as possible and not disbursing cash too quickly. Economic order quantity models of INVENTORY CONTROL can be adapted to cash management.

cash payments journal. A JOURNAL recording payments of cash out of an enterprise's bank account. The ruling of a cash payments journal depends upon the needs of the business in which it is used, but it is common to provide a separate column for payments to TRADE CREDITORS. In small businesses it is combined with the CASH RECEIPTS JOURNAL to form a CASH BOOK.

cash ratio. For a bank, the ratio between cash and deposits.

cash receipts journal. A JOURNAL recording receipts of cash into an enterprise's bank account. The ruling of a cash receipts journal depends upon the needs of the business in which it is used, but it is common to provide a separate column for receipts from TRADE DEBTORS. In smaller businesses it is combined with the CASH PAYMENTS JOURNAL to form a CASH BOOK.

cast. UK accounting term for addition, derived from the casting (throwing) of counters on an ABACUS.

Centre for Interfirm Comparison. An independent, autonomous and non-profitmaking organization set up in the UK in 1959 by the British Institute of Management in association with the British Productivity Council. It acts as an expert body conducting interfirm comparisons on a confidential basis. It has close links with trade associations.

certificate of incorporation. In the UK, a document signed by the Registrar of Companies showing that the company to which it relates has been formed. Similar documents are issued by the appropriate officials in the USA.

certified accountant. *See* ACCOUNTANCY BODIES.

certified public accountant. *See* ACCOUNTANCY BODIES.

cestui que trust. The person who has the beneficial interest or enjoyment of property, the legal ownership of which is vested in the trustee.

chairman's statement (review). A statement made by a chairman of a company at its annual general meeting and often included in the ANNUAL REPORT. The statement is not required by law and there are no regulations as to its contents but it often contains interesting and useful information. Shareholder surveys suggest that it is the most read section of an annual report, perhaps because it is in narrative form and also likely to deal with future prospects.

characteristic line. The linear relationship between the return on a security and the return on the MARKET PORTFOLIO. The slope of the characteristic line is the BETA of the security.

charge and discharge account. An account in which, under properly analysed heads, a person charges himself with certain sums or estate he or she should receive, and in the discharge, credits himself or herself with the sums paid away. Charge and discharge accounting was the basis of manorial accounting in the Middle Ages. It is still found in Scotland in relation to TRUST ACCOUNTS.

charity accounts. The financial statements published by charities. In the UK, most charities must comply with the financial reporting requirements of the Charities Act 1960 and the Charities (Statement of Account) Regulations 1960. Charities incorporated under the Companies Acts must comply with the (sometimes rather inappropriate) accounting and disclosure requirements of these Acts. The accounts of a charity usually give historical financial information and normally include one or more balance sheets (disclosing fund balances, assets and liabilities) and income and expenditure accounts. FUND ACCOUNTING is used because of the nature of a charity's income and the uses to which it can be put.

chartered accountant. *See* ACCOUNTANCY BODIES.

chartism. The use of past patterns of share price movements in an attempt to predict future prices. According to the RANDOM WALK HYPOTHESIS and the weak form of the EFFICIENT MARKET HYPOTHESIS, such predictions will not on average be successful.

chart of accounts. A list of all the accounts in an enterprise's LEDGER or ledgers, constructed in accordance with the scheme of classification adopted by the enterprise. It serves both as an index to the ledger and as a description of the accounting system.

cheque. A BILL OF EXCHANGE drawn on a banker and payable on demand.

Chernoff faces. Multidimensional graphics in the form of faces. They are used for displaying relationships between variables such as financial ratios. The faces are constructed by assigning each variable of interest to a feature of a face.

circularization of debtors. *See* CONFIRMATION.

circulating assets. Obsolete term for CURRENT ASSETS.

City Code on Take-Overs and Mergers. In the UK, a Code supervised by representatives of the City of London financial community constituted as the Panel on Take-overs and Mergers. The Code is founded not on statutory regulation but on self-regulation and does not have the force of law. It contains 14 general principles and 42 rules. The Panel is an integral part of the COUNCIL FOR THE SECURITIES INDUSTRY but is not subordinate to it. The function of the Panel is both to supervise the conduct of take-overs and mergers and to advise at all stages, both before the formal approach and in the course of the merger.

classification. An arrangement of data into classes, each class having some common significant characteristic or group of characteristics which distinguishes it from other classes. A good classification should have four properties: the distinguishing characteristic should be adhered to consistently; there should be sufficient subsets to exhaust a given universe; all subsets should be mutually exclusive; and hierarchical integrity should be preserved. Different classifications are likely to be useful for different purposes. Classification is necessary in accounting when preparing financial statements (*see* ASSET CLASSIFICATION, BALANCE SHEET FORMATS, PROFIT AND LOSS ACCOUNT FORMATS) and in designing accounting systems (*see* ACCOUNTING PLAN, CHART OF ACCOUNTS). At a different level, a number of attempts have been made to classify national systems of company financial reporting. A very broad classification can be made into micro-based systems (which include ANGLO-SAXON ACCOUNTING) and macro-uniform systems (which include most continental European financial reporting systems).

clean surplus concept. See CURRENT OPERATING PERFORMANCE CONCEPT.

clientele effect. The attraction of shareholders to companies which have a DIVIDEND POLICY which is suited to their needs. Once a particular dividend policy has been established the clientele effect makes it more difficult to alter it since this would lead to changes in shareholdings and undesirable transaction costs.

close company. A company resident in the UK which is under the control of five or fewer participators, or of participators who are directors. The definition is one of tax law not company law (a close company is not the same as a private company) and was introduced in 1965 as part of the changeover to corporation tax. It has been of little practical importance since the Finance Act 1980 which did away with the requirement that trading profits had to be treated as in part distributed to shareholders. Listed companies are required by the Stock Exchange to state whether or not they are close companies.

closing entries. Entries made at balance sheet date to close off revenue and expense accounts to the profit and loss account.

closing rate method. See FOREIGN CURRENCY TRANSLATION.

cluster sampling. In an audit context, a method of drawing a sample in which the auditor chooses one or more clusters (of, for example, files of invoices or pages of a ledger) at random and then examines all the items within the clusters. It is a limitation of cluster sampling that the sample clusters may not be representative of the whole population.

CoCoA. *See* CONTINUOUSLY CONTEMPORARY ACCOUNTING (CoCoA).

codicil. A supplement to a will, and forming part of it, generally for the purpose of making some addition or alteration.

coefficient of determination (R²). A measure of the total variance in a dependent variable that is explained by its linear relationship to an independent variable. It is usually denoted R^2 and lies between zero and unity; the closer to unity, the greater the explanatory power.

coefficient of variation. The STANDARD DEVIATION divided by the ARITHMETIC MEAN. It provides a measure of dispersion independent of the unit of measurement.

cognitive complexity. *See* HUMAN INFORMATION PROCESSING (HIP).

cognitive style. *See* HUMAN INFORMATION PROCESSING (HIP).

comfort letter. In the UK, a letter from reporting accountants in which they confirm statements by directors in a prospectus regarding the sufficiency of working capital and other financial matters. A comfort letter is addressed to the issuing house or stockbroker concerned. It is not published in the prospectus. In the USA, a comfort letter (also known as a letter for underwriters) is a letter from the auditor to the underwriter at the time of a registration of securities under the Securities Act 1933. The term comfort letters is also applied to letters requested from the auditors of subsidiary companies by the auditor of the holding company where the companies do not have the same auditor.

Commission des Opérations de Bourse (COB). The body responsible for supervising the stock exchange in France. Modelled on the US Securities and Exchange Commission, it lacks some of the SEC's powers. COB has had great influence on prospectuses and has been the driving force behind the publication of more consolidated financial statements.

commitments basis. In public sector accounting, a method of accounting which recognizes expenditure as soon as an organization is committed to it regardless of whether the necessary resources have actually been acquired.

commitments for capital expenditure. Amounts to which a company has committed itself in respect of future expenditure on fixed assets. In the UK, company law requires the disclosure in a note to the financial statements of such commitments and also of capital expenditure authorized by the directors but not contracted for. Information is thus provided relating to important projected cash outlays in the forthcoming accounting period.

committed costs. Fixed costs that arise from having fixed assets and an organization, e.g., depreciation, rates, long term lease rentals. They are controlled through a capital expenditure budget (*see* CAPITAL BUDGETING). Committed costs are long run costs whose amounts are typically large and often hard to predict.

committee of inspection. In the UK, a committee comprising creditors and shareholders for the purpose of assisting a liquidator in the winding up of a company.

Committee of Public Accounts. In the UK, a select Committee of the House of Commons with the duty of examining and reporting on central government accounts. The Committee has up to fifteen members and is chaired by a senior member of the Opposition. All accounts certified by the COMPTROLLER AND AUDITOR GENERAL and submitted to Parliament are referred to the Committee for examination, together with related reports. The Committee also offers advice to the PUBLIC ACCOUNTS COMMISSION on its examination of the annual budget of the NATIONAL AUDIT OFFICE.

Committee on Accounting Procedure (CAP). The committee of the American Institute of Certified Public Accountants responsible for the issue between 1939 and 1959 of 51 ACCOUNTING RESEARCH BULLETINS. The membership of CAP included academics as well as practitioners. It was replaced by the Accounting Principles Board (APB) in 1959.

common costs. Costs of facilities and services shared by a number of departments. Compare JOINT COSTS.

common stock. US term for ORDINARY SHARES.

companies liquidation account. In the UK, an account kept by the Department of Trade at the Bank of England into which a LIQUIDATOR in a WINDING UP by the court must pay all moneys coming into his hands, unless the COMMITTEE OF INSPECTION satisfies the Department that it is more advantageous that the liquidator should have an account at another bank.

company limited by guarantee. In the UK, a company having the liability of its members limited by the memorandum of association to such amount as the members respectively undertake to contribute to the assets of the company in the event of its being wound up.

company limited by shares. In the UK, a company having the liability of its members limited by the memorandum of association to the amount, if any, unpaid on the shares respectively held by them. The vast majority of UK companies are companies limited by shares.

comparability. Consistent accounting treatment of items in the financial statements of different entities at the same point in time so as to enable valid comparisons to be made. It is often cited as a desirable characteristic of financial statements but, in spite of the existence of ACCOUNTING STANDARDS, much DIVERSITY of treatment still exists.

complete markets. A situation in which markets exist for all commodities and claims and hence a market price for any commodity or claim is publicly observable. In other words, complete markets allow investors to engage in whatever trading they consider desirable.

compliance audit. An audit whose function is to test whether statutory obligations (e.g. to present a TRUE AND FAIR VIEW of or to present fairly a company's financial affairs) have been complied with rather than to test whether a company or other entity is being managed efficiently, effectively and economically (see VALUE FOR MONEY AUDIT).

compliance costs. The costs to the private sector of complying with tax, company and other legislation. Such costs are typically very difficult to calculate but are believed to be substantial in economies such as the UK and the USA.

compliance tests. Auditing tests the purposes of which are to obtain evidence that internal control procedures are being applied as presented and thus to indicate the necessary level of SUBSTANTIVE TESTS.

composite rate. In the UK, the rate at which building societies and banks deduct tax from interest paid to depositors. A taxpayer receiving interest from a building society or a bank does not have to pay any further tax on it (unless his or her marginal rate of tax is higher than the basic tax rate) but neither can tax be reclaimed.

composition. A SCHEME OF ARRANGEMENT.

compound discount. The difference between a future sum (S) and its present value (P), i.e., if S = 1,

$$(1+i)^n - (1+i)^{-n},$$

where i = the compound rate of interest per period and n = the number of periods. The compound rate of discount per period (d) can be calculated as

$$d = \frac{i}{(1+i)}.$$

compound interest. Interest calculated not only on the original sum (principal) invested but also on interest reinvested. An initial principal P invested at the beginning of period 1 at a compound interest rate of i per period will have an accumulated or TERMINAL VALUE (S) after n periods of $P(1+i)^n$. It follows that the PRESENT VALUE (P) of a future sum S, n periods hence, at a compound interest rate i is

$$S(1+i)^{-n}.$$

Tables of accumulated and present values can easily be calculated.

It is frequently useful to assume that interest can be compounded continuously, i.e.

that the length of the compounding period is infinitely small. The accumulated value of £1 per n periods then becomes Pe^{jn} and the present value Se^{-jn}, where e is the EXPONENTIAL CONSTANT (2.71828...) and j the nominal annual rate of interest.

See also ANNUITY.

comprehensive budget. Synonym of MASTER BUDGET.

comprehensive tax allocation. *See* DEFERRED TAXATION.

Comptroller and Auditor General (C & AG). In the UK, an independent official reporting direct to Parliament, and head of the NATIONAL AUDIT OFFICE. *See also* COMMITTEE OF PUBLIC ACCOUNTS and PUBLIC ACCOUNTS COMMISSION.

It is the duty of the C & AG to audit and certify the APPROPRIATION ACCOUNTS of all government departments; to audit the REVENUE ACCOUNTS; to audit and certify departmental trading accounts and related activities; to examine departmental store accounts; to audit and certify other accounts as laid down by the Exchequer and Audit Departments Acts and other statutes; and to report as necessary to Parliament on the results of these audits.

He may also by agreement audit and certify other accounts; have rights of access to a wide range of bodies where he is not the appointed auditor but which are largely financed by public funds; examine the economy, efficiency and effectiveness of expenditure and use of resources by bodies where he is appointed auditor or has rights of access, either under statute or by agreement; and report to Parliament on the results of these examinations.

The C & AG does not have access to the accounts of nationalized industries or local authorities.

compulsory liquidation. Synonym for a WINDING UP BY THE COURT.

compulsory winding-up. A winding up other than a VOLUNTARY WINDING-UP.

COMPUSTAT. A computerized DATA BASE containing accounting and share price data relating to US and Canadian companies. It is an extremely important source of data for empirical research in accounting in North America.

computer program. A set of instructions which specify the sequence of operations to be performed by a computer.

concept. An abstract idea forming part of the theory underlying a set of practices. *See* ACCOUNTING ASSUMPTIONS, AXIOMS, CONCEPTS, CONVENTIONS, POSTULATES AND PRINCIPLES.

conceptual framework. A set of interrelated concepts, explicit or implicit, underlying the procedures of FINANCIAL ACCOUNTING. There is no general agreement as to the contents of a conceptual framework but a possible model (based on the publications of the FINANCIAL ACCOUNTING STANDARDS BOARD) includes: a statement of objectives; a set of definitions; a specification of the desirable qualitative characteristics of financial information; a specification of what to measure; and a set of rules concerning how to measure.

It is argued in favour of a conceptual framework that it provides both a coherent set of concepts from which ACCOUNTING STANDARDS can be set and a defence against the POLITICIZATION OF ACCOUNTING. On the other hand it is argued that a conceptual framework does not in practice help much in resolving specific accounting issues, that the framework itself may be influenced by political considerations and that if standard setting is regarded as a means of settling conflicts of interest a too explicit framework may, by reducing flexibility, make setting standards more difficult rather than easier.

Only in the USA have substantial resources been devoted to the preparation of an explicit conceptual framework. The results are published by the Financial Accounting Standards Board in the form of STATEMENTS OF FINANCIAL ACCOUNTING CONCEPTS, whose predecessors include ACCOUNTING RESEARCH STUDIES Nos. 1 and 3 (1961, 1962), Statement No. 4 of the ACCOUNTING

PRINCIPLES BOARD (1970) and the TRUEBLOOD REPORT (1973). The Accounting Standards Committee in the UK has published THE CORPORATE REPORT (1975) and the Canadian Institute of Chartered Accountants, *Corporate Reporting: Its Future Evolution* (1980). The latter, written by Edward Stamp, takes a common law approach rather than the normative approach of the FASB.

See also REGULATION OF CORPORATE FINANCIAL REPORTING.

concert party. See INTERESTS IN SHARES.

Confederation of Asian and Pacific Accountants (CAPA). A regional accountancy group of (in 1983) 28 member accounting organizations from 21 countries with a secretariat in Hong Kong. The ASEAN countries (Brunei, Indonesia, Malaya, the Philippines, Singapore and Thailand) have formed within it the ASEAN FEDERATION OF ACCOUNTANTS (AFA).

confidence interval. In an audit context, a random interval which contains the true value of an audited amount with a chosen probability. The width of the confidence interval is an important determinant of sample size.

confidence level. The measure of probability associated with a CONFIDENCE INTERVAL. An auditor may, for example, wish to achieve a 95% confidence level that a reported account balance is not materially different (say, ±$5,000) from the audited amount. The range of values is a measure of PRECISION.

confirmation. An audit technique in which the auditor requests third parties (e.g. debtors, banks, employees) or the client to confirm statements made in the accounts or financial statements. A distinction can thus be made between external confirmation and internal confirmation (*see* LETTER OF REPRESENTATION). The circularization of debtors takes two forms: a positive circular requesting confirmation of the amounts shown as outstanding; and a negative circular, requesting a reply only if the debtor disputes the amount shown.

conservatism. An accounting convention which, where there is a choice of accounting treatments, chooses the one with the least favourable immediate effect on reported profit and financial position. It may lead to financial statements showing a weaker state of affairs than actually exists and to the creation of SECRET RESERVES. *See* PRUDENCE CONCEPT.

consignment accounts. Accounts recording transactions relating to goods on consignment, i.e., goods sent by a consignor to a consignee for the purpose of sale, the goods remaining the property of the consignor and the consignee receiving a commission for goods sold. Goods on consignment are part of the inventory of the consignor, not the consignee. *See also* ACCOUNT SALES.

consistency. One of the accounting principles included in the EEC FOURTH DIRECTIVE and the British Companies Act 1981. The Act requires that ACCOUNTING POLICIES shall be applied consistently from one financial year to the next. Consistency is one of the FUNDAMENTAL ACCOUNTING CONCEPTS listed in SSAP 2 in the UK and one of the FUNDAMENTAL ACCOUNTING ASSUMPTIONS set out in IAS 1.

Consistency among accounting entities at a point in time is usually referred to as COMPARABILITY.

The consistency concept does not mean that accounting treatments may never change, but such changes must be disclosed and, where material, quantified.

consolidated financial statements. Financial statements incorporating the financial position, annual results and funds flow of a holding or parent company and its subsidiaries into one set of statements. This is usually achieved by replacing the parent company's investment in its subsidiaries by the underlying assets and liabilities of the subsidiaries. Some items, e.g., share capital, are identical in holding company and consolidated statements but certain items, e.g., goodwill on consolidation and minority interest, can only occur in consolidated statements and other items, e.g., shares in subsidiary companies, can only appear in the holding company statements.

A statement of the principles followed in consolidation is required by accounting standards in the UK.

Consolidated and parent company statements can give very different indications of profitability, liquidity and capital structure. Consolidated statements are normally to be preferred on the grounds that: (1) reported profits and losses of subsidiaries will be taken into account and not merely their dividends (thus including loss-making as well as profitable subsidiaries); (2) there is disclosure of the assets and liabilities of all the companies in the group, not merely the operating assets and liabilities (if any) of the parent company plus the cost of the investments made by the parent company in its subsidiaries; (3) liquidity is measured by the current assets and current liabilities of all companies in the group, not just those of the parent company.

On the other hand, a group does not, in the UK and USA, exist as a legal entity and, unless guarantees have been given, the assets of one member of a group may not be available to settle the liabilities of another. To this extent, consolidated liquidity and gearing ratios may be misleading. Creditors and minority shareholders of a subsidiary company need to examine its accounts rather than the consolidated statements. Also, in the absence of SEGMENT REPORTING consolidated statements may conceal as well as disclose.

Consolidated statements originated in the USA in the late 19th century as a result of the development there of the holding company. They did not become popular in the UK until the 1930s and were not regulated by British law until the Companies Act 1948, which requires the publication of GROUP ACCOUNTS. They are now well established in the UK and current practice is reflected in SSAP 1 on ASSOCIATED COMPANIES and SSAP 14 on group accounts.

US practice is regulated by: (1) the rules of the SEC, which require that all companies subject to its jurisdiction file consolidated financial statements and also the statements of the parent company (but the latter are not usually included in annual reports presented to shareholders); (2) Accounting Research Bulletin (ARB) No. 51, Accounting Principles Board (APB) Opinion No. 16 (which specifies the elaborate criteria by which a purchase or acquisition is to be distinguished from a POOLING OF INTERESTS or merger) and APB Opinion No. 18, which deals with EQUITY ACCOUNTING.

Legislation and standards vary as to which subsidiaries may or must be excluded from consolidated statements. In the UK, SSAP 14 states that a subsidiary should be excluded on four grounds: dissimilarity of activity to the extent that consolidated statements would be misleading; a majority shareholding not accompanied by majority voting power or control of the board of directors; severe restrictions which significantly impair control by the holding company; or where control is intended to be temporary.

Harmonization of consolidated financial statements has been attempted by the International Accounting Standards Committee, which published a standard, IAS 3, in 1976 and the EEC which adopted its SEVENTH DIRECTIVE on the subject in 1983. There remain considerable differences throughout the world in the extent to which consolidated statements are published, in the contents of the statements and in the concepts and techniques of consolidation.

In particular, a distinction can be drawn between the 'parent company' and 'entity' concepts of consolidation, which represent in this area the difference between the PROPRIETARY VIEW and the ENTITY VIEW of accounting. The parent company concept emphasizes the viewpoint of the equity shareholders of the parent company; regards legal control arising from ownership as the reason for consolidation; does not regard the MINORITY INTEREST as part of the shareholders' equity; records only that part of GOODWILL ON CONSOLIDATION attributable to the parent company; and eliminates INTER-COMPANY PROFITS made by the subsidiary only to the extent of the parent company interest in the subsidiary. The entity concept, on the other hand, emphasizes the viewpoint of all interested parties (e.g., both parent and minority shareholders, managers, employees, trade unions and creditors); regards economic unity arising from unified management as the reason for consolidation; treats the minority interest as part of shareholders' equity; records the goodwill on consolidation relating to both parent company and minority interest; and eliminates inter-company profits completely rather than partially.

See also: ACQUISITION ACCOUNTING; EQUITY ACCOUNTING; FOREIGN CURRENCY TRANSLATION; GOODWILL ON CONSOLIDATION; INTERCOMPANY PROFITS; MERGER ACCOUNTING; MINORITY INTERESTS; PROPORTIONAL CONSOLIDATION; RESERVE ON CONSOLIDATION; SEGMENT REPORTING.

consolidated fund. In the UK, the Exchequer account into which are paid gross tax revenue, less repayments, and all other Exchequer receipts not specifically directed elsewhere.

consolidation of share capital. In the UK, the combination of shares into larger units, e.g., combining two 25p shares into one of 50p.

constant dollar accounting. US synonym for CONSTANT PURCHASING POWER ACCOUNTING. *See* CURRENT PURCHASING POWER (CPP) ACCOUNTING.

constant purchasing power accounting. A system of INFLATION ACCOUNTING in which all amounts are indexed by means of a general index reflecting changes in the purchasing power of money. In principle, purchasing power at any date can be used; in practice, current purchasing power is used: *see* CURRENT PURCHASING POWER (CPP) ACCOUNTING.

constraint. Anything that restricts or limits the production or sale of a given product. Where there is more than one constraint the use of LINEAR PROGRAMMING techniques becomes necessary.

Consultative Committee of Accountancy Bodies (CCAB). A committee established in the UK in 1970 after the failure of the proposal to integrate the six UK professional accountancy bodies. It has three main subcommittees: Parliamentary and Law; Accounting Standards; and Auditing Practices.

consumption maintenance. The maintenance intact of a STANDARD STREAM of future receipts (e.g., dividend payments to shareholders). There is a stronger element of expectations in consumption maintenance than in a CAPITAL MAINTENANCE CONCEPT, since no resort can be had to past or current market prices.

contango. On the London Stock Exchange, a charge made by a stockbroker for carrying over a position from one ACCOUNT to another without the investor paying for or delivering the stock. *See also* BACKWARDATION.

contingencies. Conditions which exist at the balance sheet date the outcomes of which will be confirmed only on the occurrence or non-occurrence of one or more uncertain future events. They do not include uncertainties connected with accounting estimates (e.g., provisions for doubtful debts). Under standard accounting practice contingent losses but not contingent gains may be accrued in financial statements. Material contingencies not so accounted for are disclosed as Notes. In the UK this includes both contingent liabilities, the disclosure of which is required by company law, and contingent assets if it is probable that the latter will be realized.

contingency theories of management accounting. Theories of management accounting which argue that accounting systems should fit the organizational context in which they are used. The relevant contingent variables may include the nature of the external environment, the type of production technology, the structure of the organization, and the strategy selected by the organization to achieve its objectives.

contingent liability. *See* CONTINGENCIES.

continuous budget. A budget which is continuously updated, a period (month, quarter) being added at the end at the same time that a period at the beginning is dropped.

continuously contemporary accounting (CoCoA). A system of accounting, associated with Professor Chambers of the University of Sydney, that defines financial position as the measure of the ability of an enterprise to adapt to a changing environment. By adaptation is meant the disposal of assets no longer appropriate and the acquisition of new assets that will serve the enterprise better. Therefore, it is argued, it is the CURRENT CASH EQUIVALENT (CCE) of assets that needs to be measured and disclosed. Assets such as GOODWILL that are not severable have a CCE of zero, as have also highly specialized assets which can be regarded as NON-VENDIBLE DURABLES.

Profit is deemed to be realized as it accrues rather than at the point of sale. By the use of price variation adjustment and capital maintenance adjustment accounts, CoCoA can be extended to take account of general price level changes.

CoCoA has received strong support in some academic circles but has not been adopted in practice. Critics of CoCoA argue that although CCEs undoubtedly provide useful information they should not be disclosed to the exclusion of other useful measures such as replacement cost.

contra accounts. Accounts which offset each other. Where two enterprises are both debtors and creditors of each other a complete or partial contra settlement may be made.

contribution. The excess of revenues over variable costs which is available to cover an enterprise's fixed costs and, if sufficiently large, to provide a profit.

contribution income statement. An income statement (profit and loss account) which discloses a CONTRIBUTION MARGIN and emphasizes the distinction between variable and fixed costs.

contribution margin. Sales less all variable costs (whether manufacturing, selling or administrative). It is to be distinguished from the GROSS MARGIN.

contribution margin ratio. The total CONTRIBUTION MARGIN divided by the total sales.

contributory. In the UK, a person liable to contribute to the assets of a company in the event of its being wound up. In the course of a winding up, the liquidator draws up a list of the present members of the company (the 'A' list) and a list of past members (the 'B' list). Calls may be made on contributories in certain circumstances.

control account. An account which contains in summary form the detailed accounts kept in a SUBSIDIARY LEDGER. For example a creditors ledger can be summarized in a creditors ledger control account to which is credited the total from the purchases journal (with a debit to purchases account) and debited with the total of the creditors column in the cash payments journal or cash book, the creditors column representing cash payments plus any cash discount. Returns outwards (purchases returns) are also debited in total to the control account. The balance on the control account should equal the sum of the balances in the subsidiary ledger.

The control account is kept in the GENERAL LEDGER (nominal ledger), the subsidiary ledger being outside the double entry system. If it is desired to make the subsidiary ledger self-balancing, this can be achieved by including within it a general ledger control account.

The use of control accounts makes possible a division of labour, improved INTERNAL CHECK and the quicker preparation of accounting reports. The general principle of control accounts is of very wide application and is used in cost accounting as well as financial accounting.

controllable costs. Costs that can be influenced by a given manager within a given time period. In the very long run almost all costs are controllable by someone.

controllership. In US usage, provision to an enterprise of some or all of the following functions: planning and control, reporting and interpreting, evaluating and consulting, tax administration, reporting to government, protection of assets and economic appraisal. It may be contrasted with TREASURERSHIP.

convention. A rule of practice adopted by common consent, express or implied. It can be distinguished from an ASSUMPTION, AXIOM or POSTULATE in that it need not represent what is thought to be a self-evident truth. For example, it is a convention (established by long usage) that debits are placed on the left hand side of a T account and credits on the right hand side. The opposite would be an equally useful convention. *See* ACCOUNTING ASSUMPTIONS, AXIOMS, CONCEPTS, CONVENTIONS, POSTULATES AND PRINCIPLES.

conversion cost. The sum of DIRECT LABOUR and FACTORY OVERHEAD, both variable and fixed.

convertible securities. Securities which may be converted at given price ratios at the option of the holder at a future date or dates into securities of a different form.

copyright. A right to published material. Copyrights are INTANGIBLE ASSETS and in the UK company law permits their capitalization and subsequent amortization if they are acquired for valuable consideration or are created by the company itself. In the USA the costs of copyright developed internally may either be written off as incurred or capitalized and amortized over its expected useful life with a maximum of 40 years. Purchased copyrights must be capitalized and amortized.

corporate modelling. The construction and use of a computer-based model of an organization to carry out the calculations required to produce results of business activities based on given sets of assumptions and predictions. The objective of the model is to assist managers to prepare effective plans for future operations. Corporate models may be based on SIMULATION or OPTIMIZATION and may be deterministic (single value inputs yielding single outputs) or probabilistic (stochastic) with ranges of values for both inputs and outputs.

Corporate Report, The. A 103 pp. discussion paper published by the UK Accounting Standards (Steering) Committee in June 1975. The compilers of the report believe that there is an implicit responsibility to report publicly (whether or not required by law or regulation) incumbent on every economic entity whose size or format renders it significant. They stress USER NEEDS and identify seven groups of users (defined as 'those having a reasonable right to information concerning the reporting entity'): equity investors; loan creditors; employees; analyst-advisers; business contacts; government; the public. Seven desirable characteristics of corporate reports are identified: relevance, understandability, reliability, completeness, objectivity, timeliness and comparability. The report recommends that six additional statements should be published in corporate reports: a statement on value added; an employment report; a statement of money exchanges with government; a statement of transactions in foreign currency; a statement of future prospects; and a statement of corporate objectives. Further study is recommended of such topics as social accounting, disaggregated (segmented) statements, value to the firm as a valuation system and multi-column reporting. *The Corporate Report* is a revolutionary document which has not been translated into legislation or accounting standards. At its date of issue it was overshadowed by the Report of the SANDILANDS COMMITTEE.

correlation coefficient (r). A measure of the strength of the linear relationship between two statistical series. It can take on values between $+1$ and -1, a value of -1 indicating a perfect negative relationship, of $+1$ a perfect positive relationship, and of zero no relationship. The correlation coefficient is the square root of the coefficient of determination (R^2). A high correlation coefficient indicates that two variables move together but does not indicate cause and effect.

cost. A term with many uses but always with the connotation of sacrifice of resources. Whereas accountants have traditionally emphasized HISTORICAL COST ACCOUNTING and the allocation of EXPIRED COSTS to accounting periods, economists have emphasized OPPORTUNITY COSTS. It is now generally recognized, however, that there is a need for DIFFERENT COSTS FOR DIFFERENT PURPOSES. Whilst the use of historical costs rather than REPLACEMENT COSTS in stewardship accounting increases objectivity it usually decreases relevance. Much of cost accounting is based upon ACTUAL COSTS but BUDGETED COSTS and STANDARD COSTS are also of great practical importance. The cost accountant classifies costs in many ways. In his scorekeeping role he measures DIRECT COSTS and INDIRECT COSTS, distinguishes between PRODUCT COSTS and PERIOD COSTS and may even attempt to allocate COMMON COSTS and JOINT COSTS. When producing information for control and decision-making he distinguishes VARIABLE COSTS from FIXED COSTS (dividing the latter into ENGINEERED COSTS, COMMITTED COSTS and DISCRETIONARY COSTS); and CONTROLLABLE COSTS from UNCONTROLLABLE COSTS. He also estimates INCREMENTAL COSTS and ignores SUNK COSTS. He recognizes a distinction between AVERAGE COST and MARGINAL COST although he usually assumes that over the relevant range of production they are equal. In pricing he may use a marginal cost approach but is more likely to use FULL COST PRICING. If he is an academic he will increasingly find it difficult to ignore references to AGENCY COSTS.

cost absorption. The application of costs accumulated by a department to the physical units (or other measures of output) that pass through the department.

cost accounting. In its original meaning, the accumulation and assignment of historical costs to units of product and departments, primarily for purposes of stock (inventory) valuation and profit (income) measurement.

In its modern meaning, it is difficult to distinguish from MANAGEMENT ACCOUNTING, but may be considered to combine parts of both management accounting and FINANCIAL ACCOUNTING in that it serves stewardship as well as control and decision-making purposes.

Cost Accounting Standards Board. A board established by the US Congress in 1970 and wound up in 1981. Its standards had the full force of law and applied to all US federal government procurement contracts exceeding $100,000.

cost accumulation. The collection of cost data in an organized way by means of an accounting system.

cost behaviour pattern. Synonym for COST FUNCTION.

cost benefit analysis. An analysis of the costs and benefits of a project including the SOCIAL COSTS and SOCIAL BENEFITS. The phrase is also loosely used to mean any comparison of costs and benefits.

cost centre. The smallest segment of activity or area of responsibility for which costs are accumulated. A cost centre may be a department but one department may contain several cost centres.

cost effectiveness. Achievement of a particular objective at the least cost. A cost effectiveness approach is most useful where outcomes cannot easily be quantified in monetary terms whereas costs can be.
See EFFECTIVENESS, COST BENEFIT ANALYSIS.

cost estimation. The attempted measurement of historical costs.

cost flow assumptions. In the context of INVENTORY VALUATION, assumptions made about the flow of individual items of inventory (stock) which cannot be physically identified. The most common assumptions are FIRST IN FIRST OUT (FIFO), WEIGHTED AVERAGE COST and LAST IN FIRST OUT (LIFO). Mainly for tax reasons, LIFO is much more popular in the USA than in the UK. Cost flow assumptions are not strictly necessary under current cost accounting (CCA) as distinct from historical cost accounting (HCA) but, in the UK, CCA accounts are usually prepared by first recording stocks at their FIFO cost and then adjusting them to current cost by means of a COST OF SALES ADJUSTMENT (COSA).

cost function. The relationship, expressed as an equation, between a cost and one or more variables. In choosing a cost function both economic plausibility and GOODNESS OF FIT are relevant.

cost of capital. The minimum required rate of return on new investment. It is usually calculated as the weighted average cost of the long term sources of finance available. The weights should ideally be market values based on a company's optimum CAPITAL STRUCTURE. The specific cost of each source is the minimum rate of return required by the suppliers of that source and can be decomposed into the riskless interest rate plus a premium for risk. The specific cost of debt is equal to its after-tax REDEMPTION YIELD after allowing for flotation costs; that of preference shares (preferred stock) is higher because preference dividends are not tax deductible. The cost of retained earnings is equal to the cost of ordinary shares with an adjustment for flotation costs. The cost of ordinary shares can be calculated in a number of ways; for example, by use of the EARNINGS YIELD, a DIVIDEND GROWTH MODEL, or by use of the CAPITAL ASSET PRICING MODEL (CAPM). The CAPM can also be used to calculate the specific cost of other sources of capital.

cost of goods sold. See COST OF SALES.

cost of sales. The cost of goods sold during a period, calculated by adjusting cost of goods purchased or manufactured by the change in stocks (inventories). In the UK, disclosure of the cost of sales is required by two out of the four PROFIT AND LOSS ACCOUNT FORMATS. Cost of sales is synonymous with cost of goods sold. The latter term is usual in the USA and is also common in the UK. See also COST OF SALES ADJUSTMENT.

cost of sales adjustment (COSA). An adjustment in CURRENT COST ACCOUNTING (CCA) systems to eliminate STOCK APPRECIATION from reported profit. In principle the adjustment should be made each time a sale takes place in order to base cost of sales on the cost current at the date of consumption instead of at the date of purchase. A number of approximations are used in practice, e.g., the averaging method in which the COSA is equal to the difference between (a) the FIFO cost of opening stock (inventory) less the FIFO cost of closing stock, and (b) the average current cost of the opening stock less the average current cost of the closing stock.

cost-plus pricing. Synonym for FULL COST PRICING.

cost prediction. The attempted measurement of expected future costs.

cost savings. Those HOLDING GAINS that represent the excess of the current cost over the historical cost of inputs used in producing outputs sold. They measure the effects of buying goods in advance of a price rise.

Council for the Securities Industry (CSI). A self-regulating body set up by the financial institutions of the City of London. The CSI has published a code of conduct for dealers in securities and rules governing substantial acquisitions of shares (see DAWN RAID). See also CITY CODE ON TAKE-OVERS AND MERGERS.

coupon rate. The rate of return on a bond or debenture expressed as a fixed percentage of the face value. It is not necessarily equal to the EFFECTIVE ANNUAL RATE or YIELD TO MATURITY.

covariance. A measure of the relation between two variables. The correlation coefficient is equal to the covariance of x and y divided by the product of the standard deviation of x and the standard deviation of y.

CPP accounting. *See* CURRENT PURCHASING POWER (CPP) ACCOUNTING.

creative accounting. The use of accounting to mislead rather than help the intended user. Creative accounting deliberately takes advantage of areas where there is no standard treatment or where there are ambiguities or arbitrary cut-off points.

credit entry. An entry in a double-entry bookkeeping system recording an increase in a liability; an owner's equity item or a revenue; or a decrease in an asset or an expense. Credit entries are conventionally made on the right-hand side of T ACCOUNTS.

credit management. The management of an enterprise's debtors (accounts receivable). It involves the credit rating of customers, deciding on credit terms and discounts, collection policies and procedures, AGE ANALYSIS of debtors and FACTORING.

creditors. In the UK, amounts (representing either cash or a claim to services) owed to an accounting entity. The BALANCE SHEET FORMATS distinguish between amounts falling due within one year (*see* CURRENT LIABILITIES) and amounts falling due after more than one year. The US term is ACCOUNTS PAYABLE and does not include accrued expenses and other current liabilities not arising out of trading transactions.

creditors ledger. The subsidiary ledger in which creditors' accounts are recorded. Also known as the bought ledger or purchase ledger. Each creditor's account is credited with purchases and debited with cash paid, discounts received and returns outward. The detail in the creditors ledger is summarized in the creditors ledger control account kept in the general ledger.

creditors' voluntary winding up. In the UK, a VOLUNTARY WINDING UP in which a DECLARATION OF SOLVENCY has not been made.

criterion of regret. *See* DECISION TABLE.

critical path method (CPM). A form of NETWORK ANALYSIS suited to projects where past experience provides a useful guide to the future and the relevant information can be fairly accurately estimated. The activities comprising a project are set out in a network diagram showing the sequence in which each activity can be commenced and its duration. The critical path is that path through the network that provides the minimum time for the project, obtained by summing the activity times of the path having the longest duration. The only way in which the duration of a project can be shortened is to reduce the time allotted to activities on the critical path.

See also PROGRAMME EVALUATION AND REVIEW TECHNIQUE (PERT).

cross-cast. UK accounting term for addition horizontally. *See* CAST.

cum. A Latin word meaning with. Thus: cum dividend, cum rights, etc.

cumulative preference shares. *See* PREFERENCE SHARES.

current account. In the UK, an account kept at a bank on which cheques can be drawn and on which interest is not usually paid; also, an account in the books of sole traders and partnerships recording fluctuating amounts of proprietorship interest (i.e., shares of profit less drawings).

current asset. In UK company law any ASSET other than a FIXED ASSET, i.e. a current asset is one which is not intended for use on a continuing basis in an enterprise's activities. The UK BALANCE SHEET FORMATS subdivide current assets into stocks (inventories), debtors, investments and cash at bank and in hand. Prepayments and accrued income may also be shown under this heading.

In the USA, current assets are defined by Accounting Research Bulletin No. 43 as cash and other assets or resources commonly identified as those that are reasonably expected to be realized in cash or sold or consumed during the normal operating cycle of a business. Apart from cash, current assets therefore include marketable securities held as short-term investments, accounts receivable, short-term notes receivable, inventories and prepayments.

current cash equivalent (CCE). The measure of assets and liabilities used in CONTINUOUSLY CONTEMPORARY ACCOUNTING (CoCoA). For assets CCE is equal to NET REALIZABLE VALUE (NRV) in the ordinary course of business. It is argued that CCEs enable owners to satisfy themselves that managers have maintained adaptive capacity; provide useful measures of SOLVENCY and credit-worthiness; and enable owners to compare the rate of return on total assets with the rate which could be earned by selling the assets and switching to some alternative activity. The CCEs of non-severable assets such as GOODWILL and of unsaleable highly specialized assets (NON-VENDIBLE DURABLES) are zero.

current cost accounting (CCA). An accounting system based on the matching of current revenues with current costs (usually current REPLACEMENT COSTS) and the maintenance of physical capital intact. CCA takes account of changes in SPECIFIC PRICES and produces different figures from HISTORICAL COST ACCOUNTING (HCA) even in the absence of changes in the GENERAL PRICE LEVEL. Unlike CURRENT PURCHASING POWER (CPP) ACCOUNTING, it is based on an ENTITY VIEW of enterprise.

There are many variations of detail both in what is practised and in what is recommended in authoritative accounting standards and in the literature. It is generally agreed that if current cost accounts are drawn up by adjustments to HCA it is necessary to adjust HCA profit by a COST OF SALES ADJUSTMENT (COSA) and a DEPRECIATION ADJUSTMENT. There is less agreement about the necessity for a MONETARY WORKING CAPITAL ADJUSTMENT (MWCA) and a GEARING ADJUSTMENT.

In the balance sheet, MONETARY ASSETS are valued as under HCA but NON-MONETARY ASSETS are shown at current replacement cost (RC) or, if VALUE TO THE BUSINESS is combined with CCA, at RC or the RECOVERABLE AMOUNT, whichever is the lower. To achieve this an appropriately named reserve is credited on the other side of the balance sheet.

Empirical research has found no impact of CCA upon share prices. This suggests that either CCA information was already available to the stock market or that it was not considered relevant. Other research has shown that investment analysts do make a limited use of CCA information.

Forms of CCA were recommended in the Reports of the UK SANDILANDS COMMITTEE, the Australian MATHEWS COMMITTEE and the New Zealand RICHARDSON COMMITTEE and CCA exposure drafts were issued by the relevant standard setting bodies. In the UK, attempts to produce an acceptable CCA accounting standard based on CCA proved difficult but eventually resulted in SSAP 16 (1980), which has, however, received less than full support from UK companies. A new exposure draft (ED 35, 'Accounting for the Effects of Changing Prices') was issued in 1984. CCA is perhaps most extensively used in the UK by nationalized industries (which do not, however, incorporate a gearing adjustment in their CCA accounts).

In the USA, replacement cost data have been favoured by the SEC, and FAS 33 (1979) requires not only CPP data but also estimates of income from continuing operations on a current cost basis (including current cost of goods sold and depreciation); current cost amounts of inventory and property, plant and equipment at the end of the fiscal year; and increases or decreases in current cost amounts of inventory and property, plant and equipment gross and net of changes in the general price level.

current cost depreciation. Depreciation based on current costs rather than historical costs. Current cost depreciation may be based on the cost of a MODERN EQUIVALENT ASSET or of replacing the services received from the existing asset. Current costs may be either those at the end of the accounting period or the average for the period. In practice specific price indexes may be used. *See also* DEPRECIATION ADJUSTMENT, BACKLOG DEPRECIATION.

current cost of goods sold. COST OF GOODS SOLD in current cost (normally REPLACEMENT COST) terms rather than historical cost. It can be calculated directly or by an end-of-year adjustment: see COST OF SALES ADJUSTMENT (COSA). SSAP 16 in the UK and FAS 33 in the USA require disclosure of a current cost of goods sold figure.

current cost operating profit. In the UK, conventional accounting profit after making a COST OF SALES ADJUSTMENT (COSA), a DEPRECIATION ADJUSTMENT and a MONETARY WORKING CAPITAL ADJUSTMENT (MWCA). It is equivalent in principle to the CURRENT OPERATING PROFIT recommended by some US accountants, but the latter do not usually incorporate a MWCA.

current liability. A LIABILITY which is expected to have been paid within one year from the date of the balance sheet. The UK BALANCE SHEET FORMATS refer to current liabilities as 'creditors: amounts falling due within one year'. They include trade creditors, bills of exchange payable, amounts owed to group and related companies, taxation and social security creditors, proposed dividends, accruals and deferred income, payments received on account, and, to the extent that they are due for repayment within one year, bank overdrafts, bank loans and debenture loans.

In the USA, current liabilities include amounts payable, short-term notes payable, interest payable, dividends payable, accrued expenses, income and other taxes payable, and the current portion of long-term debt.

current/non-current method. See FOREIGN CURRENCY TRANSLATION.

current operating performance concept. The inclusion in the profit and loss account (income statement) of items relating only to the normal activity of each year, i.e., extraordinary items and prior year adjustments are excluded. Such a concept has been considered by standard setters in both the UK and USA as giving too much discretion to management. Also known in the USA as the CLEAN SURPLUS CONCEPT, it can be contrasted with the ALL-INCLUSIVE CONCEPT.

current operating profit. The profit that results from the matching of current revenues from operations with the current cost of those operations. It can be derived from conventional accounting profit by deducting a COST OF SALES ADJUSTMENT (COSA), a DEPRECIATION ADJUSTMENT and, according to some accountants, a MONETARY WORKING CAPITAL ADJUSTMENT (MWCA).

current purchasing power (CPP) accounting. A system of INFLATION ACCOUNTING in which nominal pounds or dollars are replaced by constant pounds or dollars. In principle, current purchasing power (CPP) accounting can be applied to both HISTORICAL COST ACCOUNTING (HCA) and CURRENT COST ACCOUNTING (CCA) but in practice it is mainly confined to the former; for its application to the latter see RELATIVE PRICE CHANGE ACCOUNTING.

As applied to HCA, CPP accounting is based on a PROPRIETARY VIEW of income and wealth, the former being regarded as the difference between the generalized purchasing power of an enterprise's owners at the beginning and end of an accounting period. Thus, a financial CAPITAL MAINTENANCE CONCEPT is retained but money is replaced by purchasing power.

In the balance sheet, monetary assets and liabilities are carried at the same amount as in HCA but non-monetary assets are valued at historical cost adjusted by a general price index (except that, in accordance with the PRUDENCE concept, stocks are not recorded at a higher amount than their net realizable value). All profit and loss account (income statement) items are restated in terms of the general price level prevailing at the end of the accounting period. In addition the profit and loss account is debited or credited with a PURCHASING POWER LOSS OR GAIN. The owner's equity is not adjusted directly but by means of the adjusted retained profit transferred from the profit and loss account. In order to compare, say, this year's CPP financial statements with those of last year, the previous year's statements must be updated for the further change in a general price index.

CPP accounting is dependent on the reliability of the GENERAL PRICE LEVEL indexes used. In most developed countries government-calculated indexes are published at fairly frequent intervals. In principle, the index should be constructed so as to reflect the consumption patterns of a particular company's shareholders. In practice, more general indexes have to be used.

CPP accounting provides figures that are slightly easier to manipulate (but not perhaps significantly so) than HCA figures and less easy to manipulate than the figures produced by CURRENT VALUE ACCOUNTING systems. CPP accounting is rather more complicated than HCA, its figures take longer to produce and fit less obviously into the double entry process. Unlike HCA, it does not ignore changes in general prices but specific price changes are still ignored. Profits are less likely to be overstated and assets are less likely to be understated but may bear no relation to current values. ADDITIVITY is achieved within an historical cost framework. But CPP accounts are no more relevant to decision-making than historical cost accounts.

CPP is most popular in countries with highly inflationary economies (as in some parts of Latin America). It has been tried and abandoned in the UK, where a provisional accounting standard recommending supplementary CPP financial statements was issued in 1974 but later withdrawn, as a result of the Report of the SANDILANDS COMMITTEE, in favour of CURRENT COST ACCOUNTING. In the USA, the FASB issued a CPP exposure draft in 1974 but was then confronted by an SEC preference for replacement costs. FAS 33 (1979) requires some CPP information (income from continuing operations adjusted for the effects of general inflation and the purchasing power gain or loss on net monetary items) but also requires current cost data.

Empirical research suggests that stock markets ignore CPP figures. This may be either because such data are regarded as irrelevant or because the market has already made its own assessment of the effects of inflation.

current ratio. The ratio of current assets to current liabilities. It is a widely used test of liquidity, of a less short-term nature than the QUICK RATIO. The inclusion in the numerator of stocks (inventories), if they are slow-moving, may give a false impression of liquidity.

current value accounting. A general term for accounting systems that take account of changes in SPECIFIC PRICES rather than changes in the GENERAL PRICE LEVEL and in which assets are valued at current REPLACEMENT COST, NET REALIZABLE VALUE, NET PRESENT VALUE or some combination thereof. The underlying CAPITAL MAINTENANCE CONCEPT may be either physical or financial. Whilst CURRENT PURCHASING POWER (CPP) ACCOUNTING substitutes constant for nominal monetary units, current value accounting retains nominal units but substitutes current for historical ASSET VALUATIONS.

See also BUSINESS PROFIT, CAPITAL MAINTENANCE CONCEPT, CURRENT COST ACCOUNTING, RELATIVE PRICE CHANGE ACCOUNTING.

Customs and Excise. The agency responsible for the assessment and collection within the UK of CUSTOMS DUTIES, EXCISE DUTIES and VALUE ADDED TAX.

customs duties. Taxes levied on imported goods and some goods manufactured from them. They may also be levied on some exports. They are sometimes designed to protect local industries from foreign competition as well as to raise revenue.

cybernetics. The study of the nature of SYSTEMS.

D

dangling debit. A debit balance on GOOD-WILL account deducted from shareholders' funds instead of being shown as an asset.

data. Things which are known or assumed to be true. Accounting data are expressed in the form of numbers and words which can be stored and processed. Data is the plural of datum, a singular noun.

data base. A collection of data on a particular subject. Examples in an accounting context include the London Business School share price data base, the University of Cambridge data base on company accounts and, in North America, COMPUSTAT.

dawn raid. A sudden acquisition of substantial shareholdings in a company in circumstances which appear to deny to some shareholders the opportunity of selling their shares at the price offered.

day book. In the UK, one of the specialized JOURNALS; in the USA, a memorandum book of transactions to be subsequently entered in a journal.

death duties. A general term for taxation of wealth at death, including in particular ESTATE DUTY as it existed in the UK from 1894 to 1975.

debenture. In the UK, an instrument acknowledging an interest-bearing loan, usually, but not necessarily secured on the assets of a company. 'Debentures' are always for fixed or ascertainable sums whereas 'debenture stock' can be transferred in fractional amounts. Debenture stock is generally created by a trust deed in which a trustee for the debenture stockholders is appointed.

debenture discount. In the UK, the discount which arises from issuing debentures (as is normal) at less than their par value.

It is disclosed in the balance sheet to the extent that it is not written off.

debenture redemption reserve. A CAPITAL RESERVE set up voluntarily by transfers out of profits. By the date of redemption the amounts transferred should be equal to the redemption value of the debentures. The establishment of a reserve limits the amount of distributable profits but does not provide the cash needed on redemption. To do this it is also necessary to establish by means of periodic SINKING FUND payments a debenture redemption reserve fund matched among the assets by investments earmarked to the fund.

debit entry. An entry in a double-entry bookkeeping system recording an increase in an asset or an expense, or a decrease in a liability, owner's equity item or revenue. Debit entries are conventionally made on the left-hand side of T ACCOUNTS.

debt. A near synonym for LIABILITIES. In the context of GEARING (LEVERAGE), debt excludes CURRENT LIABILITIES but includes PREFERENCE SHARES (preferred stock).

debtors. In the UK, amounts representing either cash or a claim to services owing to an accounting entity. The BALANCE SHEET FORMATS include the following debtors: trade debtors (arising from the sale of a good or service), amounts owed by group and related companies, prepayments and accrued income, and called up share capital not paid. The US term is ACCOUNTS RECEIVABLE and does not include prepaid expenses and other current assets not arising out of trading transactions.

debtors ledger. The subsidiary ledger in which debtors' accounts are recorded. Also known as the sold ledger or sales ledger. Each debtor's account is debited with sales and credited with cash received, discounts allowed and returns inward. The detail in the debtors ledger is summarized in the debtors ledger control account kept in the general ledger.

decision model. A method for deciding

among courses of action. A formal decision model requires an OBJECTIVE FUNCTION, a set of alternative actions to be considered, a set of probabilities of each state of nature occurring, and a set of outcomes or payoffs. All of these may be set out in a DECISION TABLE.

decision support system. A man/machine system designed to help managers make decisions. The components of a decision support system are a manager, DECISION MODELS, a computer (usually an interactive mini or micro), a communication device linking manager and computer, and a DATA BASE.

decision table. A systematic statement in table form of the contemplated actions, states of nature, probabilities and outcomes contained in a DECISION MODEL. In a situation of complete uncertainty where no probabilities are available the following criteria can be used: the optimistic maximax, i.e., select the action with the largest maximum outcome; the pessimistic maximin, i.e., select the action with the largest minimum outcome; the criterion of regret, i.e., select the action that minimizes regret (defined as the difference between the actual outcome and the outcome that could have been achieved if the decision maker had known that that state would occur); and the Laplace criterion, which assigns equal probabilities to each state of nature.

If uncertainty is not complete, subjective or objective probabilities can be assigned to each state of nature and the outcome with the highest expected monetary value (or, if the decision maker is not risk neutral, the highest utility) selected.

decision tree. A diagram setting out possible actions, their outcomes and associated probabilities in tree form.

declaration of solvency. In the UK, a statutory declaration by the directors, where it is proposed to wind up a company voluntarily, that they have made a full enquiry into the affairs of the company and, that having done so, they have formed the opinion that the company will be able to pay its debts in full within a specified period not exceeding 12 months from the commencement of the winding up.

declining balance method. US term for the reducing balance method of depreciation. *See* DEPRECIATION METHODS.

deep discount bond (DDB). A bond carrying a low or zero interest coupon and issued at a substantial discount. Tax benefits may arise from lack of symmetry in the treatment of borrowers and lenders.

defective units. Goods that are not up to standard and are subsequently reworked for sale.

defensive interval. A measure of how many days' operating expenses can be paid out of quick assets. Also known as the no credit interval, it is an attempt to treat liquidity as something to be measured over a period rather than at a point in time (as do the QUICK RATIO and CURRENT RATIO). The calculation can be made using actual or forecast data.

deferred charge. An expenditure carried forward to be written off in future periods.

deferred credit. *See* DEFERRED INCOME.

deferred income. Income received or recorded before it is deemed to be earned, a portion of which is transferred annually to the credit of the profit and loss account, the balance being shown in British balance sheets as a separate item or under creditors (amounts falling due after more than one year or within one year, according to circumstances). Government grants received in respect of expenditure on fixed assets may be treated in this manner.

deferred revenue. *See* DEFERRED INCOME.

deferred shares. In the UK, shares conferring, for example, a right to a fixed percentage dividend after all other classes of shares have received a fixed percentage dividend. Such shares are now very rare.

deferred taxation. The taxation attributable to TIMING DIFFERENCES, i.e., to differences between profits as computed for taxation purposes and profits as stated in financial statements. Unlike PERMANENT DIFFERENCES, timing differences are capable of being reversed in future periods. The treatment of deferred taxation has caused considerable controversy and there are differences in UK and US standard accounting practice and terminology.

In the USA, APB Opinion No. 11 distinguishes between partial tax allocation and comprehensive tax allocation. According to the former view, the tax charge for a period should be based on the profits of the taxes payable for an accounting period; according to the latter view (adopted by Opinion No. 11), the tax charge for a period should be based upon the taxes associated with the reported accounting profit (excluding amounts for permanent differences) even if the amounts are not payable on the current accounting period.

If comprehensive allocation is adopted it becomes necessary to choose a method for determining the amount of taxation deferred. The 'deferred' (or 'deferral') method, adopted by the APB, treats deferred taxation balances as DEFERRED CREDITS or DEFERRED CHARGES depending upon the direction of the difference, and requires no adjustments if tax rates change. The liability method, on the other hand, which is favoured in the UK, treats deferred taxation balances as amounts ultimately due to or by the company and therefore requires these amounts to be adjusted as tax rates change. The first method may be thought of as an income statement approach; the second as a balance sheet approach.

Timing differences were very large in the 1970s in the UK and resulted both in very large items in the balance sheet whose status was unclear and a tax charge in the profit and loss account consisting almost entirely of deferred taxation. This led eventually to a standard requiring the provision of deferred taxation in relation to all material timing differences to the extent that it is probable that a liability will crystallize. The potential amount of deferred tax for all timing differences has to be disclosed as a contingent liability.

It can be argued that UK practice produces more relevant deferred taxation figures than that of the USA, but that the figures are more subjective.

The discounting of deferred tax liabilities to their present values is not general practice and has not been adopted in any accounting standard.

deficiency or surplus account. In the UK, an account required by law to be attached to a STATEMENT OF AFFAIRS. It explains how the deficiency or surplus revealed by the statement has arisen over the previous three years or more.

degrees of freedom. The number of pieces of information that can vary independently of each other.

Delphi technique. A technique for arriving at the collective opinion of a group of recognized experts on a particular topic. Each expert gives his or her opinion independently in writing and is then asked if he or she wishes to modify it in the light of the written answers of the other participants.

demonstrative legacy. See LEGACY.

departmental accounting. Accounting for a division of an enterprise. Departments have varying degrees of autonomy, but are not usually separated geographically from the rest of the business. They may be concerned with manufacturing or, in the case of a department store, with retailing. Departmental accounts usually include a trading account and may also include a profit and loss account to which overheads are allocated or imputed. *See also* TRANSFER PRICES.

de Paula, Frederic Rudolf Mackley (1882-1954). The most influential British writer on accounting in the 1930s and 1940s, de Paula qualified as an English chartered accountant in 1906 and was in public practice until 1929, apart from a break during World War I in the Ministry of Munitions and in the army. He succeeded DICKSEE as part-time professor of accounting at the London School of Economics in 1926 but resigned in 1929 when he joined the Dunlop Rubber Co. as chief accountant, and later as financial controller. In 1943 he became the first non-practising member of the council of the Institute of Chartered Accountants in England and Wales.

De Paula was a strong opponent of the use of secret reserves and an advocate of consolidated accounts and of more disclosure generally. His arguments were strengthened by the revelations in the ROYAL MAIL CASE of 1931. He was able to put his ideas in these areas, and in management accounting, into practice at Dunlop.

He was the main progenitor of the Recommendations on Accounting Principles, issued by the Institute of Chartered Accountants in England and Wales from 1942 onwards, which strongly influenced both the Cohen Report (1945) on company law amendment and the accounting and disclosure provisions of the Companies Act 1948.

De Paula's most important books were *Principles of Auditing* (1914 and many later editions) and *Developments in Accounting* (1948).

depletion accounting. A method of DEPRECIATION appropriate to WASTING ASSETS in which the cost or other valuation amount of the asset is apportioned over accounting periods in proportion to the rate of extraction.

depreciation. A measure of the wearing out, consumption or other loss of value of a FIXED ASSET, arising from use, effluxion of time or OBSOLESCENCE. Depreciation as a term is sometimes restricted to fixed tangible assets but in the UK is usually regarded as a general term that also includes the AMORTIZATION of INTANGIBLE ASSETS and of assets such as leases whose useful life is determined in advance, and the DEPLETION of WASTING ASSETS such as mines. Deprecia-

tion involves the systematic allocation over time of the historical cost or other measure (e.g., replacement cost) of an asset in financial statements. At least in HISTORICAL COST ACCOUNTING, the purchase price of a fixed asset is regarded as a prepayment for services to be received over the accounting periods constituting the asset's estimated economic life. By historical cost is meant either purchase price (including expenses incidental to acquisition) or production cost. Company law in the UK allows the inclusion in the latter of a reasonable proportion of direct costs and interest on capital borrowed to finance production.

In order to make the allocation it is necessary to estimate not only a historical or current replacement cost but also the asset's useful economic life and its residual or scrap value. The latter is difficult to estimate and in practice is often regarded as zero. Useful life may be predetermined, as in leaseholds; governed by extraction (as in mines) or consumption; dependent on the extent of use (as for motor vehicles); or in part dependent on physical deterioration or obsolescence through technological and market changes. Estimates of useful life may be influenced by guidelines laid down by tax authorities.

There are many different ways of allocating the cost of a fixed asset over its useful life (*see* DEPRECIATION METHODS) but in practice, given the uncertainties involved, they tend to be heavily influenced by considerations of simplicity or of taxation. In the UK, where CAPITAL ALLOWANCES often reflect the government's economic policy rather than an attempt to measure capital consumption, the straight line method is by far the most widely used. The straight line method is also very popular in the USA but changes in tax laws in recent years have encouraged declining balance methods. In many continental European countries depreciation charges in financial statements must equal those granted for tax purposes unless fiscal benefits are to be lost.

Depreciation is a measure, however inaccurate, of a reduction in the use value of a fixed asset, so that, except in accounting systems avowedly based on exchange values (see CONTINUOUSLY CONTEMPORARY ACCOUNTING), the written-down value (WDV) of an asset is not meant to represent its net realizable value (NRV). For some assets, NRV may be greater than WDV based on historical costs. For such assets revaluations are permitted (and not unusual) in the UK but not in the USA.

Depreciation accounting is not intended to provide a fund for replacement and is not a source of funds, even though the adding back of depreciation in a source and application of funds statement may give the misleading impression that it is. Cash to purchase a new fixed asset depends not on the allocation of a historical, or even a replacement cost, but on making profits and budgeting for cash to be available when required. Profit after tax is, of course, increased by taking advantage of generous capital allowances.

In the UK, company law requires both the charging of depreciation and its disclosure. Standard accounting practice (SSAP 12) requires disclosure, for each major class of depreciable asset, of the depreciation methods used, the useful lives or the depreciation rates used, total depreciation allocated for the period, and the gross amount of depreciable assets and the related accumulated depreciation. INVESTMENT PROPERTIES are, however, required by accounting standard (SSAP 19) not to be depreciated but to be included in the balance sheet at their OPEN MARKET VALUE.

In the USA, Accounting Principles Board Opinion No. 12 requires disclosure of depreciation expense for the period; balances of major classes of depreciable assets, by nature or function, at balance sheet date; accumulated depreciation, either by major classes of depreciable assets or in total, at balance sheet date; and a general description of the method or methods used in computing depreciation with respect to major classes of depreciable assets.

depreciation adjustment. An adjustment in CURRENT COST ACCOUNTING (CCA) systems to eliminate from reported profit the difference between current cost depreciation and historical cost depreciation. It can be based

on either the average current value of the fixed asset during an accounting period or the current value at the end of the period. *See also* BACKLOG DEPRECIATION. Indexes of SPECIFIC PRICES may be used to estimate current values.

depreciation methods. Methods of allocating the cost or revalued amount (less estimated residual value) of a FIXED ASSET systematically over its estimated economic life. Depreciation methods may be based on time or on use. Possible methods based on time include: immediate write-off; allocation of an equal amount to each period; allocation of a decreasing amount to each period; allocation of an increasing amount to each period. In both the UK and the USA, the straight-line method (linear depreciation) is the most popular method. Under this method the cost or revalued amount less estimated residual value is divided by the estimated economic life, i.e.,

$$D = \frac{C-R}{n}$$

where D is the depreciation charge, C the cost or revalued amount, R the estimated residual value, and n the estimated economic life. The reason for the popularity of straight-line depreciation is probably simplicity of operation in the face of uncertainty.

Allocation of a decreasing amount to each period can be achieved by the reducing balance method (US, declining balance method) and the sum of the years digits method (rare in the UK). Under the reducing balance method, the second most popular in the UK, the amount of depreciation charged each year decreases over the life of the asset, a constant percentage rate being applied to the written down value. The rate can be obtained from the formula

$$1 - \sqrt[n]{\frac{R}{C}}$$

but approximations are often used instead since the formula is very sensitive to changes in the value of R (which cannot be zero). In the USA, the rate used is often the maximum permitted for tax purposes. Since this is usually twice the straight-line rate, the method is then called the double declining balance method.

Under the sum of the years digits method, the depreciation charge is determined by applying to the cost or other amount (less estimated residual value) a fraction based on the sum of the number of periods of the estimated economic life. For example, an asset with a ten-year life would be depreciated 10/55 in year 1, 9/55 in year 2 and so on $(1+2+ \ldots +9+10 = 55)$.

All of the depreciation methods described so far ignore the TIME VALUE OF MONEY and lead (misleadingly, it can be argued) to increasing rates of RETURN ON INVESTMENT on constant net cash flows. This anomaly can be avoided by the use of COMPOUND INTEREST depreciation methods. If equal net cash flows are assumed, increasing depreciation charges result. The charge in the first year is equal to

$$\frac{C-R}{Sn\rceil i}$$

i.e., the sum that accumulated at a rate i will amount to $(C-R)$ at the end of n years, i being the COST OF CAPITAL. The charge in the second year is equal to that of the first year plus interest at the rate i on the first year's charge, and so on. Thus, in the illustration below the first year's charge is

£1,000/15.937 = £63, and the second year's charge £63 (1.1) = £69. Because of the method of calculation this method is often called the sinking fund method.

An alternative compound interest method is the annuity method under which the charge in each year is equal to

$$\frac{C-R}{An\rceil i}$$

where $An\rceil i$ is an annuity factor. Since $1/Sn\rceil i = An\rceil i-i$, it is necessary also to credit the profit and loss account each year with interest on the written-down value. The net charge is the same as under the sinking fund method. (See under ANNUITY for an explanation of $Sn\rceil i$, $An\rceil i$ and the relationship between their reciprocals.)

These compound interest methods do not assume an actual investment of depreciation 'funds', but they can be adapted to such an assumption and if desired the amounts charged for depreciation can be invested in secondary assets and held for replacement purposes.

The depreciation methods described so far are illustrated in the following example, where the cost of the asset is £1,100, the estimated residual value £100, the estimated economic life ten years and the cost of capital 10%.

Method	Annual Depreciation Charge (nearest £)									
	1	2	3	4	5	6	7	8	9	10
	£	£	£	£	£	£	£	£	£	£
Straight-line	100	100	100	100	100	100	100	100	100	100
Reducing balance (21%)	231	182	144	114	90	71	56	45	35	28
Double declining balance (20%)	220	176	141	113	90	72	58	46	37	29
Sum of the years digits	182	164	145	127	109	91	73	55	36	18
Sinking fund	63	69	76	84	92	101	111	122	134	148
Annuity – (dep'n)	163	163	163	163	163	163	163	163	163	163
(int.)	(100)	(94)	(87)	(79)	(71)	(62)	(52)	(41)	(29)	(15)

N.B. Since the double declining balance is an approximation, the total depreciation charges over ten years add up to £982 not £1,000. The reducing balance depreciation charges add up to £996 owing to rounding.

Depreciation methods

Methods of depreciation based on usage rather than time are possible with some assets. Trucks, for example, can be depreciated on the basis of so much per mile, the depreciation charge per mile being $(C-R)$ divided by the estimated total number of miles. Plant and machinery can similarly be depreciated on a units-of-production basis. The depletion of mines and oil and gas wells is also normally calculated in this manner. These methods assume that depreciation is a variable rather than a fixed cost.

A few fixed assets are 'depreciated' on a renewals basis, i.e., all expenditure on maintenance and renewals of parts is charged to revenue, or to a maintenance equalization account which is credited with constant annual transfers from profit and loss account.

For tax purposes enterprises tend to choose depreciation methods (known in the UK as CAPITAL ALLOWANCES) that write off fixed assets as quickly as possible.

deprival value. Synonym for VALUE TO THE BUSINESS.

depth testing. The retracing by an auditor of the chronological sequence of documents related to a transaction. For example, the purchase of raw materials may involve the following documentary references: copy of official order; delivery note from supplier; copy of internal goods inwards note; invoice received from supplier; entry in purchases journal or equivalent; ledger postings; supplier's statement; counterfoil of cheque issued in supplement; cash book entry; entry on bank statement; returned cheque; postings from cash book.

Depth testing is facilitated by the use of FLOW CHARTS and is related to the concept of an AUDIT TRAIL.

devise. A gift of REALTY made by will.

Dicksee, Lawrence Robert (1864-1932). The most prolific and influential of the early British writers on accounting (as distinct from bookkeeping) and auditing and the first professor of accounting (part-time) in a British university. Dicksee came from a family of successful artists and qualified as a chartered accountant in 1886, being one of the first to do so by examination. He was in public practice throughout his life but his contributions to accounting were mainly through teaching and authorship.

He was part-time professor of accounting at the University of Birmingham 1902-06 and part-time lecturer (later professor) at the London School of Economics from 1902 to 1926.

The most important of his many books, which went through numerous editions, were *Auditing* (1892), *Depreciation, Reserves and Reserve Funds* (1897), and *Advanced Accounting* (1903). It has been said that he provided a literature for accounting single-handed. An American edition of *Auditing* was published in 1905 and forms the original basis of the leading text *Montgomery's Auditing*.

different costs for different purposes. The philosophy, now widely accepted, that a measure of cost is dependent upon the purpose for which it is required. In particular, costs for stewardship purposes may be different from those required for control or for decision-making purposes.

differential cost. The difference in expected total cost if a given decision is made.

dilution. The decrease in control and EARNINGS PER SHARE suffered by existing shareholders on a new issue of shares or a conversion of other securities into shares in which they have a less than proportionate share.

direct costing. US term for what is usually referred to in the UK as MARGINAL COSTING. A more precise term is VARIABLE COSTING. Direct costing can be contrasted with ABSORPTION COSTING.

direct costs. Costs that can be traced to a finished good in an economically-feasible manner.

direct debit system. A system for periodical

payments (both fixed and variable) in which the debit to the purchaser's account is initiated by the seller not the purchaser.

directive. Instructions to member states of the EEC to amend domestic laws in the interests of harmonization. They have been especially important in the fields of company law (see FOURTH DIRECTIVE, SEVENTH DIRECTIVE and EIGHTH DIRECTIVE) and taxation.

direct labour. All labour that can be identified with a manufactured good and can be traced to it in an economically feasible manner. Contrast INDIRECT LABOUR.

direct materials. All materials that can be identified with a manufactured good and can be traced to it in an economically feasible manner. Contrast INDIRECT MATERIALS.

directors' report. In the UK, a report to shareholders required by the Companies Acts. The items to be disclosed may be summarized as follows:

(1) A fair review of the development of the business of the company and its subsidiaries during the financial year and of their position at the end of it.
(2) Proposed dividend.
(3) Proposed transfers to reserves.
(4) Names of directors.
(5) Principal activities of the company and of its subsidiaries and any significant changes therein.
(6) Significant changes in fixed assets of the company, or any of its subsidiaries.
(7) An indication of the difference between the book and market values of land and buildings of the company, or any of its subsidiaries, if significant.
(8) In relation to the company and its subsidiaries:
   (a) particulars of any important events which have occurred since the end of the financial year.
   (b) an indication of likely future developments in the business, and
   (c) an indication of any activities in the field of research and development.
(9) Interests in shares or debentures of group companies of each person who was a director of the company at the end of the financial year (this may be given, instead, in the notes to the accounts).
(10) Totals of UK political and charitable contributions of the company (or, if any made by subsidiaries, of the group), unless together not more than £200. The amount and name of political party or person paid for each contribution for political purposes over £200.
(11) Where the company's average number of employees over the financial year exceeds 250, the company's policy as to:
   (a) employment of disabled persons,
   (b) continued employment and training of persons who become disabled while in the company's employment, and
   (c) otherwise for the training, career development and promotion of disabled people.
(12) Comprehensive particulars of the acquisition and disposal by a company of its own shares.

direct tax. A tax which is assessed on and collected from those who are intended to bear it. Examples are income tax, corporation tax, capital transfer tax and capital gains tax. Unlike an INDIRECT TAX, it can take individual circumstances into account.

disclaimer of opinion. *See* AUDIT OPINION.

discounted cash flow. The discounting of expected future cash flows to take account of the TIME VALUE OF MONEY. It is the basis of two methods of CAPITAL INVESTMENT APPRAISAL: NET PRESENT VALUE and INTERNAL RATE OF RETURN.

discovery sampling. In an audit context, a sampling plan designed to control the level of beta risk, i.e., the risk that an auditor will accept a population when he should have rejected it. The auditor must specify a minimum unacceptable error rate together with a predetermined level of beta risk. Discovery sampling leads to smaller sample sizes than ACCEPTANCE SAMPLING but at the expense of a much higher level of alpha risk.

discovery value accounting. Synonym for reserve recognition accounting. *See* OIL AND GAS ACCOUNTING.

discretionary costs. FIXED COSTS that arise from periodic appropriation decisions. It is difficult to establish a best relationship between inputs and outputs in relation to discretionary costs and the value and quality of the outputs may be difficult to ascertain. An obvious example is advertising of which one managing director is supposed to have said: 'half these costs are a waste of money, but I am not sure which half'. An example from the public sector is the costs of travel grants to university researchers. As the latter are painfully aware, discretionary costs can be cut quite sharply and quickly in times of acute financial stress. Control of discretionary costs is difficult and has to be done through NEGOTIATED STATIC BUDGETS. The feedback time is longer than for ENGINEERED COSTS. A favourable discretionary cost variance, unlike a favourable engineered cost variance, may indicate not less costly performance but less output or output of a lower quality.

Not all costs are innately engineering or discretionary and discretionary costs have sometimes been successfully transformed into engineered costs. A discretionary cost may behave as if it were variable if managers are allowed to incur costs in accordance with a formula arbitrarily linked to output. Discretionary costs may be fixed or decision making purposes but variable for control purposes.

dispersion. A measure of the variation of a group of numerical data from a central tendency (e.g., an ARITHMETIC MEAN). Measures of dispersion include the RANGE, the AVERAGE DEVIATION and the STANDARD DEVIATION.

distributable reserves. In the UK, a company's REALIZED PROFITS so far as not previously distributed or capitalized, less its accumulated realized losses so far as not previously written off in a reduction or reorganization of capital. PUBLIC COMPANIES are subject to the further restriction that they may only pay a dividend if their net assets are not less than the aggregate of the called-up share capital and undistributable reserves.

distribution costs. In the UK, an expenditure heading required by two of the four PROFIT AND LOSS ACCOUNT FORMATS. Distribution costs are distinguished from ADMINISTRATIVE EXPENSES but no definitions are provided.

district auditor. In England and Wales, auditors appointed by central government to carry out external audits of local authorities. Local authorities have the right to choose between district auditors and private sector approved auditors, both of whom are responsible to the AUDIT COMMISSION. The duties of district auditors are laid down in the Local Government Finance Act 1982 and include VALUE FOR MONEY AUDITS as well as COMPLIANCE AUDITS.

diversity. The opposite of UNIFORMITY and one of the basic concepts of Grady's 'Inventory of Generally Accepted Accounting Principles for Business Enterprises' (*Accounting Research Study 7*, 1965). Diversity leaves each accounting entity to choose the accounting policies most appropriate to it but requires disclosure of those methods and CONSISTENCY in their application from year to year.

dividend. That part of the profits of a company that is distributed to shareholders. Dividends may be either interim (and normally paid during the financial year) or final (and recommended by the directors for approval by the shareholders at the annual general meeting). Dividends are shown in the appropriation section of the profit and loss account (income statement). A proposed final dividend is shown in the balance sheet as a current liability and in the profit and loss account, even though it is not a legal obligation at the date of the balance sheet. Preference share dividends may be either cumulative or non-cumulative. If they are non-cumulative, shareholders are not entitled to receive later a dividend which has been passed through lack of profits. Arrears of cumulative dividends, on the other hand, must be disclosed in the notes to the accounts and paid before dividends on the ordinary shares are resumed.

dividend control. Limitation of dividend payments by government regulation. Such control has been practised a number of times in the UK. It is not necessarily against the interest of shareholders since the money not paid out may be invested in profitable projects.

dividend cover. The ratio between EARN-INGS PER SHARE (EPS) and ordinary dividend per share. It is a measure of the extent to which current dividends are covered by current earnings and may help in forecasting future dividends. In the UK, where the calculations are complicated by the tax system, SSAP 3 prescribes the calculation of EPS, and hence dividend cover, on the NET BASIS, but the *Financial Times* calculates and reports dividend cover (but not EPS) on a MAXIMUM BASIS.

dividend growth model. A model which makes an assumption about the future growth of dividends. If, for example, the dividends of a company are expected to grow at a constant rate g, which is less than the expected rate of return r, the latter rate can be shown to be equal to

$$\frac{D_1}{P_o} + g$$

where D_1 is the expected dividend at the end of the first period and P_o the share price at the beginning of that period. Dividend growth models are often used in the calculation of a company's COST OF CAPITAL.

dividend policy. A company's policy on the division of its profits between distribution to shareholders as dividends and retention for investment. It has been shown by Miller and Modigliani that the price of a company's ordinary shares is independent of its dividend policy in a perfect CAPITAL MARKET in which there are no risks, no flotation or transaction costs, no government controls and no differential taxation of income and capital gains, and information is freely and immediately available. In practice the capital market is not perfect, retained profits are cheaper than new issues (thus encouraging retention), dividends have informational content (i.e. they alter or confirm investors' beliefs about the future prospects of a company), and investors may for tax reasons prefer capital gains to dividends. Investors may also prefer stable dividends even where earnings fluctuate. Since companies may also wish to avoid having to cut a dividend in a bad year, current dividends become a function not only of current earnings but also of past dividends. Existing shareholders may prefer to limit dividends in order to avoid new issues which would dilute control. In the UK, a number of governments have placed statutory limitations on the size of company dividends. The effect of inflation on dividend policy is uncertain. Directors have to choose between the conflicting needs of retaining a higher proportion of historical cost earnings in order to maintain operating capacity and paying dividends whose value to shareholders does not fall in real terms.

dividend reinvestment plan. A procedure whereby shareholders can automatically reinvest in the same company part or all of the dividends to which they are entitled.

dividend washing. Buying a security just after dividends have been paid and selling it just before the next payment so as to avoid tax on income as distinct from capital gains.

dividend yield. The ratio between a company's dividend per ordinary share and the market price per share. Dividend yields are usually calculated gross of tax and are published daily in newspapers such as the *Financial Times*.

dollar-unit sampling (DUS). US term for MONETARY UNIT SAMPLING (MUS).

dollar value LIFO. In the USA, a form of LIFO used for items that are not physically identical units. To achieve this, dollar value LIFO is based on dollars of constant purchasing power invested in goods. Dollar value LIFO was developed in order to make available to retail enterprises tax benefits already available, in times of rising prices, to manufacturing enterprises.

donated capital. In the USA, the account credited to recognize on the capital and liabilities side of a balance sheet the donation to a company of an asset. In the UK the credit would normally be to a capital reserve.

donationes mortis causa. Gifts made in expectation of death and conditional on the subsequent death of the donor. Unlike GIFTS INTER VIVOS they are revocable during the lifetime of the donor.

dormant companies. In the UK, companies that during any accounting period have had no significant accounting transactions. Such a company, provided that it is a SMALL OR MEDIUM COMPANY and notwithstanding that it is a member of a group, need not appoint auditors. This privilege is granted to no other UK companies.

double account system. In the UK, a method of presenting financial statements formerly used by railways and public utilities. It was mandatory for railway companies from 1868, gas companies from 1871 and electric lighting companies from 1882. It was also used voluntarily by some water, dock and mining companies. The system is no longer used, most of the companies using it having been nationalized after World War II.

Companies using the system were those where a large initial expenditure was necessary but followed only by a need to finance current operations. The main characteristic of the system was the division of the conventional balance sheet into a capital account, setting out the capital raised from issuing shares and debentures and the amount spent on fixed assets, and a general balance sheet setting out the current assets and current liabilities.

double declining balance method. A declining (reducing) balance method of depreciation used in the USA. *See* DEPRECIATION METHODS.

double entry. A system of recording financial events which recognizes that each event has a dual aspect, one of which gives rise to a debit entry, the other to a credit entry. Double entry was first used about the year 1300 in the city states of Northern Italy and first described in a printed book by LUCA PACIOLI in 1494. It remains one of the principal techniques used by accountants.

The rules of double entry can be explained by reference to the ACCOUNTING IDENTITY, or in terms of flows into and out of accounts.

If the accounting equation is written as assets = liabilities + capital then increases on the left-hand side are called debits (abbreviated to Dr.) and increases on the right-hand side are called credits (abbreviated to Cr.). Similarly, decreases on the left-hand side are credits and decreases on the right-hand side debits. The capital item can be broken down into its component parts, so that increases in expenses, taxes charged and dividends (all of which reduce capital) are debits and increases in revenues, retained profits and reserves (all of which increase capital) are credits.

A second way of generating the rules of double entry is to define flows into an account as debits and flows out of an account as credits. The rules in expanded form are: for PERSONAL ACCOUNTS, debit the receiver and credit the giver; for REAL ACCOUNTS, debit what goes in, credit what goes out; and for NOMINAL ACCOUNTS, debit losses and expenses and credit gains.

Debits and credits can also be recorded in MATRIX form. This approach demonstrates that it is the dual aspect rather than making an entry twice which is fundamental. Debits may be represented by rows and credits by columns or vice versa so that an event is represented by one cell in the matrix.

double-entry bookkeeping. A recording system making use of DOUBLE ENTRY. There are many variations but the essentials of double-entry bookkeeping are the analysis of TRANSACTIONS or other EVENTS into DEBIT ENTRIES and CREDIT ENTRIES in one or more JOURNALS; the POSTING of entries from the journals into one or more LEDGERS; and the taking out of a TRIAL BALANCE from which, after the making of appropriate ADJUSTING ENTRIES, a PROFIT AND LOSS ACCOUNT (INCOME STATEMENT) and a BALANCE SHEET can be drawn up. Forms of double-entry bookkeeping have been in use since about 1300 A.D. In the 20th century double-entry bookkeeping has been adapted for use with accounting machines and computers.

double taxation agreements. Agreements between countries to avoid the taxation of the same income in more than one jurisdiction.

doubtful debts. Amounts owing that an enterprise is doubtful of receiving. The debts are not written off as bad (*see* BAD DEBT) but a provision for doubtful (or bad) debts is established by a combination of examination of individual debtors' accounts and of past experience. The provision for doubtful debts may thus be a percentage of gross debtors rather than referring to particular debts. Debtors subsequently recognized as bad are debited to the provision. In the balance sheet the provision is deducted from gross debtors.

dual aspect. *See* DOUBLE ENTRY.

dynamic programming. A technique for solving a series of sequential decisions, so as to optimize over the series of decisions. The models used can be linear or non-linear, deterministic or probabilistic.

E

earned income. In the UK, for tax purposes, income other than INVESTMENT INCOME. Earned income has traditionally been taxed less heavily than 'unearned' investment income.

earnings per share (EPS). The earnings of a company attributable to the ordinary shareholders (common stockholders) divided by the number of ordinary shares. Disclosure of EPS is required by SSAP 3 in the UK and APB Opinion No. 15 in the USA. Both earnings attributable and number of shares are open to many interpretations. It is generally agreed, however, that earnings should be calculated for this purpose before the deduction or addition of EXTRAORDINARY ITEMS but after the deduction of tax and preference dividends and that the weighted average number of ordinary shares in issue during the period should be used.

In the UK, the main problems arise from the imputation system of corporation tax as a result of which there are both constant and variable components in the tax charge (variable, that is, in relation to the proportion of profit distributed by way of dividend). The constant components are corporation tax on taxable income, tax attributable to dividends received, and overseas tax unrelieved because the rate of overseas tax exceeds the rate of UK corporation tax. The variable components are irrecoverable ADVANCE CORPORATION TAX (ACT) and overseas tax unrelieved because dividend payments restrict the double taxation credit available. Earnings may thus be calculated on a net basis (taking account of both constant and variable components), a nil basis (taking account only of the constant components) and a maximum basis (on the assumption that a company has distributed all its earnings and is liable to pay ACT on them). The net basis has the advantage that all the relevant facts are taken into account; the nil basis and the maximum basis that they

are independent of the level of dividend distribution. In practice the net and nil bases give (except for companies relying heavily on overseas income) the same result for most companies. SSAP 3 requires the net basis to be used, and the nil basis EPS also to be shown where the difference is material. The standard does not refer to the maximum basis but this is used by the London *Financial Times* in its calculation of DIVIDEND COVER.

SSAP 3 devotes less attention to the problem of dilution, which is mainly dealt with in attached Guidelines which do not have the force of standard accounting practice. The standard does require, however, the disclosure of 'fully diluted' EPS where this is materially different from 'basic' EPS. Dilution may arise from the existence of shares that may rank for dividend in the future; debentures, loans or preference shares convertible into equity; and options and warrants.

In the USA, the calculation of EPS is not affected by tax complications but the calculation of both 'primary' EPS (which is not the same as 'basic' EPS in the UK) and fully diluted 'EPS' is very complicated. The former requires adjustment for common stock equivalents (i.e., securities whose beneficial value arises from their capability of being converted into, or exchanged for, common stock, instead of for their own periodic cash yields over time, e.g., stock options and warrants); the latter requires adjustment for both common stock equivalents and for other potentially dilutive securities.

earnings yield. The ratio between a company's EARNINGS PER SHARE and the market price per share. It is more usual to express the same relationship in the form of a PRICE-EARNINGS RATIO.

economic consequences of accounting. The impact of accounting reports and especially regulation of their contents on the decision-making behaviour of managers, government, trade unions, investors and creditors. Economic consequences arise in that changes in ACCOUNTING POLICIES may produce changes in the costs incurred and benefits enjoyed by different interested parties. For example, the distribution of wealth among investors may change as may also the allocation of wealth between consumption and investment. It can be argued that law makers and standard setters should overtly take these consequences into account. Interested parties are in any case likely to bring pressure to bear if they feel that their interests are being threatened. An alternative point of view is that yielding to such 'political' pressures removes the credibility of accounting reports as unbiased and neutral representations of operating results and financial position.

It was alleged in the USA, for example, that FAS 8 encouraged companies to hedge against artificial accounting exposure rather than against real economic risks. Partly as a result of pressure from multinational companies FAS 8 has been replaced by FAS 52 (*see* FOREIGN CURRENCY TRANSLATION). In relation to LEASE ACCOUNTING, the capitalization of finance leases has been opposed in the UK and the USA on the grounds that it adversely affects calculations under borrowing power clauses; inhibits some companies from entering into finance (capital) leases by denying them the opportunity of OFF BALANCE SHEET FINANCING; and prejudices their favourable tax treatment. Fear of the last of these held up approval of SSAP 21 by the Institute of Chartered Accountants in Ireland.

economic order quantity. *See* INVENTORY CONTROL.

economic value. An alternative and rather imprecise term for NET PRESENT VALUE in the context of ASSET VALUATION. It is sometimes represented as the ideal measure for which REPLACEMENT COST or NET REALIZABLE VALUE may act as surrogates.

economy. In the context of a VALUE FOR MONEY AUDIT, the acquisition of resources of an appropriate quality at minimum cost. Contrast EFFICIENCY and EFFECTIVENESS.

EEC Accountants Study Group. *See* GROUPE D'ETUDES.

effective annual rate. The relationship between the interest earned or paid in a year and the principal outstanding at the beginning of the year. The effective rate compounded annually produces the same accumulated amount after any specified time as the corresponding nominal rate with more frequent compounding. *See also* ANNUAL PERCENTAGE RATE, FLAT RATE.

effectiveness. The degree of attainment of a predetermined goal. Contrast EFFICIENCY and ECONOMY.

efficiency. Maximization of the amount of output per unit of input. Efficiency can be viewed from a number of aspects, e.g., the minimal use of physical units to achieve a given level of production or service (productive efficiency); optimal allocation of national resources (allocative efficiency); and optimal use of a firm's internal resources (x-efficiency). It can be difficult to reconcile these three approaches to efficiency, especially in the case of publicly owned enterprises such as the nationalized industries in the UK. Efficiency is used in yet another sense in relation to stock markets (*see* EFFICIENT MARKET HYPOTHESIS).

See also EFFECTIVENESS, ECONOMY.

efficiency frontier. A graphical representation in the form of an envelope curve of the EFFICIENT PORTFOLIOS available to an investor.

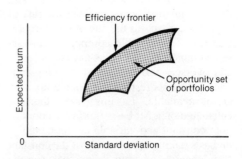

efficiency variance. A variance arising as the result of the actual quantity of inputs differing from the budgeted or standard quantity. The variance is usually calculated by multiplying the quantity difference by the budgeted or standard price. Efficiency variances may be calculated for direct labour, direct materials (where the term usage variance is more common) and variable overhead. A fixed overhead efficiency variance is also sometimes calculated but it is misleading since in the short run fixed costs are not affected by efficiency of operation.

See also JOINT VARIANCE, PRICE VARIANCE, VOLUME VARIANCES.

efficient market hypothesis (EMH). The hypothesis that the stock market is a highly efficient pricing mechanism. Efficiency in this context does not refer to the organizational and operational aspects of the market or to the efficient allocation of resources within the economy but to the capacity of the market to convert information into share prices. There are three forms of the hypothesis:

(a) weak efficiency: share prices move independently of previous movements (also known as the RANDOM WALK HYPOTHESIS);

(b) semi-strong efficiency: share prices respond instantaneously and in an unbiased manner to all information publicly available;

(c) strong efficiency: share prices fully reflect all relevant information including that not publicly available.

The empirical evidence is generally thought to give strong support to hypotheses (a) and (b) but not to (c). If the market is efficient in the semi-strong sense it must also be efficient in the weak sense; if it is efficient in the strong sense it must also be efficient in the weak and semi-strong senses.

Acceptance of hypothesis (a) means rejection of CHARTISM; of hypothesis (b) rejection of the FUNDAMENTAL ANALYSIS of corporate financial reports and other relevant information publicly available; of hypothesis (c) that it is not possible to beat the market by the use of INSIDER DEALING.

Acceptance of the EMH does not mean a belief that the market can predict the future, rather that it takes account of all the uncertainties about the future, i.e., efficiency is not the same as clairvoyance.

A paradox of market efficiency is that those who make the market efficient by responding rapidly and with sophistication to new information substantially eliminate the opportunity to profit personally from their analytical skills. The continuing efficiency of the market may depend on the efforts of analysts who act on the basis that the market is inefficient.

The EMH has implications for both investment strategy and financial reporting. The implications for investment are that a risk-averse investor who wishes to hold equities should hold a well-diversified portfolio (i.e., a combination of shares that, by their interaction with one another, produce efficient diversification) and that once the portfolio has been established the investor should buy and hold since switching securities involves unnecessary transaction costs. The implications for financial reporting by listed companies are that full disclosure to the market and to sophisticated analysts is more important than comprehensibility and simplicity (see SIMPLIFIED FINANCIAL STATEMENTS).

It can be argued that corporate financial reports of listed companies should be divided into a stewardship report for the NAIVE INVESTOR and a market report for the SOPHISTICATED INVESTOR. The latter, but not the former, could contain information which is technically complex, probabilistic and unprocessed and could use MULTI-COLUMN REPORTING.

efficient portfolio. A combination of securities which maximizes the expected return on the securities for a given variance (standard deviation) or, equivalently, minimizes risk for a given expected return. See also EFFICIENCY FRONTIER.

Eighth Directive. A DIRECTIVE on company law approved by the EEC in 1984. The directive, which applies to all member states of the EEC, deals with various aspects of the qualification of professionals who may be authorized to carry out legally required audits. The directive does not deal with freedom of establishment and gives a discretionary power to member states to determine the conditions of independence for a statutory auditor.

electronic funds transfer (EFT). Systems for the transfer of money in which processes based on paper are replaced by electronic techniques. On-line EFT systems make possible the instantaneous transfer of funds (which has implications for CASH MANAGEMENT) and calculation of account balances. Electronic funds transfer at the point of sale (EFTPOS) enables retail customers and others to pay for goods by instantaneous bank transfer. The spread of EFT thus has important implications for accountants and auditors.

employee report. A corporate financial report to employees, published either separately or as a supplement to a house magazine. Employee reports are often also made available to shareholders and to other interested parties. They should not be confused with EMPLOYMENT REPORTS. It is argued that employee reports influence employee behaviour by improving motivation and job satisfaction and helping to avoid industrial conflict; influence employee attitudes by improving understanding of the business; satisfy the employees' right to know about the company; and influence outsiders by demonstrating the progressiveness of the company. There is little empirical evidence about these suggested influences.

Not much is known about how, if at all, the employees' need for information differs from that of investors. It is sometimes suggested that in addition to the type of information provided to investors, employees need information about their own work unit and the security of their jobs and about the labour force of the company as a whole (as may be provided in an employment report).

Employee reports in practice tend to give prominence to value added statements and funds statements rather than to profit and loss accounts and balance sheets and to present information in simplified and graphic form (*see* SIMPLIFIED FINANCIAL STATEMENTS). Employee reports are not audited, although they may be based largely on information taken from audited accounts.

employment report. A report, included in a company's annual report, giving details of such matters as numbers of employees, their age and sex distribution, their geographical location, the costs (including pensions and fringe benefits) of employing them, training schemes and costs, recognized trade unions, and health and safety measures. The publication of an employment report is recommended in THE CORPORATE REPORT but it is not common practice in the UK. Legislation requires, however, the publication of some employment and health and safety information in the DIRECTORS' REPORT and notes to the accounts.

The publication of employment reports has progressed further in France where, as a result of a recommendation in the SUDREAU REPORT followed by the law of 12 July 1977 and related decrees, companies with 300 or more employees are required to publish a *bilan social* (literally, social balance sheet), i.e., to provide information on employment (in great detail), wages and related costs, health and safety conditions, other working conditions, training, industrial relations and other matters relating to the quality of life at work.

Employment reports may be considered as one aspect of SOCIAL RESPONSIBILITY REPORTING. They should not be confused with EMPLOYEE REPORTS.

engagement letter. *See* LETTER OF ENGAGEMENT.

engineered costs. Costs that have an explicit specified relationship with a selected measure of activity. The value and quality of the outputs that result are usually relatively easy to ascertain. An example of an engineered cost is the cost of direct materials. Engineered costs are controlled through the use of flexible budgets and standards. The history of control systems is in part the history of attempts, sometimes successful, to turn DISCRETIONARY COSTS into engineered costs.

entity view. A view of an enterprise or

group of enterprises that stresses the importance of the enterprise itself rather than its owners, i.e., in terms of the ACCOUNTING IDENTITY, assets equals claims on assets, whether by proprietors or creditors. The distinction between the entity view and the PROPRIETARY VIEW is of great importance in such areas as INFLATION ACCOUNTING, where it gives support to CURRENT COST ACCOUNTING rather than CURRENT PURCHASING POWER ACCOUNTING, and CONSOLIDATED FINANCIAL STATEMENTS. An entity view of enterprise appeals more to managers and employees than to proprietors.

entropy. In CYBERNETICS, the tendency of any closed system to move from a less to a more probable state.

entry. The record of a TRANSACTION or other EVENT in a JOURNAL or a LEDGER.

entry values. In the context of ASSET VALUATION, values based on purchase prices in a market either at the date of acquisition (HISTORICAL COST) or at the date of a balance sheet (current REPLACEMENT COST). Contrast EXIT VALUES.

equities. A synonym for ordinary shares (UK) and common stock (USA).

equity. Normally used as a synonym for OWNERS' EQUITY but a distinction can be made between the EQUITIES of owners and creditors, especially if one takes an ENTITY VIEW of an enterprise.

equity accounting. A method of accounting for investments in ASSOCIATED COMPANIES (broadly companies in which an investor company has a minority ownership but exercises a significant influence) in which credit is taken for a share of profits (or losses) rather than dividends and the investment is carried not at cost but at cost plus a share of undistributed profits (with or without an adjustment for GOODWILL). Equity accounting is sometimes known as one-line consolidation. Since assets, liabilities and profits are not brought in 100%, no figure for minority interest arises under this method.

The use of equity accounting in consolidated financial statements produces the same EARNINGS PER SHARE as would full consolidation and decreases the scope for manipulation of results by slight variations in shareholdings but CREATIVE ACCOUNTING is still possible on the borderline between associated companies and investments.

A distinction can be made (although the terms are not in common use in the UK or the USA) between the 'cost based equity method', in which an investment is valued at cost plus a proportionate share of the retained profits (or accumulated losses) since the date of acquisition, and the 'pure equity method' in which the cost figure is decreased or increased by the goodwill element (positive or negative) at the date of acquisition. In the UK, SSAP 1 (as revised) requires use of the former method, but with disclosure of the amount which represents goodwill. In the USA, Accounting Principles Board Opinion No. 18 requires use of the latter method and the amortization of the goodwill.

In the UK, equity accounting can only be implemented in consolidated financial statements. In the USA, however, it can also be used in the accounts of the investor company.

Equity accounting is also used in the case of subsidiaries excluded from full consolidation.

equity capital. A synonym for ORDINARY SHARES. EQUITY SHARE CAPITAL has a legal definition which includes participating preference shares as well as ordinary shares.

equity method. *See* EQUITY ACCOUNTING.

equity share capital. In the UK, the issued share capital of a company except shares limited to a specified amount as regards dividend and capital. Thus, in law if not always in business practice, equity share capital includes participating preference shares as well as ordinary shares.

equivalent units. Output expressed in terms not of physical quantities but the amount of resources (materials, labour, overhead) applied. Equivalent units are used mainly in PROCESS COSTING.

error. A FUNDAMENTAL ERROR, a departure from an INTERNAL CONTROL procedure or a clerical error. Departures from internal control procedure should be discovered by an auditor through COMPLIANCE TESTS. Clerical errors may be errors of principle, errors of original entry, errors of omission, errors of commission or compensating errors (*see* TRIAL BALANCE). It is necessary for an auditor to decide that level of error which he is prepared to accept.

estate duty. A tax on wealth passing at the time of death, introduced in the UK in 1894 and abolished in 1975. The tax was regarded as relatively easy to avoid and never formed a large part of total tax revenue. It was replaced by CAPITAL TRANSFER TAX.

estimation sampling. In an audit context, estimating the population values of variables (e.g., total sales), or attributes (e.g., the proportion of particular types of sales to total sales) from a sample.

ethics. *See* PROFESSIONAL ETHICS, QUESTIONABLE PAYMENTS.

European currency unit (ECU). A notional currency based upon a basket of the currencies of the member states of the European Monetary System (EMS), which dates from 1979. The member states are those of the European Community (EC) except the UK and Greece. The accounts of the EC bodies are kept in ECUs and currency amounts in directives and regulations are denominated therein.

European economic interest grouping. A proposed EEC business organization based upon the French *groupement d'interêt économique*. It is of the nature of a joint venture.

event. In an accounting context, a TRANSACTION or other internal or external change recognized by a recording system. Which events are recorded depends upon whether HISTORICAL COST ACCOUNTING (HCA) or some form of INFLATION ACCOUNTING is used. Unmodified HCA, for example, does not regard as events a change in the NET REALIZABLE VALUE or REPLACEMENT COST of a FIXED ASSET or a change in the GENERAL PRICE LEVEL. All events can be expressed in terms of DEBIT ENTRIES and CREDIT ENTRIES.

evidence. *See* AUDIT EVIDENCE.

ex. A Latin word meaning without. Thus: ex dividend, ex rights, etc.

'except for'/'with the exception of' opinion. *See* AUDIT OPINION.

exceptional items. Items which are exceptional on account of size and/or incidence but derive from the ordinary activities of a business. In the UK, SSAP 6 refers to size *and* incidence, whereas the Companies Act 1981, which requires their disclosure, refers to size *or* incidence. In practice they cannot always be sharply distinguished from EXTRAORDINARY ITEMS. In particular there is no uniformity of practice in the UK in the treatment of sales of fixed assets and redundancy costs.

excess burden of taxation. A cost arising from a tax which is not compensated for by a benefit, thus leading to a loss of economic welfare.

Exchequer and Audit Department. Former name of NATIONAL AUDIT OFFICE.

excise duties. Taxes levied on goods manufactured and consumed within a country. An excise duty may be imposed as a unit tax or may be AD VALOREM. In the UK the most important excise duties are those levied on such goods as hydrocarbons, tobacco, spirits, beer and wine.

executor (executrix). The person appointed by a will to administer the estate of a deceased testator.

executorship accounts. Accounts relating to the estate of a deceased person. The form of accounts is similar to that of TRUST ACCOUNTS in general.

executory contract. A mutually unexecuted contract, i.e., one in which two parties have agreed to make a transfer of resources but neither has yet done so. Examples are contracts for the future supply of raw materials and some leasing contracts. According to conventional accounting, such contracts do not give rise to assets and liabilities.

exempt private company. A category of company established in the UK by the Companies Act 1948. It was essentially a family company which had the privilege of not filing its financial statements with the REGISTRAR OF COMPANIES. Exempt private companies were abolished by the Companies Act 1967, but the Companies Act 1981 created a class of 'small companies' that need only file an abridged balance sheet with the Registrar.

exit values. In the context of ASSET VALUATION, values based on sale prices in a market at the date of a balance sheet, i.e., NET REALIZABLE VALUES. Contrast ENTRY VALUES.

expected value of imperfect information. The maximum amount that a decision maker should be willing to pay for imperfect information. It is equal to the expected value with imperfect information (i.e., extra but not perfect information) less expected value with existing information.

expected value of perfect information (EVPI). The maximum amount that a decision maker should be willing to pay for perfect information. It is equal to expected value with perfect information less expected value with existing information. EVPI is the weighted average cost of PREDICTION ERROR where the weights are the probabilities of the various events occurring.

expenditure tax. A tax based on consumption expenditure rather than on income. A form of expenditure tax was recommended by the UK Meade Committee in 1978.

expired cost. An historical cost whose utility has expired and which is therefore written off against income.

exponential constant. The base of natural or Napierian logarithms, denoted by e, and equal to 2.71828. Its use is necessary whenever continuous compounding of interest is assumed.

exposure draft. A draft of, for example, a proposed accounting standard, published for comment by interested parties.

external financing limit (EFL). In the UK, the total of grants, net borrowing, capital value of leases and public dividend capital made available annually to a nationalized industry, i.e., a CASH LIMIT on spending during a financial year. The EFL takes account of the capital requirements of the industry and the internal resources (gross of depreciation) that it can generate.

externalities. Benefits and costs which are not received or borne by the enterprise responsible for them and hence do not usually appear in their accounting records. An example of an external cost is a factory polluting the surrounding environment. Externalities arise because of the existence of MARKET FAILURE.

extraordinary items. Items that derive from events or transactions outside the ordinary activities of a business and which are both material and expected not to recur frequently or regularly (the UK definition in SSAP 6; APB Opinion No. 30 in the USA refers in rather similar terms to events and transactions that are distinguished by their unusual nature and by the infrequency of their occurrence). Extraordinary items are shown BELOW THE LINE in the profit and loss account (income statement) and thus do not affect the calculation of EARNINGS PER SHARE. They are distinguished in principle from EXCEPTIONAL ITEMS, which are shown ABOVE THE LINE.

In the UK, the Companies Act 1981 requires the separate disclosure, where material, of extraordinary income, extraordinary charges, extraordinary profit or loss and tax on extraordinary profit or loss.

In practice in the UK extraordinary and exceptional items are not sharply distinguished; in particular, companies differ in their treatment of sales of fixed assets and redundancy costs. This may be due to lack of a clear definition of what are ordinary activities. The US definition is more precise, stating that 'the underlying event or transaction should possess a high degree of abnormality and be of a type clearly unrelated to, or only incidentally related to, the ordinary and typical activities of the entity, taking into account the environment in which the entity operates'.

US standard accounting practice is to show the disposal of a business segment and unusual or infrequent items separately from extraordinary items. The profit or loss on terminated activities is usually classified as extraordinary in the UK.

F

factor analysis. The statistical analysis of a multivariate set of observations in terms of a set of hypothetical components or factors.

factoring. The sale by an enterprise of its debts to a factor who not only collects the debts but may also provide administrative and bookkeeping services and credit insurance facilities. In deciding on whether to factor debts, the enterprise must weigh the advantages of improved liquidity, less uncertainty and a smaller administrative load against the charges made by the factor.

factory burden. Synonym for FACTORY OVERHEAD.

factory overhead. All costs associated with a manufacturing process other than direct materials and direct labour. They are also referred to as indirect manufacturing costs, factory burden, manufacturing overhead and manufacturing expenses. Variable factory overhead is usually distinguished from fixed factory overhead.

feedback. In an accounting context, information about performance furnished to the persons responsible for that performance. It is especially important when PARTICIPATIVE BUDGETING is used. The comparison of planned and actual performance enables corrective adjustments to be made in objectives or performance or both. Feedback is an important factor in motivating organizationally desirable actions in future periods.

fellow subsidiaries. Companies that are subsidiaries of the same company but not of each other.

fiar. The Scottish equivalent of the English REMAINDERMAN.

fiat measurement. A measurement which is arrived at in an apparently arbitrary manner.

Finance Act. An Act of the British Parliament imposing and changing central government taxes. There is at least one Finance Act each year.

finance lease. *See* LEASE ACCOUNTING.

financial accounting. That part of accounting which is concerned mainly with external reporting to shareholders, government and other users of accounting outside the enterprise. It emphasizes the stewardship rather than the control or decision-making aspects of accounting and is heavily constrained by legal regulation (e.g., company law in the UK and the rules of the SEC in the USA) and ACCOUNTING STANDARDS. It may be contrasted with MANAGEMENT ACCOUNTING.

Financial Accounting Foundation. In the USA, a body whose responsibilities include raising funds to support the FINANCIAL ACCOUNTING STANDARDS BOARD (FASB), appointing members of the FASB and the FINANCIAL ACCOUNTING STANDARDS ADVISORY COUNCIL, and periodically reviewing the standard-setting process.

Financial Accounting Standards Advisory Council. In the USA, the body that advises the FINANCIAL ACCOUNTING STANDARDS BOARD on establishing priorities and reviews proposed standards. It has an advisory role only.

Financial Accounting Standards Board (FASB). Since 1973, the board responsible for developing accounting standards in the USA. Its predecessors were the COMMITTEE ON ACCOUNTING PROCEDURE (1936-59) and the ACCOUNTING PRINCIPLES BOARD (1959-73). Unlike its predecessors and the UK ACCOUNTING STANDARDS COMMITTEE, membership of the FASB is small (seven), full-time, and well paid. The board is not wholly composed of practising CPAs. Members are appointed by the FINANCIAL ACCOUNTING FOUNDATION and advised by the FINANCIAL

ACCOUNTING STANDARDS ADVISORY COUNCIL. In developing standards the FASB follows a complex due process procedure that for major projects includes task forces, discussion memoranda, public hearings and exposure drafts. The FASB issues Statements of Financial Accounting Standards, which are officially recognised as authoritative by the SECURITIES AND EXCHANGE COMMISSION and by the American Institute of Certified Public Accountants, STATEMENTS OF FINANCIAL ACCOUNTING CONCEPTS, Interpretations, and Technical Bulletins.

financial budget. That part of the MASTER BUDGET of an organization which deals with such matters as cash and capital expenditures, and *pro forma* balance sheets and funds statements.

financial capital maintenance. *See* CAPITAL MAINTENANCE CONCEPT.

financial failure. A term covering both 'economic failure', i.e. achieving a rate of return, adjusted for risk, significantly lower than the prevailing rate of interest, and 'legal failure' (i.e. INSOLVENCY, the use of the word legal being rather a misnomer).

financial intermediaries. Persons and institutions who collect funds and invest them on behalf of others, e.g., unit trusts (US: mutual funds), investment trusts, pension funds.

financial leverage. *See* GEARING (LEVERAGE).

financial mathematics. The mathematics of COMPOUND INTEREST and ANNUITIES.

financial modelling. That part of CORPORATE MODELLING concerned with the construction and use of computer-based models to carry out the calculations necessary to produce financial statements based on given sets of assumptions and predictions. *See also* FINANCIAL PLANNING MODELS.

financial planning. That part of long-range planning concerned with the financial aspects of a company's objectives, and strategies for meeting those objectives. It involves forecasting future capital expenditures and working capital and their financing from operations or from new issues of shares or debentures, i.e., forecasting, for several years ahead, profit and loss accounts, balance sheets and funds statements. Such forecasting usually involves many uncertainties. These can be better appreciated, but not removed, by the use of computer-based SENSITIVITY ANALYSIS and FINANCIAL MODELLING.

financial planning models. Mathematical statements of the relationships among all the operating and financial activities of an organization, account being taken of relevant outside factors. Financial planning models are usually computer-based and give the opportunity to test (by SENSITIVITY ANALYSIS) the effects of changes in assumptions and forecasts. They may be general purpose or specially tailored to a particular organization. *See also* FINANCIAL MODELLING.

financial ratio. Relationships among items in financial statements. They are normally expressed in either ratio form, e.g.,

current assets/current liabilities = 2.0

or in percentage form (e.g., current liabilities are 50% of current assets). Which form is chosen is a matter of convenience and convention. Financial ratios are used in the assessment of profitability, liquidity and capital structure and are widely recognized as useful guides to business performance. A financial ratio should not, however, be used in isolation and the limitations of conventional accounting should be borne in mind. Financial ratios are most useful in comparisons: actual ratios may be compared with budgeted ratios; a series of ratios for a business may be compared over time; ratios for one business may be compared with those of others or with the average ratios for an industry.

financial risk. Risk which results from an increase in GEARING (LEVERAGE). Contrast BUSINESS RISK.

Financial Statement and Budget Report. A summary of the central government accounts published annually by the UK government.

financial statements. Statements giving financial information about an accounting entity. The traditional financial statements are the BALANCE SHEET and the PROFIT AND LOSS ACCOUNT (income statement). Many enterprises in the UK and the USA also publish a FUNDS STATEMENT. The UK CORPORATE REPORT recommended the publication of six additional statements of which only the VALUE ADDED STATEMENT has proved to be popular. *See also* GENERAL PURPOSE FINANCIAL STATEMENTS; SIMPLIFIED FINANCIAL STATEMENTS. In the UK, financial statements are often referred to as ACCOUNTS.

financial structure. Synonym for CAPITAL STRUCTURE.

***Financial Times* share indices**. Measures of the behaviour of the London stock market published daily by the London *Financial Times*. The best known is the *Financial Times* Industrial Ordinary Share Index (the 'FT Index'), which has 30 constituent companies. The index is calculated as an unweighted geometric mean. The FT-Actuaries All Share Index covers the whole of the UK equity market and is published together with about 40 component indices. There are also FT-Actuaries Fixed Interest Indices. A real-time *Financial Times*-Stock Exchange (FTSE) 100-share index was introduced in 1984.

financial year. An accounting period of twelve months or (sometimes) 52 weeks. For many companies in the UK and USA the financial year coincides with the calendar year. The financial year for UK corporation tax runs from April 1 to March 31 of the subsequent year, whereas the income tax year runs from April 6 to April 5. The explanation of this curiosity is that the most important financial days in England and Wales were originally the quarter days, including March 25 (Lady Day). April 5 is eleven days after March 25, the eleven days

being those 'lost' when the calendar was reformed in 1752. In UK company law a financial year is any period (not necessarily of 12 months) in respect of which a profit and loss account is drawn up. In the USA the term FISCAL YEAR is commonly used instead of financial year.

first in first out (FIFO). In the context of INVENTORY VALUATION, the calculation of the cost of inventories (stocks and work in progress) on the basis that the quantities in hand represent those most recently purchased or produced. FIFO is the most popular method in the UK of calculating the historical cost of stocks and work in progress. Compared with the LAST IN FIRST OUT (LIFO) method, FIFO normally results, in times of rising prices, in a lower cost of goods sold figure (and therefore a higher profit figure) and in a higher asset valuation in the balance sheet.

first year allowance. In the UK, a CAPITAL ALLOWANCE granted in the first year of purchase of plant and machinery. First year allowances from 1970 onwards were as high as 100% but the Finance Act 1984 introduced a new and less generous policy. In subsequent years an annual WRITING-DOWN ALLOWANCE is granted.

fisc. The persons and institutions responsible in any country for the assessment and collection of taxes.

fiscal drag. The action of a progressive tax system in taking an increasing portion of the national income as nominal incomes rise over time (whether from inflation or an increase in real output per head or both). Fiscal drag can be countered by INDEXATION.

fiscal year. US term for what is usually called FINANCIAL YEAR in the UK, where fiscal year refers to the tax year.

Fisher effect. The hypothesis, named after the economist Irving Fisher, that the nominal rate of interest embodies in it an inflation premium sufficient, on a one-for-one basis, to compensate lenders for the expected loss of purchasing power associated with inflation. In an international context, the hypothesis is that, between two countries, the differential in interest rates earned on similar financial assets is equal to the expected change in the exchange rate.

Fitzgerald, A.A. (1890-1969). A leading Australian practitioner and academic who was the first professor of accounting at an Australian university. Sir Alexander Fitzgerald was also editor of *The Australian Accountant* from 1936 to 1954, a prolific writer and chairman of many government committees. A chronology of his life and a list of his writings (from 1928 to 1965) is given in R.J. Chambers, L. Goldberg and R.L. Mathews, *The Accounting Frontier* (Melbourne: F.W. Cheshire, 1966). Fitzgerald's writings reflect a knowledge of and a keen interest in British and American accounting as well as Australian.

fixed assets. ASSETS that are intended for use on a continuing basis in an enterprise's activities. This definition, long accepted in practice, has received legal recognition in Britain in the Companies Act 1981. Since that Act, any asset which is not a fixed asset is deemed to be a CURRENT ASSET. In particular, investments must be classified in company balance sheets as either fixed or current. The compulsory BALANCE SHEET FORMATS of the Act sub-divide fixed assets into INTANGIBLE ASSETS, TANGIBLE ASSETS and INVESTMENTS. In US usage intangibles are not regarded as fixed assets.

fixed charge. A charge which is attached to some specific asset or assets. *See also* FLOATING CHARGE.

fixed cost. A cost which remains unchanged for a given time period and over a RELEVANT RANGE of activity. Contrast VARIABLE COST. *See also* COMMITTED COSTS, DISCRETIONARY COSTS.

flat rate. A rate of interest applied to the original sum in a contract rather than to the reducing balance, and therefore potentially misleading. For example, if the cash price of a household item is £400 and it can be purchased for 12 monthly instalments of £35 each (£420 in all), the flat rate is 5% p.a. but the monthly rate of interest is approximately ¾% and the EFFECTIVE ANNUAL RATE approximately 9.4%. Consumer credit regulations in the UK require the disclosure of this rate, known as the ANNUAL PERCENTAGE RATE (APR).

flat yield. A yield which does not take account of the REDEMPTION value of an investment.

flexible budget. A BUDGET that is adjusted for changes in volume over a RELEVANT RANGE of activity. It is usually based on linear cost-volume-profit relationships.

floating assets. Obsolete term for CURRENT ASSETS.

floating charge. A charge which is not attached to any specific asset but to all assets or to a class of assets (e.g. stock and work in progress). A floating charge, unlike a FIXED CHARGE, allows a company to dispose of the assets charged in the usual course of business without obtaining special permission from the lender.

flotation costs. The costs arising from an issue on a stock exchange of shares or other securities.

flow chart. In general, a graph displaying the sequence of operations. More particularly, a diagram showing the operations to be performed by a computer.

flow of funds accounts. In the context of NATIONAL ACCOUNTING, accounts showing both financial and non-financial flows through the sectors of an economy. They measure changes in the financial structure of the economy and in the financial relationships between different sectors and illustrate the dependence of financial and non-financial flows. Barter transactions and depreciation are not recorded, since they do not involve financial flows. For each sector, uses of funds (debits) and sources of funds (credits) are shown. Flow of funds accounts are analogous to the FUNDS STATEMENTS of business enterprises.

folio. The name (derived from the Italian *foglio*) used by accountants to denote a page of a JOURNAL or LEDGER.

forecast reporting. The reporting of projected data to external users of financial statements. Forecast reporting is recommended in both the UK CORPORATE REPORT (1975) and the US TRUEBLOOD REPORT (1973), the former proposing as an additional statement a statement of future prospects, showing likely future profit, employment and investment levels. These recommendations have not been followed up by the FASB or the ASC.

The publication of forecasts has never been prohibited in the UK. Detailed, quantitative forecasts are provided in PROSPECTUSES and during takeover battles. In the annual financial statements they tend to be brief and mainly qualitative; to the extent that they are quantitative they contain ORDINAL NUMBERS rather than CARDINAL NUMBERS. Forecasts in prospectuses are reviewed by auditors who report whether they have been properly compiled on the bases and assumptions made by the directors and whether they are presented on bases consistent with the accounting policies normally adopted by the company. Forecasts in the annual financial statements are not audited. Forecast reporting is becoming more popular in the USA and the AICPA now permits audits of financial forecasts, i.e., those based on the 'most probable' financial figures of an accounting entity in one or more future periods.

The US empirical evidence suggests that investors view managerial forecasts as providing useful information; UK empirical evidence suggests that forecasts are reasonably accurate.

Foreign Corrupt Practices Act. A US federal Act passed in 1977 ostensibly to combat corporate bribery and illegal business practices. The Act requires companies under SEC jurisdiction (whether or not they do business outside the USA) to maintain proper books, records and accounts and an adequate system of INTERNAL CONTROL. Documentation of the evaluation of internal control by management has thus been made mandatory.

foreign currency translation. The restatement of accounts or transactions in one currency into another currency. The translation may be of a set of financial statements, prepared in a local currency, of a foreign subsidiary or branch which has to be consolidated with the statements, prepared in the home currency, of a parent company. Alternatively, the translation may be of transactions involving a currency other than the one in which a company's own accounts are kept (*see* FOREIGN EXCHANGE TRANSACTION). Translation has become an important practical problem in recent years because of the increase in overseas operations by companies and the severe fluctuations in exchange rates especially since 1971.

If exchange rates are not fixed the accountant must decide what rate or rates of exchange to use in translation and how to account for any gain or loss that may arise. The choice of rates is between historic (i.e. at the date the balance was established) and closing (also known as current, i.e. at the date the translation is being made).

The three traditional translation methods used for balance sheets are (a) the closing rate method, which uses the closing rate for all assets and liabilities; (b) the current/non-current method, which uses the closing rate for current assets and current liabilities, and the historic rate for all other assets and liabilities; and (c) the monetary/non-monetary method, which uses the closing rate for monetary items and the historic rate for non-monetary items. Method (a) assumes that all assets and liabilities are subject to translation gain or loss; method (b) only current assets and liabilities; and method (c) only monetary assets and liabilities. The three methods can produce widely different translated balance sheets, profit figures and translation gains or losses.

Translation gains and losses can be accounted for in three ways: in the income statement, as an ordinary item affecting earnings per share; in the income statement, as an extraordinary item; or in the balance sheet.

A possible way to choose translation rates is to use the temporal principle, which states that the valuation methods used in the local currency balance sheet should be retained in the translated statements. Applied to conventional statements prepared on a basis of historical cost modified by prudence, the temporal principle produces results very similar to those of the monetary/non-monetary method, the main difference being that stocks (inventories) measured at net realizable value are translated at a closing rate and not at an historic rate. In 1975 the US Financial Accounting Standards Board issued FAS 8 which made the temporal method (i.e. the application of the temporal principle to conventional statements) obligatory and required exchange gains and losses to be treated as ordinary items in the income statement.

FAS 8 became very unpopular with US companies since it coincided with a weakening of the dollar and obliged them to record translation losses on foreign currency borrowings (even long-term borrowings) whilst no translation gain could be recorded in respect of foreign fixed assets acquired with the proceeds of the borrowings. It was claimed that this did not accord with economic reality and would lead management to make incorrect decisions.

The UK and other countries have been slower to issue accounting standards in this area, the UK Accounting Standards Committee, for example, being unwilling to ban either the temporal method, given its adoption in FAS 8, or the closing rate method since this is the one used by most UK companies.

As a result of the dissatisfaction with FAS 8, the need in an area of vital concern for multinational companies for harmonization between countries, and an unwillingness to abandon historical cost accounting, the net investment concept has been developed. Under this concept it is argued that the investment of a company is in the net worth of its foreign subsidiary rather than a direct investment in the individual assets and liabilities. The foreign subsidiary will normally have partly financed its net assets by local currency borrowings and its day-to-day operations will not normally be dependent on the reporting currency of the investing company. (*See* FUNCTIONAL CURRENCY.) The difficulty with this approach is that it appears to remove the rationale for full consolidated statements. In the absence of consolidation, foreign currency translation becomes unnecessary. The accounting standards issued by the USA, the UK and the IASC (see below) thus appear to have shaky conceptual foundations but they may perhaps be regarded as successful in removing the undesirable economic consequences of FAS 8.

The US, UK and international accounting standards on foreign currency translation (FAS 52, SSAP 20 and IAS 21) differ only slightly. If the operations of the foreign entity are not regarded as an integral part of those of the parent, assets and liabilities are to be translated at the closing rate and income statement items at the average rate for the period (SSAP 20 and IAS 21 also allow closing rate). In general, translation gains and losses are not passed through the income statement.

If the operations of the foreign entity are regarded as integral to those of the parent, the temporal method is to be used, with all gains and losses taken to the income statement except that deferral of gains and losses on long-term monetary items is permitted.

Fluctuations in exchange rates have been accompanied by high rates of inflation in many countries, hence there has been a need to combine currency translation with inflation accounting. It is not satisfactory to use the former as a substitute for the latter since in the short run changes in exchange rates and internal prices take place at different rates. Two procedures are possible: translate/restate, i.e. translate the local currency statements into the home currency and then restate them to take account of price changes; and restate/translate, the reverse procedure. Which procedure is appropriate depends on the method of inflation accounting that is used: translate/restate is appropriate for current purchasing power (constant dollar) accounting; restate/translate for current cost accounting. This is because the purchasing power of the home (reporting) currency is relevant to the shareholders of the holding company whilst replacement reporting costs in the home country are not relevant for local assets.

FAS 52, SSAP 20 and IAS 21 all refer to the translation of non-monetary assets in hyper-inflationary economies. FAS 52 requires the use of historical rates; SSAP 20 calls for restatement for inflation followed by use of the closing rate; IAS 21 prefers restatement/translation but permits historical rates.

foreign exchange risk. The risk of loss from carrying out operations, or holding assets and liabilities, in a foreign currency. The size of the risk has increased in recent years because of the growth in international trade and financing and the increased magnitude of exchange rate fluctuations, especially since 1971. Also, foreign currency losses and gains have become more visible in published company financial statements. A company's exposure to foreign exchange risk may be measured in economic terms using discounted cash flows, or in conventional accounting terms. It is the latter which are reported in published financial statements.

It is necessary for a company to decide whether to be a risk minimizer adopting a defensive strategy or a profit maximizer adopting an aggressive strategy. The techniques for managing foreign exchange exposure, i.e., for avoiding risk, may be classified as internal or external.

The internal techniques include the following: (a) minimizing the number of foreign currency transactions by bilateral or multilateral netting of payments and receipts with trading partners; (b) the matching of currency inflows and outflows and of assets and liabilities; (c) leading and lagging, i.e., prepaying or delaying payment in line with forecast exchange rate movements; (d) adjusting pricing policies; (e) trying to invoice exports in relatively strong currencies and imports in relatively weak currencies (if adopting an aggressive strategy) or invoicing in the home currency (if adopting a defensive strategy); (f) trying to ensure that exposed assets, revenues and cash flows are denominated in strong rather than weak currencies (if adopting an aggressive strategy) or seeking to minimize exposure in any foreign currency (if adopting a defensive strategy).

The external techniques available include: (a) hedging by the use of FORWARD EXCHANGE CONTRACTS and short-term borrowing; (b) discounting foreign currency bills receivable; (c) factoring foreign currency receivables; (d) taking advantage of government exchange risk guarantees; (e) swaps, i.e., the simultaneous buying and selling of a foreign currency for different maturities.

Some of the above techniques may be prohibited or made difficult in certain circumstances by exchange control or tax regulations.

foreign exchange transaction. An accounting transaction involving a currency other than that in which an enterprise's accounts are kept. Such transactions are normally translated using the rate of exchange at the date of the transaction. Where there is a related or matching FORWARD EXCHANGE CONTRACT the rate of exchange specified in the contract may be used. Exchange gains and losses on settled transactions are reported as part of the profit or loss for the year from ordinary activities.

forfeited shares. In the UK, shares forfeited, in accordance with a company's ARTICLES OF ASSOCIATION, for non-payment of CALLS. A public company may sell forfeited shares or cancel them and reduce the share capital accordingly. A private company may, subject to its articles, treat forfeited shares as it pleases.

Form 10-K. An annual report required to be filed under the US Securities Acts. Part 1 contains information about the registrant and his business. Part II contains financial statements and other related information. *See also* SECURITIES AND EXCHANGE COMMISSION.

Form 10-Q. A quarterly report required to be filed under the US Securities Acts. Its most important contents are INTERIM FINAN-CIAL STATEMENTS.

formation expenses. Synonym for PRELIMINARY EXPENSES.

forward exchange contract. An agreement to exchange different currencies at a specified future date and at a specified rate. The difference between the specified rate and the spot rate ruling on the date the contract was entered into is the discount or premium on the contract.

founders' shares. Synonym for DEFERRED SHARES.

Fourth Directive. A directive on company law approved by the EEC in 1978 and being implemented by the member states in the 1980s (in the UK by the Companies Act 1981). The directive changes the law relating to company accounting considerably in all member states, but its harmonizing effects are limited by the large number of options allowed (e.g., in relation to inflation accounting) and by its lack of applicability to consolidated financial statements. It covers both public and private companies and deals with valuation rules, formats of financial statements and disclosure requirements. The amount of disclosure required is governed by three size criteria (turnover, balance sheet total and number of employees).

franked investment income (FII). Dividends received by companies from other UK resident companies and paid out of income which has borne corporation tax. FII is not taxable in the hands of the recipient company but neither can the company benefit from the accompanying tax credit, since companies do not pay income tax. The recipient company can, however, use FII to reduce its payment of ADVANCE CORPORATION TAX (ACT) on distribution of a dividend.

In accordance with UK standard accounting practice (SSAP 8), FII is grossed up in the profit and loss account of the recipient company and the corporation tax charge increased accordingly.

franked SORPs. In the UK, statements of recommended practice (SORPs) prepared by a body other than the Accounting Standards Committee (ASC) and franked (i.e., approved) by the ASC. They usually relate to topics of limited application.

free riders. Users of PUBLIC GOODS who do not pay for them but cannot be easily excluded from consuming them. Once a company has published accounting information, for example, it becomes freely available to everyone. Since the users of the information do not have to pay for it, the price mechanism does not operate and they are likely to ask for more and more information. In an unregulated economy, providers of information are likely to provide only such amounts as deemed necessary to attract investment and it may therefore be under-provided. It can be argued, therefore, that regulation is necessary to protect the interests of, especially, NAIVE INVESTORS.

full costing method. See OIL AND GAS AC-COUNTING.

full cost pricing. Basing prices on the full costs of products, i.e., on product costs based on ABSORPTION COSTING and NORMAL VOLUMES, plus a mark-up. Full cost pricing is more common in practice than MARGINAL COST PRICING, possibly because whilst the latter provides a minimum price, full cost pricing provides a relatively safe starting point from which management can use its judgment as to how much, in the light of anticipated demand, can be added to full cost. At the same time, full cost can be defended before government price commissions. It is argued against full cost pricing that it ignores demand (in that it assumes a normal level of production and sales); that it is partly based on irrelevant past costs; that it involves the allocation of fixed costs; and that a business may not be operating at normal volume.

functional currency. In the context of

FOREIGN CURRENCY TRANSLATION, the currency which a foreign subsidiary handles on a day to day basis and in which it generates net cash flows. It is usually the currency of the country in which the subsidiary operates, but may be the currency of the parent company if the subsidiary's operations are regarded as integral to those of the parent. Gains and losses arising from the translation of financial statements in the functional currency into the reporting currency are not passed through the consolidated income statement.

functional fixation. The tendency of a person to attach a certain meaning to a title or an object and his or her inability to perceive other possible meanings or uses.

fund. In public sector accounting a separate pool of monetary and other resources established to support specified activities. The fund is an accounting entity and is operated and accounted for independently of other funds. In principle, the use of the resources of the fund is restricted to the specified activities. In practice, some resources may be common to two or more funds or transfers may be permitted between funds.

fund accounting. In the public sector, stewardship accounting in which a FUND forms the accounting entity. In the UK, fund accounting is usually operated on a cash basis. The main central government funds are the CONSOLIDATED FUND and the NATIONAL LOANS FUND.

fundamental accounting assumption. One of three assumptions set out in IAS 1, i.e., GOING CONCERN, CONSISTENCY and ACCRUALS.

fundamental accounting concept. In the UK, one of the four concepts set out in SSAP 2, i.e., GOING CONCERN, ACCRUALS, CONSISTENCY and PRUDENCE. They are described as the broad basic assumptions which underlie the periodic financial accounts of business enterprises and as having general acceptability.

The concepts were included in the EEC

FOURTH DIRECTIVE and the British Companies Act 1981. The first three concepts, but not prudence, are termed FUNDAMENTAL ACCOUNTING ASSUMPTIONS in IAS 1.

fundamental analysis. The study of corporate financial reports and other relevant information to try and gain an insight into the 'real worth' of a company's shares, in the expectation of identifying ones that the market has over- or under-valued. According to the semi-strong form of the EFFICIENT MARKET HYPOTHESIS such attempts will not on average be successful.

fundamental errors. In the context of PRIOR YEAR ADJUSTMENTS in the UK, errors of such significance as to destroy a TRUE AND FAIR VIEW and hence the validity of the financial statements and which would have led to the withdrawal of the statements had the errors been recognized at the time.

funds statements. Statements that show the sources and applications of funds of an enterprise for a period. In their simplest form they consist simply of the differences between two successive balance sheets, but the items are usually rearranged and adjusted. Published funds statements take a variety of forms in an attempt to serve such overlapping and even conflicting objectives as: showing the relationship between liquidity and profitability; reporting on liquidity and solvency; aiding the prediction of future cash flows; highlighting financing and investing activities as distinct from operating activities; disclosing changes in balance sheet items; and reporting transactions with outsiders (as distinct from internal transactions).

The concept of 'funds' used is not always made explicit. The most common concepts are working capital and cash (or NET LIQUID FUNDS). Under the working capital concept, funds are increased by, for example, selling fixed assets for cash or on credit, and issuing shares (stock) for cash or other current assets. Generating profits before tax also increases funds but depreciation and losses on sale of fixed assets must be added back and profits on the sale of fixed assets subtracted since none of these involves a change in a working capital item. Funds are decreased by, for example, buying fixed assets for cash or on credit, redeeming debentures, proposing or paying dividends, and providing for tax. Transactions such as the issue of BONUS SHARES, which involve no movement of funds, are omitted. Sources of funds less uses of funds during the period is represented by the change in working capital (usually analyzed into its component parts).

Under the cash concept, funds are increased by, for example, selling fixed assets for cash (but not on credit unless the cash has been received during the period), and issuing shares for cash. To profits before tax must be added not only depreciation and losses and profits on the sale of fixed assets but also changes in inventories (stock and work in progress), debtors and creditors. Funds are decreased by the expenditure of cash, including dividends paid and taxes paid. Sources of funds less uses of funds during the period is represented by the change in cash balances.

Funds can also be defined as all financial resources, in which case sources of funds equals application of funds. An advantage of this definition is that a significant transaction (e.g., a build-up in inventories financed by short-term loans and thus not affecting the total of working capital) is not excluded simply because it affects only working capital or cash items.

In the UK, statements of source and application of funds are required by SSAP 10 to be published by all companies with a turnover or gross income of £25,000 p.a. or more. They form part of the audited financial statements. The definition of funds is not made clear but appears to be a mixture of working capital and cash. The increase or decrease in working capital must be shown, subdivided into its component parts, as must also net liquid funds.

In the USA, audited statements of changes in financial position are required by Accounting Principles Board Opinion No. 19, which in effect defines funds as working capital but also requires disclosure of the financing and investing aspects of exchanges or conversions of non-current items not affecting working capital.

fungible assets. Assets that are substantially indistinguishable from one another, e.g., some stocks (inventories) and investments. The term was introduced into UK company law via the FOURTH DIRECTIVE.

future costs. Costs based on expectations of the future. Future costs, not past costs, are relevant in decision-making, although the latter often form the basis for prediction.

G

gain on borrowing. A gain that results from repaying a loan in monetary units of a lower purchasing power (either of commodities in general or of specific commodities) than those at the date of borrowing. *See also* GEARING ADJUSTMENT, PURCHASING POWER LOSS OR GAIN.

game theory. The theory of making the best choice from among available strategies given imperfect information. *See also* NON-ZERO SUM GAME, ZERO SUM GAME.

Garner v. Murray, rule in. A rule in PARTNERSHIP ACCOUNTS applicable to insolvent partnerships where the ratio of capital contributions is not the same as the profit-sharing ratio. The rule is that where one partner has both a deficiency on his separate estate and a final debit balance on his capital account, whilst the other partners are solvent, the debit balance of the insolvent partner is to be apportioned to the solvent partners in proportion to their capital contributions.

gearing. *See* GEARING (LEVERAGE) RATIOS.

gearing adjustment. In UK inflation accounting practice, an adjustment intended to indicate the benefit to shareholders of the use of long-term debt, measured by the extent to which the net operating assets are financed by borrowing. As calculated in SSAP 16 it reduces the sum of the three current cost adjustments (cost of sales, monetary working capital, depreciation) by the proportion which has been financed by borrowing. Nationalized industries (which are financed differently from private sector companies) do not adjust profit in this way but disclose in a Note the amount the adjustment would have been.

Rather different gearing or financing adjustments have been adopted in some other countries. Gearing adjustments have been criticized as uneasy mixtures of the proprietary and entity views of capital maintenance.

gearing (leverage). The relationship between the funds provided to a company by its ordinary shareholders (common stockholders) and the long-term sources of funds carrying a fixed interest charge or dividend (e.g. unsecured loans, debentures and preference shares). The degree of gearing can be measured in terms of either capital or income. A company's CAPITAL STRUCTURE is said to be highly geared when the fixed charges claim an above average proportion of either capital or income. There is a number of ways in which GEARING (LEVERAGE) RATIOS can be calculated.

The effect of gearing is to increase or decrease more than proportionately the return to the ordinary shareholder resulting from an increase or decrease in earnings before interest.

gearing (leverage) ratios. Ratios based on either balance sheet or income data measuring the degree of a company's gearing (leverage). Gearing ratios based on balance sheets may be defined in different ways, e.g. as debt/equity or as debt/(debt and equity). Preference capital in this context is treated as debt. If calculated using book values the equity figure usually includes reserves and undistributed profits as well as ordinary share capital. Deferred taxation should strictly be apportioned between the numerator and the denominator depending on the extent to which it represents a liability. Ideally, market values should be used. Debt should include bank overdrafts thought to be permanent.

Income gearing may be measured by calculating TIMES INTEREST EARNED, i.e. (profit before interest and tax)/interest (gross). This calculation ignores the existence of undistributed profits, as does also the method of priority percentages in which a calculation is made of the percentage of earnings that is required to service each category of loan and share capital.

general journal. *See* JOURNAL.

general ledger. The LEDGER containing those accounts not contained in the SUBSIDIARY LEDGERS. Also known in the UK as the NOMINAL LEDGER.

general legacy. *See* LEGACY.

generally accepted accounting principles (GAAP). In the USA, the definitions, concepts, methods and procedures used in preparing financial statements. US audit reports specifically state whether or not the financial statements are in conformity with GAAP applied on a consistent basis.

The concept of GAAP has not been adopted in the UK but company law in the context of realized profits refers to 'principles generally accepted . . . at the time when those accounts are prepared' and GAAP have also been referred to in case law relating to price control legislation.

generally accepted auditing standards (GAAS). In the USA, AUDITING STANDARDS approved and adopted by the American Institute of Certified Public Accountants. There are ten standards, which may be summarized as follows:
General standards
1. Technical proficiency
2. INDEPENDENCE
3. Due professional care
Standards of field work
1. Adequate planning and supervision
2. Proper study and evaluation of INTERNAL CONTROL
3. Sufficient AUDIT EVIDENCE
Standards of reporting
1. Whether financial statements are presented in accordance with GENERALLY ACCEPTED ACCOUNTING PRINCIPLES
2. Whether such principles have been consistently observed
3. Information disclosure adequate unless otherwise stated in report
4. An expression of opinion or an assertion that an opinion cannot be expressed.

general price level. A measure of the purchasing power of money, as represented by a general index. The available indexes in the UK include the Retail Price Index and the GNP deflator (which measures the price level of all the components of GROSS NATIONAL PRODUCT); and in the USA the Consumer Price Index for All Urban Consumers (CPI-U) and the Gross National Product Implicit Price Deflator. Retail price indexes have the advantage that they are calculated and published more frequently and it is these which, on practical grounds, have been advocated for use by standard setters in both the UK (provisional SSAP 7) and the USA (FAS 33). The UK SANDILANDS REPORT, however, rejected the view that a general index can be a measure of the rate of inflation equally appropriate to all individuals and entities and claimed that there is no such thing as a general price level.

The major problem in the construction of general price level indexes is the selection of commodities to be included and the relative weights to be attached to them. In practice there may be a high rate of correlation between different index numbers.

general price level accounting. Synonym for CURRENT PURCHASING POWER (CPP) ACCOUNTING.

general purchasing power accounting. Synonym for CURRENT PURCHASING POWER (CPP) ACCOUNTING.

general purpose financial statements. Financial statements prepared for all potential users rather than just one user. Such statements are the norm in the UK and the USA but the needs of equity investors predominate in law and in practice. *See* USER NEEDS.

geometric mean. The nth positive root of the product of n values. The FT Index (*see* FINANCIAL TIMES SHARE INDICES) is calculated as an unweighted geometric mean.

geometric progression. A series of numbers in which each number is increased or decreased by a constant ratio, as for example, in the calculation of the present value of an ANNUITY. The sum of a geometric progression is given by the expression

$$a\frac{(x^n - 1)}{(x - 1)}$$

where a is the first term, x the constant ratio and n the number of terms.

Gesellschaft mit beschränkter Haftung (GmbH). The approximate German equivalent of a UK private company.

gifts inter vivos. Gifts made between living persons.

GIGO. Garbage in, garbage out. An expression used (especially in a computing context) to emphasize the fact that the reliability of outputs (e.g., financial statements) depends upon the reliability of inputs (e.g., accounting data).

goal congruence. Co-ordination of the personal and group goals of subordinates and superiors with those of the organization of which they are a part. The goals of an organization may include maximization of profits or share of the market; the goals of a group, shared values and mutual commitments; and the goals of an individual, an aspiration to succeed.

goal programming. An extension of LINEAR PROGRAMMING in which one or more goals are formulated as constraints and the objective function seeks to minimize the sum of the absolute deviations from these goals. Goals can be ranked in order of importance and trade-offs made between them. If not all goals are attainable, the minimum additional resources required to realize all goals can be calculated.

going concern. One of the accounting principles included in the EEC FOURTH DIRECTIVE and the British Companies Act 1981. The Act requires that a company shall be presumed to be carrying on business as a going concern. Going concern is one of the four FUNDAMENTAL ACCOUNTING CONCEPTS of STATEMENT OF STANDARD ACCOUNTING PRACTICE No. 2 in the UK and one of the three FUN-DAMENTAL ACCOUNTING ASSUMPTIONS of International Accounting Standard No. 1. An audit report may be qualified if the continuance of a company as a going concern is dependent upon, say, government monetary help which cannot be guaranteed. The going concern concept can be regarded as supporting the valuation of assets at historical cost or replacement cost rather than net realizable value.

goodness of fit. The extent to which an estimated equation fits the data. It may be measured by the COEFFICIENT OF DETER-MINATION.

goodwill on consolidation. GOODWILL which arises on a BUSINESS COMBINATION when ACQUISITION ACCOUNTING as distinct from MERGER ACCOUNTING is used. It does not arise, however, when the EQUITY METHOD or PROPORTIONAL CONSOLIDATION is used. If the assets of the company acquired are retained at their book values and not adjusted to their fair (current market) values part of the figure for goodwill on consolidation will represent this lack of adjustment rather than goodwill proper. The latter will be positive if it is thought that the company acquired possesses unrecorded goodwill of its own or if the SYNERGY of the combination is expected to make the group itself more valuable than the sum of its parts. If shares are issued as the purchase consideration they are valued at the fair value (market price if listed) of the shares issued or the fair value of the property acquired, whichever is the more objectively determinable.

The treatment of goodwill on consolidation is not covered by company law or accounting standard in the UK but the SEVENTH DIRECTIVE, which must eventually be incorporated into British law, requires either amortization over economic life or, in the case of positive goodwill, an immediate and clear deduction from reserves. NEGATIVE GOODWILL may be transferred to profit and loss account in certain circumstances but this option is unlikely to be taken up in the UK (*see* RESERVE ON CON-SOLIDATION).

In the USA, goodwill on consolidation

must be systematically amortized over the period expected to benefit from the acquisition, up to a maximum of 40 years. Negative goodwill on consolidation must be allocated proportionately against the assigned values of the fixed assets, excluding listed securities. If as a result any asset value is reduced below zero, the balance of negative goodwill must be recorded as a deferred credit, which must then be systematically amortized.

goodwill (other than goodwill on consolidation). An INTANGIBLE ASSET that is not specifically identifiable and relates to the business as a whole. Conceptually, goodwill represents the difference between the value of a business as a going concern and the sum of the values of its net assets taken individually. It may also be regarded as the present value of expected superior earnings over a normal return on investment. It arises from such attributes of a business as good reputation, customer loyalty, advantageous location and good management. Under UK company law only goodwill purchased for valuable consideration may be capitalized. If so capitalized it must be systematically written off to profit and loss account over a period not greater than its economic life. The Accounting Standards Committee has proposed that purchased goodwill (other than NEGATIVE GOODWILL) should normally be written off immediately against reserves. It may, however, be amortized over its useful economic life. Negative goodwill should be credited to reserves. In the USA only GOODWILL ON CONSOLIDATION can be capitalized.

Government Accounting Service (GAS). In the UK, the professional accountants who provide accounting advice to central government departments. Members of the GAS (which was formed in 1974) work within a department, but may move to other departments in the course of their careers.

government grants. In the UK, cash grants made to companies that acquire certain types of fixed assets. The standard accounting treatment (SSAP 4) of these grants is to credit them to revenue over the expected useful life of the asset by either (a) reducing the cost of the acquisition of the asset by the amount of the grant, or (b) treating the amount of the grant as a deferred credit (the written down amount being disclosed, if material, in the balance sheet), a portion of which is transferred to reserve annually. The two methods, which give rise to the same reported earnings but different amounts in the balance sheet, are equally popular in UK practice.

gross margin. The excess of sales over the cost of goods sold (i.e., for a manufacturing company using ABSORPTION COSTING, all manufacturing costs, both fixed and variable, relating to goods sold).

gross national product (GNP). A measure of the production of the goods and services of an economy shown in NATIONAL INCOME AND EXPENDITURE ACCOUNTS. It can be obtained by recording incomes, expenditures or outputs. It is stated to be gross because no deduction is made for depreciation or CAPITAL CONSUMPTION. GNP may be measured at market prices or, if indirect taxes and subsidies are excluded, at factor cost. Domestic product as distinct from national product excludes the effect of net property income from abroad.

gross profit. See GROSS MARGIN.

group accounts. In the UK, the financial statements required by company law and accounting standard (SSAP 14) to be presented to the parent company shareholders of a group constituted by a holding company and its subsidiaries. One company is the subsidiary of another if the latter is *either* a member of it and controls its board of directors *or* holds more than half in nominal value of its EQUITY SHARE CAPITAL.

Group accounts must be published where a company has a subsidiary at the end of its financial year, and is not itself a wholly owned subsidiary of another company incorporated in Great Britain.

Group accounts is a wider term than CONSOLIDATED FINANCIAL STATEMENTS. In Britain, other forms are permissible if, in the opinion of the directors, a better presentation of the same or equivalent information can be achieved that can readily be appreciated by shareholders. In particular, group accounts may take the form of one of the following: (a) more than one set of consolidated accounts dealing respectively with the company plus one group of subsidiaries and other groups of subsidiaries; (b) separate accounts dealing with each of the subsidiaries; (c) statements expanding the information about the subsidiaries in the company's own accounts; or (d) any combination of the above. In UK practice, group accounts containing other than one set of consolidated statements are very rare and will not be permissible once the EEC SEVENTH DIRECTIVE is made part of UK law. SSAP 14 (1978) is firmly in favour of a single set of consolidated statements except in exceptional circumstances. In accordance with SSAP 10, companies provide a consolidated statement of source and application of funds as well as a consolidated profit and loss account and balance sheet.

group companies. Companies that are subsidiaries or holding companies of other companies.

Groupe d'Etudes **(EEC Accountants Study Group)**. A committee of accountants from each member state of the EEC formed in 1966 at the request of the EC Commission. It is based in Brussels and its official language is French. The UK representative is appointed by the CONSULTATIVE COMMITTEE OF ACCOUNTANCY BODIES and the Irish representative by the Institute of Chartered Accountants in Ireland. The function of the *Groupe d'Etudes* is to represent with one voice the views of European professional accountants to the EEC bodies. Its influence on EEC directives on company law and accounting has been considerable.

guarantee, company limited by. *See* COMPANY LIMITED BY GUARANTEE.

H

harmonization. The process of increasing the compatibility of accounting practices by setting bounds to their degree of variation. The word 'harmonization' is commonly used for this process only in an international context, 'STANDARDIZATION' being preferred otherwise. Rather confusingly, international harmonization can lead to INTERNATIONAL ACCOUNTING STANDARDS.

Harmonization is felt to be necessary when financial statements prepared in one country cannot properly be compared with those prepared in another because of major differences in accounting practices. Such comparisons are most likely to be attempted by the shareholders (and their financial advisers), managers, creditors and employees of multinational companies and also by those whose job it is to audit them, to levy taxes on them, or to attempt to regulate their activities.

It should not necessarily be assumed that harmonization is desirable. Differences in accounting practices may reflect real and fairly permanent economic, social and cultural differences and it is disputable to what extent harmonization should be extended to business organizations operating in only one country.

The obstacles to harmonization are many, notably the dichotomy between the role of financial statements in, e.g., the UK and USA, as presenting a fair view to shareholders and their role, e.g., in most of continental Europe, of presenting a prudent view to creditors and tax collectors; a lack of agencies to enforce international standards; the diversity of national enforcement agencies; nationalistic beliefs in the superiority of one's own practices; and the different ECONOMIC CONSEQUENCES of standards in different countries.

Attempts at harmonization have been made more especially by the EC Commission and the INTERNATIONAL ACCOUNTING STANDARDS COMMITTEE. It has been suggested that worldwide harmonization will only succeed if supported by six 'vital countries', viz. France, Japan, the Netherlands, the UK, the USA and West Germany. Regional harmonization is being attempted by such bodies as the EC Commission and the ASEAN FEDERATION OF ACCOUNTANTS.

Hatfield, Henry Rand (1866-1945). One of the earliest American academic accountants; on the staff of the University of California at Berkeley from 1904 to 1937. He was president in 1919 of the predecessor body of the American Accounting Association. His major work was *Modern Accounting*, first published in 1909 and issued in a revised form in 1927 as *Accounting: Its Principles and Some of its Problems*. In 1938 he was co-author with Sanders and Moore of *A Statement of Accounting Principles*. His 'Historical Defense of Bookkeeping', first published in the *Journal of Accountancy* in 1924 has been widely anthologized. His Dickinson Lectures at Harvard University in 1941-42 were published in 1943 as *Surplus and Dividends*. Hatfield is one of the most readable of accounting writers, writing with clarity and wit and making detailed references to authorities.

Hawthorne studies. Research carried out by Elton Mayo and others at the Hawthorne, Illinois, plant of Western Electric from 1927 to 1932. The research findings emphasize the organization as a social unit and members of organizations as social beings with social needs to be satisfied.

heuristics. Simplified rules used for processing information on a rule of thumb, trial and error basis.

Hicksian income concepts. Concepts of income put forward by the economist J.R. Hicks in his book *Value and Capital* (2nd ed. 1946). Hicks's chapter on income in this book is often referred to in the accounting literature. His three *ex ante* concepts are:

> No. 1: 'the maximum amount which can be spent during a period if there is to be an expectation of maintaining intact the capital value of

prospective receipts (in money terms)'

No. 2: 'the maximum amount the individual can spend this week, and still expect to be able to spend the same amount in each ensuing week'

No. 3: 'the maximum amount of money which the individual can spend this week, and still expect to be able to spend the same amount *in real terms* in each ensuing week.'

Each of these definitions has an *ex post* equivalent, but even these involve an estimation of future events. Thus the Hicksian concepts are more subjective than those of accounting which place more emphasis on past and current transactions and other events.

Income No. 1 is a CAPITAL MAINTENANCE CONCEPT; incomes 2 and 3 are CONSUMPTION MAINTENANCE concepts.

hidden reserves. *See* SECRET RESERVES.

hierarchy of needs. *See* MOTIVATION.

highlights. Brief summaries of financial and operating data, especially those included in ANNUAL REPORTS to shareholders.

high-low method. A crude approximation to LEAST SQUARES using only representative highest and lowest points on a SCATTER DIAGRAM to fit a straight line.

hire purchase. In the UK, the supply of goods on hire with an option to purchase at the end of the hire period. Ownership remains with the supplier until the last payment is made but the customer enjoys full possession and use of the goods. The economic consequence as distinct from the legal status of a hire purchase contract is therefore very similar to that of an INSTALMENT SALE and the accounting treatment of the two tends to be identical.

See also HIRE PURCHASE AND INSTALMENT SALE ACCOUNTING.

hire purchase and instalment sale accounting. Accounting for HIRE PURCHASE and INSTALMENT SALES in the books of finance companies, dealers and purchasers.

The common practice in the UK is for the finance company to purchase goods from the dealer, which then hires or sells them to the purchaser. The dealer usually makes the agreement with the purchaser on the finance company's behalf and often also collects the instalments. Each instalment collected is normally recognized as a partial recovery of the cost of goods sold and a partial realization of deferred income. The Consumer Credit Act 1974 requires disclosure of the effective interest rate included in the financing of the transaction (*see* ANNUAL PERCENTAGE RATE). The deferred income can be apportioned by using ANNUITY factors, by the rule of 78 (i.e., by a method akin to the sum of the years digits DEPRECIATION METHOD: $1+2+\ldots+11+12=78$, instalments usually being collected monthly), or by the straightline method. In the balance sheet, hire purchase (or instalment) debtors are shown gross with a deduction for deferred income not yet recognized (the details are usually relegated to the notes). Provisions for doubtful debts are also usually necessary.

The profit of the dealer attributable to his activities as a dealer can either be recognized in its entirety when an agreement is made or spread over the life of the agreement. If the dealer acts as his own financier it is necessary to decide how much of the excess over cost is trading profit and how much is income from financing.

In the books of the purchaser, the asset acquired is debited with the price at which it could have been bought for cash, the supplier is credited with the total amount and a hire purchase (or instalment sale) interest suspense account is debited with the interest to be apportioned over the period of the agreement. In the balance sheet the asset is shown gross (but described as being under hire purchase) less accumulated depreciation (as for any other fixed asset). The credit balance remaining on the hire purchase interest suspense account is either set off against the amount still owing to the supplier or divided between current and other liabilities.

For US practice *see* INSTALMENT METHOD OF ACCOUNTING.

histogram. A graphical representation of a frequency distribution showing the class intervals horizontally and the frequencies vertically.

historical cost accounting. A system of accounting based on HISTORICAL COSTS but modified in practice by PRUDENCE (as, for example, in the valuation of stocks or inventories at the lower of cost or market) and, in the UK but not in the USA, by revaluations of fixed assets. Historical cost accounting (HCA) is at the basis of US generally accepted accounting principles; in the UK the Companies Acts require the adoption of either HCA principles or ALTERNATIVE ACCOUNTING RULES. During periods of high inflation HCA is the subject of many attacks but appears to have the capacity to survive them all.

The strengths of HCA are that it is 'harder' and less easily manipulated than accounting systems based on REPLACEMENT COSTS, NET REALIZABLE VALUES or NET PRESENT VALUES; can be produced more quickly and more cheaply; and fits more easily into the double entry recording process. It can also be argued in favour of HCA that unlike systems of inflation accounting it is based on the recording of events that have actually occurred, rather than on contingent events, and is thus more appropriately used when there are claims on a company's resources by different partners.

The weakness of HCA is that it ignores changes in both general and specific prices. This leads to a number of problems: CAPITAL MAINTENANCE is based on the nominal amount of the original money capital invested rather than on purchasing power or operating capability; monetary gains and losses are ignored; profits are overstated as historical costs are matched against current revenues; assets may be understated in terms of current prices; and hence RETURN ON INVESTMENT is likely to be overstated (with the numerator too high and the denominator too low). There is also a loss of ADDITIVITY since 1985 pounds or dollars are added to, say, 1975 pounds or dollars.

These weaknesses of HCA make it less useful as a TAX BASE than it would otherwise be. Taxation authorities have, however, tended to continue to favour HCA because of its relative freedom from manipulation.

If prices both general and relative are reasonably stable HCA provides quite a good basis for stewardship (ACCOUNTABILITY) and control (PERFORMANCE EVALUATION) but is less suitable for decision-making, where the emphasis is on future differential costs.

historical cost accounting rules. The rules set out in the British Companies Act 1981 requiring the application to company financial statements of the conventional accounting procedures based on historical cost modified by prudence. Companies must follow either these rules or the ALTERNATIVE ACCOUNTING RULES based on current cost.

holding company. In the UK, a company which is either a member (shareholder) of another company and controls its board of directors or which holds more than half in nominal value of the EQUITY SHARE CAPITAL of the other company. More narrowly, a holding company is defined in some countries as one which has no operating activities but exists solely to hold shares in other companies.

holding gain. A gain that results from holding assets rather than using them in operations. Holding gains can be classified into the overlapping categories of realizable holding gains and realized holding gains. Realizable holding gains represent the increase during an accounting period in the current value of assets held by a firm, some of which will be realized during the period and some of which will remain unrealized. Realized holding gains include not only the realizable and realized gains of the period but also gains which first accrued in previous periods but have been realized in the current period.

Realized holding gains can also be classified into realized capital gains (the excess of proceeds over depreciated historical costs on the irregular sale or disposal of fixed assets) and realized COST SAVINGS (the excess of the current cost over the historical cost of inputs used in producing outputs sold).

Holding gains can also be divided into real holding gains and fictitious holding gains. A real holding gain results from a rise in a SPECIFIC PRICE greater than a rise in the GENERAL PRICE LEVEL.

BUSINESS PROFIT is defined by Edwards and Bell as the sum of CURRENT OPERATING PROFIT and realizable holding gains. Both conventional accounting profit and REALIZED PROFIT are equal to the sum of current operating profit and realized holding gains.

homemade gearing (leverage). GEARING (LEVERAGE) of investors as distinct from the gearing of the company in which they have invested. See CAPITAL STRUCTURE.

horizontal equity. The tax principle that equal people in equal circumstances should be treated in an equal way. It can be argued, for example, that a WEALTH TAX as well as an INCOME TAX is necessary for horizontal equity to be achieved.

hotchpot. The bringing into account of any ADVANCEMENT made to a child during the parent's lifetime. At the death of the testator such advances will, if brought into hotchpot, form part of the estate to be distributed.

human assets. The wealth tied up in human beings, including the investment in time and money spent to allow individuals to acquire education, training and skills. Human assets are not conventionally recorded in financial statements except insofar as they are included under GOODWILL. See HUMAN RESOURCE ACCOUNTING (HRA).

human capital. See HUMAN ASSETS.

human information processing. The ways in which decision makers make use of information under uncertainty. Improvements in HIP may be achieved by altering the information provided, by improving the ability of decision makers, and by the construction of formal models of human decision making. The major approaches used by researchers in HIP are the Bayesian (see BAYES' RULE); the LENS MODEL; the cognitive complexity and cognitive styles approaches; and process tracing. Cognitive complexity reflects a decision maker's capacity to differentiate and integrate stimuli; cognitive style reflects how decision makers prefer to approach and solve various tasks. The aim of process tracing is to understand the processes occurring between the introduction of stimuli and the final choice of the decision maker (see also PROTOCOL ANALYSIS).

human resource accounting (HRA). Accounting for the human resources of an enterprise (e.g., loyal and efficient employees, an established clientele and reliable suppliers) that are excluded from conventional financial statements except insofar as they are included under GOODWILL. A distinction can be made between internal human resources (employees) and external human resources (customers, suppliers, etc.). The latter are ignored in most discussions of HRA.

Advocates of HRA contend that money spent on human beings represents an asset not an expense and that recognition of such assets provides useful data for management decision-making and for stewardship. On the other hand it can be argued that human beings (other than slaves and perhaps footballers) cannot represent assets and that in any case the practical measurement problems are too great.

If it is decided to measure and record internal human resources a number of valuation methods are in principle available. These include: capitalizing recruiting and training costs incurred; current replacement costs; opportunity cost; the present value of future wages and salaries; and the present value of the enterprise's future earnings attributable to its human resources.

hygiene factors. See MOTIVATION.

hyper-inflation. An extremely high rate of increase in the GENERAL PRICE LEVEL. In the USA, for the purpose of FOREIGN CURRENCY TRANSLATION, a hyper-inflationary environment is defined as one where the inflation rate is 100% or more in a three year period (FAS 52). Hyper-inflation may render a national monetary unit unsuitable as a unit of account and lead to the substitution therefor of a commodity (e.g., gold) or the monetary unit of another country.

I

idle time. Wages paid for unproductive time caused by, for example, machine breakdowns, shortages of material or inefficient scheduling. It is classified as an indirect rather than direct labour cost.

imprest system. *See* PETTY CASH BOOK.

imputation system. A system of taxation of companies and shareholders which attempts to avoid the double taxation of distributed profits. Most countries within the EEC have such a system but the details vary. *See* ADVANCE CORPORATION TAX, MAINSTREAM CORPORATION TAX, TAX CREDITS.

incidence of tax. The way in which the burden of tax eventually falls, as distinct from the apparent burden.

income and expenditure statement/account. A financial statement and ledger account prepared by bodies whose major objective is other than making profits. It shows the income, expenditure and surplus or deficit for an accounting period.

income gearing. *See* GEARING (LEVERAGE) RATIOS.

income in kind. Income in the form of goods and services rather than cash. Income in kind is more difficult to tax adequately and fairly than income in cash. Non-taxation of income in kind encourages individuals towards 'do-it-yourself' work and trade by barter.

income statement. US term for PROFIT AND LOSS ACCOUNT.

income tax. A DIRECT TAX on income, as distinct from capital. In the UK individuals pay income tax and companies corporation tax; in the USA both pay income tax. Taxable income often differs from income as computed for the purpose of reporting to owners. In the UK, income tax is by far the largest source of revenue to the central government. It was introduced in 1799, withdrawn in 1802, re-imposed in 1803, abolished in 1815, but re-introduced in 1842. The INCOME TAX SCHEDULES, cumulative PAY AS YOU EARN (PAYE) system, and long basic rate band are not found in other countries, but there is no system of SELF-ASSESSMENT as in the USA and Australia. *See also* TAXABLE INCOME, TAX ALLOWANCES.

In the USA there is both a federal income tax and local income taxes. A local income tax was recommended in the UK Layfield Report of 1976.

income tax schedules. The division in the UK of income tax assessment and collection under six (formerly five) schedules. The system was introduced in 1803 so as to avoid the need for a taxpayer to disclose his total income on one tax return. The six schedules are as follows:

Schedule A: income from property

Schedule B: income from commercial woodlands

Schedule C: interest and annuities payable out of public revenue

Schedule D: income from trades, professions, business, property and other annual profits

Schedule E: income from employment

Schedule F: dividends subject to higher rates of tax.

The rules under the various schedules are not necessarily the same. For example, under Schedule E expenses to be deductible must have been incurred 'wholly, exclusively and necessarily in the performance' of the employment while under Schedule D expenses need only be incurred 'wholly and exclusively' for the purposes of the trade, profession or vocation. There may thus be incentives to be taxed under one schedule rather than another.

incomplete records. Accounting records that are incomplete in some way and fall short of a full double entry system. A business may, for example, record only transactions affecting cash and persons. With ingenuity and perseverance, profit and loss accounts and balance sheets of reasonable reliability can usually be constructed from incomplete records by analysing the cash book.

incremental budget. A NEGOTIATED STATIC BUDGET that takes the previous year's budget and actual results as the starting point, the budget amounts then being changed in accordance with the experience of the previous period and expectations for the period under consideration. *See also* PRIORITY BUDGET, ZERO-BASE BUDGETING.

incremental cost. Synonym for DIFFERENTIAL COST.

independence (of the auditor). The ability of an auditor to act with integrity and objectivity, both as an individual practitioner and as a member of a profession. To be independent, an auditor needs to be free from (i) controls or pressures concerning audit techniques and procedures to be used and the extent of their application; (ii) restrictions relating to examination of any source of information and any personal interests discouraging such examination; (iii) pressures to suppress facts or modify the audit report. The profession to which the auditor belongs should not be, or give the impression of being, dependent in any way upon its clients.

Threats to independence may arise or be perceived to arise from the following:
(i) although a company auditor is (in the UK but not always in the USA) appointed by shareholders and remunerated on their instructions, both these tasks may in fact be under the control of the management which is subject to audit;
(ii) auditors may have to compete with each other to persuade management to recommend their appointment;
(iii) any audit fee representing a large proportion of an auditor's income;
(iv) the provision of non-auditing services (e.g., accounting, secretarial, tax, management consultancy, personnel selection) to an audit client;
(v) the holding of shares in, or being a loan creditor of, a client.

The independence of an auditor can be strengthened by:
(i) regulation, e.g., the UK Companies Acts give the auditor a right of access at all times to books and accounts and the right to demand from the officers of a company such information and explanation as the auditor considers necessary; and the right to speak generally at annual general meetings and in particular if reappointment is not proposed. In addition, the Acts require a statutory auditor to be a member of a recognized body of accountants;
(ii) professional ethics, which require, for example, communication between incoming and outgoing auditors.

independent project. A capital investment project the acceptance or rejection of which has no effect on any other capital project.

indexation. The adjustment of the terms of contracts by a price index in order to allow for inflation. Contracts are thus fixed in real rather than money terms. It has been adopted to some degree in a number of Latin American countries. In the UK, public sector pensions, some government securities and (unless the government explicitly decides otherwise in its annual budget) income tax personal allowances are indexed, and wages were partially indexed in 1973-74. CURRENT PURCHASING POWER (CPP) ACCOUNTING may be regarded as a form of indexation of accounts although it does not directly affect the money amount of contractual payments.

indifference curve. A curve showing the combinations of two goods (including, for example, expected return and risk measured by standard deviation) for which an individual is indifferent. Sets of indifference curves can be drawn, the higher indifference curves indicating higher levels of utility.

indirect costs. Costs that cannot be traced to a finished good in an economically feasible manner.

indirect labour. Labour that cannot be identified with a manufactured good or traced to it in an economically feasible manner. Contrast DIRECT LABOUR.

indirect manufacturing costs. Synonym for FACTORY OVERHEAD.

indirect materials. Materials that cannot be identified with a manufactured good or traced to it in an economically feasible manner. Contrast DIRECT MATERIALS.

indirect tax. A tax that is not assessed on and collected from those who are intended to bear it. Examples are value added tax, sales tax, payroll tax and excise duties. Unlike a DIRECT TAX, it cannot take individual circumstances into account. Although levied on producers, the burden of an indirect tax may be 'shifted' to consumers.

inductance hypothesis. *See* INFORMATION INDUCTANCE.

industry ratios. Average ratios, calculated from financial statements, for an industry. There can be difficulties in obtaining comparable data across companies and in defining an industry. These are reduced when an interfirm comparison scheme exists.

inflation accounting. A rather imprecise term denoting any system of accounting that attempts to take account of changes in the GENERAL PRICE LEVEL, SPECIFIC PRICES or both, and to avoid the disadvantages of HISTORICAL COST ACCOUNTING (HCA). It includes CURRENT PURCHASING POWER (CPP) ACCOUNTING (US: constant dollar accounting) and CURRENT COST ACCOUNTING (CCA) and their variants and also RELATIVE PRICE CHANGE ACCOUNTING. The varieties of inflation accounting can be classified on the basis of the unit of measurement (nominal or constant pounds or dollars), the ASSET VALUATION method adopted (HISTORICAL COST, REPLACEMENT COST, NET REALIZABLE VALUE, NET PRESENT VALUE) and the underlying CAPITAL MAINTENANCE CONCEPT (financial or physical). The following table can then be drawn up. It does not attempt to cover all the possibilities (in particular, CONTINUOUSLY CONTEMPORARY ACCOUNTING is not included).

No general agreement has been reached about which form, if any, of inflation accounting should be adopted. In some countries, e.g., the German Federal Republic, any form of inflation accounting is illegal in published financial statements except as a supplementary statement. In the UK, inflation accounting is permitted under the ALTERNATIVE ACCOUNTING RULES set out in company law but historical cost figures must

Method	Unit of measurement	Asset valuation method	Capital maintenance concept
HISTORICAL COST	Nominal	Historical cost	Financial (money)
CURRENT COST	Nominal	Replacement cost	Physical
BUSINESS PROFIT	Nominal	Replacement cost	Financial (money)
CURRENT PURCHASING POWER	Constant	Historical cost	Financial (purchasing power)
CURRENT COST/CURRENT PURCHASING POWER	Constant	Replacement cost	Financial (purchasing power)

Note: Under certain circumstances (*see* VALUE TO THE BUSINESS) net realizable and net present value can also be used under the current cost and business profit methods.

Inflation accounting

also be provided. In Anglo-Saxon countries generally, there has been a reluctance to accept the forms of inflation accounting laid down in accounting standards. One probable reason for this is that there is no theoretically ideal solution and different forms of inflation accounting may be appropriate in different situations. The US accounting standard (FAS 33), but not the UK standard (SSAP 16), recognizes this in that it requires the reporting of more than one type of inflation accounting measure.

Some writers have argued for eclectic financial statements which reflect both HCA and various inflation accounting measures. Whether or not these would present even sophisticated investors with INFORMATION OVERLOAD is a matter which has not been adequately researched. It can be claimed that the usefulness of such a procedure to investors is supported by the EFFICIENT MARKET HYPOTHESIS.

information. Often used as a synonym for DATA but may be defined more narrowly as the data relevant to a particular decision.

informational asymmetry. A situation in which some users of financial statements have superior information to others.

information economics approach to accounting. An approach to accounting that concentrates on the demand for and supply of information in a setting in which there are a set of alternative acts by decision makers (normally investors), a set of possible STATES OF NATURE, ECONOMIC CONSEQUENCES, investor preferences, investor beliefs regarding the probability of states, and an objective function (the maximization of expected utility). The accountant is seen as operating in a world in which there are neither PERFECT MARKETS nor COMPLETE MARKETS and his role is to provide 'noisy communication' rather than precise measurement. The reports he provides alter the beliefs of investors and the 'best' financial reporting system is the one associated with the highest level of expected utility. ACCRUAL ACCOUNTING, for example, is 'better' than CASH FLOW ACCOUNTING if it provides more information and does so in a cost-effective manner.

information inductance. The process by which a person's behaviour is affected by the information that he or she is required to communicate.

information intermediaries. Persons and institutions engaged in the gathering, processing, analysing and interpreting of financial information on behalf of others. Examples are financial analysts, investment advisory services, credit agencies, and stockbrokers. Information intermediaries search for information that is not publicly available, use information to predict, and interpret events ex post.

information overload. The provision of more information than readers of financial statements are capable of absorbing. Empirical evidence suggests that this may happen to non-expert readers but not to sophisticated analysts.

initial allowance. In the UK, a CAPITAL ALLOWANCE granted in the first year of purchase of industrial buildings.

Inland Revenue. The board responsible within the UK for the assessment and collection of income tax, corporation tax, capital gains tax, capital transfer tax and stamp duties.

input-output tables. In the context of NATIONAL ACCOUNTING, tables (matrices) which show the flows of goods and services among the different sectors and industries of an economy. In accounting terms they may be regarded as an alternative method of recording flows of income and expenditure.

insider dealing. The use of information not publicly available to acquire shares at less than their 'real worth'. The strong form of the EFFICIENT MARKET HYPOTHESIS, but not the semi-strong and weak forms, predicts that such an attempt will not be successful.

In the UK, insider dealing in listed securities is prohibited by company law. In the USA an insider is defined by the Securities and Exchange Act 1934 as a corporate director, officer or owner of more than 10% of a registered security who acquires knowledge through his or her official position. Insiders are forbidden to use such information for their personal gain and any 'insider' profits belong to the corporation.

insolvency. The inability of a debtor (whether an individual or a corporate body) to pay debts as they fall due. Insolvency is a question of fact, not of law. A person can be insolvent without being bankrupt (*see* BANKRUPTCY) but he or she cannot be bankrupt without being insolvent.

instalment method of accounting. In the USA, a method of recording revenue from an INSTALMENT SALE in which the dealer's gross profit (including any financing element) is recognized in a financial year in proportion to that part of the selling price collected during the year. Alternative methods of accounting for instalment sales are to recognize the full amount of the gross profit at the date of sale or to regard all cash received up to the amount of the cost of the goods as a recovery of cost and all cash received thereafter as revenue.

instalment sale. A credit sale in which payments are made by instalments. Unlike HIRE PURCHASE (not found in the USA), title to the goods passes from the supplier to the customer when delivery is made. In practice, the accounting treatment of instalment sales and hire purchase tends to be identical. *See also* HIRE PURCHASE AND INSTALMENT SALE ACCOUNTING, INSTALMENT METHOD OF ACCOUNTING.

institutional investors. Shareholders other than persons, industrial and commercial companies, the public sector and the overseas sector, i.e., financial institutions such as insurance companies and pension funds. The importance of institutional investors in UK stock markets has steadily risen in recent years. Institutional investors are more likely than private shareholders to be SOPHISTICATED INVESTORS.

in-substance defeasance of debt. In the USA, the removal of a debt from a balance sheet where a company has placed a sufficient amount of essentially risk-free monetary assets in trust solely to pay for the debt and where it is unlikely that the company will have to make further payments. This treatment is required by the FASB.

intangible assets. Assets such as GOODWILL, PATENTS, TRADE MARKS and COPYRIGHTS which have no tangible form. Conceptually, intangible assets can be classified as purchased or non-purchased and as identifiable or non-identifiable. In the UK they are by company law a sub-division of fixed assets. Identifiable intangibles include some, such as patents and trade marks, which can be sold separately. Non-identifiable intangibles, of which goodwill is the obvious example, cannot be sold except as part of the enterprise, i.e. they are non-severable.

Under UK company law, goodwill can only be capitalized if purchased for valuable consideration, but other intangibles (except research costs) can be capitalized when created by the company itself. In the USA, specifically identifiable and internally developed assets, such as trade marks and copyrights, but excluding research and development costs, can either be capitalized and subsequently amortized (over a period of not more than 40 years) or written off as incurred. Specifically identifiable and externally acquired intangibles must be capitalized and amortized. Intangibles which are internally developed but not specifically identifiable must be written off as costs are incurred. Intangibles which are externally acquired but are not specifically identifiable are considered to be goodwill and must be capitalized and amortized. Straight line amortization is in general required. The US requirements relating to intangibles have little in the way of theoretical justification but have produced uniformity of treatment.

integer. A whole number containing neither fractional nor decimal components.

integer programming. Mathematical

programming for which only INTEGER solutions are acceptable.

integrated test facility. A computer audit test in which the auditor integrates into the operating system a test person, department or activity in order to determine whether the computer processes the information in the way prescribed.

Inter-American Accounting Association. A regional accountancy group of South and North American accountancy bodies from (in 1983) 21 member countries. It publishes a quarterly newsletter, *Boletín Interamericano de Contabilidad*, as well as committee reports and other technical items.

inter-company profits. Profits earned by one company at the expense of another company in the same group because TRANSFER PRICES are set higher than cost. In order to present fairly the results of the operations of the group as a whole, such profits need to be eliminated to the extent that they remain in unsold stocks (inventories) or in fixed asset balances. It is controversial whether, in the case of less than wholly owned subsidiaries selling to their parent companies, the elimination should be 100% or proportional to the parent's holding. The former is probably the more common in practice but it follows from the generally accepted parent company concept of consolidation (*see* CONSOLIDATED FINANCIAL STATEMENTS) that the elimination should be proportional. Complete elimination is supported by the entity concept. If the elimination is not complete, the unsold stocks (inventories) or fixed assets in the balance sheet will be valued at a figure that includes a profit unrealized by sale to third parties (unless the minority shareholders are so considered).

The amount of deferred taxation to be provided in the consolidated balance sheet may be affected by the existence of inter-company profits.

inter-company transactions. Transactions between the member companies of a group. They are eliminated or otherwise adjusted for during the preparation of CONSOLIDATED FINANCIAL STATEMENTS. They include inter-company sales and purchases, inter-company charges and may give rise to INTER-COMPANY PROFITS. Each company in the group needs to keep a record of such transactions.

interests in shares. In the UK, significant shareholdings in a public company that must be notified by the shareholder to the company. A 5% interest is regarded as significant. Notification must also be given by persons acting together (so-called 'concert parties'). A register of interests in shares must be kept as a STATUTORY BOOK. In certain circumstances companies have powers to investigate the ownership of their own shares and shareholders the power to require a company to carry out such an investigation.

interim dividend. A dividend paid or proposed to be paid in the course of a financial year.

interim financial statements. Financial statements issued for a period shorter than the normal statutory year, e.g., half-yearly, quarterly. There are no laws or accounting standards covering this matter in the UK but the Stock Exchange requires listed companies to report important trading figures half-yearly. It does not require balance sheet amounts; CCA figures in addition to historical cost figures are recommended but not required. Publication typically takes the form of a two- or three-page circular sent to shareholders and a paid newspaper advertisement of highlights. In the USA the SEC requires quarterly reporting and disclosure of balance sheet items and contingencies as well as income figures. It also requires that all reported figures for interim periods are set out in the annual financial statements, together with the figures for the full year.

An interim period can be regarded either as a separate, discrete, self-contained accounting period, or as an integral but incomplete part of a full accounting year. The discrete basis matches costs and revenues of each period insofar as these are known at the end of the period; the integral basis allocates to each period its appropriate proportion of the matched costs and revenues as anticipated for the whole year. The integral basis is the more subjective and is open to artificial smoothing of results. Most companies appear to follow the discrete basis in practice. This basis tends to lead to the reporting of greater fluctuations from period to period.

Interim reports are usually unaudited. The British Companies Act 1980 states that an interim financial statement used as a basis for a dividend distribution need not have been audited but must have been 'properly prepared'.

internal audit. An element of the INTERNAL CONTROL system set up by the management of an enterprise in order to review accounting, financial and other operations and to determine whether prescribed policies are being adhered to. An external auditor takes account of the work done by an internal auditor having regard to the extent of the latter's INDEPENDENCE, staff resources, the tests made, and the influence on management action.

internal check. That aspect of INTERNAL CONTROL which is exclusively concerned with the prevention and early detection of errors and fraud. It involves the arrangement of bookkeeping and other clerical duties in such a way as to ensure that no single task is executed from beginning to end by only one person and that the work of each clerk is subject to an independent check in the course of another's duties. Such checks are more difficult to arrange in a computerized accounting system than in a manual one.

internal control. The whole system of controls, financial and otherwise, established by management in order to carry on the business of an enterprise in an orderly and efficient manner, ensure adherence to management policies, safeguard the assets, and secure as far as possible the completeness and accuracy of the records. Internal control is thus a very wide term and includes within it INTERNAL AUDIT and INTERNAL CHECK.

Important elements of an internal control system include the following:

(i) separation of duties and in particular segregation of the functions of authorization, custody and recording;

(ii) clear definition and allocation of responsibilities and lines of delegation and reporting;

(iii) procedures and security measures designed to ensure that access, both direct and via documentation, to assets is limited to authorized personnel;

(iv) authorization and approval of all transactions by an appropriate responsible person, with specification of the limits for the authorizations;

(v) checks of arithmetical accuracy, reconciliations, control accounts, trial balances, etc.;

(vi) procedures to ensure that personnel have capabilities commensurate with their responsibilities;

(vii) supervision by responsible officials of day-to-day transactions and the recording thereof;

(viii) review of management functions and comparison with budgets.

The nature and extent of internal controls are the responsibility of management and depend on such factors as the nature, size and geographical spread of the business; the number of staff; the nature of the transactions entered into; and management style. In particular small, family-owned and operated businesses may have little in the way of a formal internal control system.

The external auditor tests the internal control system by means of COMPLIANCE TESTS in order to determine the extent of SUBSTANTIVE TESTS necessary.

internal control questionnaire. A standardized form, designed by the audit firm using it, comprising a series of questions, each of which raises an enquiry on INTERNAL CONTROL.

internal rate of return (IRR). The discount rate that equates the present value of the expected cash outflows of an investment with the present value of the expected inflows, i.e., it is the rate r, such that

$$\sum_{t=0}^{n} \frac{A_t}{(1+r)^t} = 0$$

where A_t is the cash flow (in or out) for period t and n is the number of periods. It is one of the DISCOUNTED CASH FLOW methods of CAPITAL INVESTMENT APPRAISAL.

Internal rates of return can be calculated iteratively (using a computer) or by trial and error. Some projects have more than one IRR, i.e., there are multiple rates of return, but the number of distinct IRRs cannot exceed the number of sign changes in the expected cash flows. This ambiguity can be avoided by the discounting back of negative cash flows to previous periods at the required rate of return.

Internal Revenue Service (IRS). The agency responsible for the assessment and collection of income and other direct taxes in the USA.

international accounting. The international aspects of accounting, including such matters as accounting principles and reporting practices in different countries and their classification; patterns of accounting development; international and regional HARMONIZATION; FOREIGN CURRENCY TRANSLATION; FOREIGN EXCHANGE RISK; international comparisons of consolidation accounting and inflation accounting; accounting in developing countries; accounting in communist countries; performance evaluation of foreign subsidiaries; TRANSFER PRICING across frontiers; capital budgeting in an international context; international financial markets; disclosures by multinational companies; and international taxation.

international accounting standards. In general any ACCOUNTING STANDARDS agreed upon internationally; in particular the standards issued by the INTERNATIONAL ACCOUNTING STANDARDS COMMITTEE.

International Accounting Standards Committee (IASC). A committee founded in 1973 with the objectives of formulating and publishing ACCOUNTING STANDARDS to be observed in the presentation of financial statements, promoting their worldwide acceptance and observance, and of working generally for the improvement and HARMONIZATION of regulations, accounting standards and procedures relating to the presentation of financial statements. The IASC was founded by the professional accountancy bodies of Australia, Canada, France, West Germany, Japan, Mexico, the Netherlands, the UK and Ireland, and the USA. Professional accountancy bodies in about 50 countries are members. As at 1 July 1984 the IASC had issued 24 international accounting standards (IASs).

The IASC has no direct authority and works through national accountancy bodies. Whilst the UK bodies control the ACCOUNTING STANDARDS COMMITTEE, the American Institute of Certified Public Accountants influences but does not control the FINANCIAL ACCOUNTING STANDARDS BOARD and in many countries standards, insofar as they exist at all, are controlled by governments or regulatory bodies. The authority of the IASC thus varies considerably from country to country. The IASC's secretariat is in London. Its standards tend to follow or to be compromises between American and British practice and to allow a wider range of practices.

International Auditing Practices Committee (IAPC). A committee of the INTERNATIONAL FEDERATION OF ACCOUNTANTS (IFAC) which issues international auditing guidelines (IAG). Thirteen had been issued as at 1 October 1983. IAPC has members from 13 countries.

international congresses of accountants. Meetings of accountants from around the world that have been held at five-year intervals since 1952. Congresses have been held as follows: St. Louis (1904), Amsterdam (1926), New York (1927), London (1933), Berlin (1937), London (1952), Amsterdam (1957), New York (1962), Paris (1967), Sydney (1972), Munich (1977), Mexico City (1982). The Sydney congress led to the formation of the INTERNATIONAL CO-ORDINATION COMMITTEE FOR THE ACCOUNTANCY PROFESSION (ICCAP) and the

INTERNATIONAL ACCOUNTING STANDARDS COMMITTEE (IASC). The Munich congress led to the formation of the INTERNATIONAL FEDERATION OF ACCOUNTANTS (IFAC).

International Co-ordination Committee for the Accountancy Profession (ICCAP). A committee composed of national accountancy bodies founded in 1972 at the International Congress of Accountants held in Sydney and superseded in 1977 by the INTERNATIONAL FEDERATION OF ACCOUNTANTS (IFAC). The members of ICCAP were Australia, Canada, Federal Republic of Germany, France, India, Japan, Mexico, the Netherlands, the Philippines, United Kingdom and Ireland, and the USA.

International Federation of Accountants (IFAC). A body formed in 1977, at the International Congress of Accountants held in Munich, which aims to develop a co-ordinated international accountancy profession with harmonized standards. Its predecessor was the INTERNATIONAL CO-ORDINATION COMMITTEE FOR THE ACCOUNTANCY PROFESSION (ICCAP, 1972-77). IFAC has a secretariat in New York and a 1983 membership of 83 accountancy bodies from 62 countries. It works through committees on education, ethics, financial and management accounting, INTERNATIONAL AUDITING PRACTICES (IAPC), regional organizations and IFAC/IASC Co-ordinating. The education committee produces guidelines and statements of guidance; the ethics committee, statements of guidance on ethics; the IAPC, international auditing guidelines. IFAC contributes 10% of the annual budget of the INTERNATIONAL ACCOUNTING STANDARDS COMMITTEE (IASC) and organizes the INTERNATIONAL CONGRESSES OF ACCOUNTANTS. IFAC does not issue standards, this being the function of the IASC.

interperiod tax allocation. US term for the allocation of tax over accounting periods when TIMING DIFFERENCES exist. *See* DEFERRED TAXATION.

intestate. A person who dies without leaving a WILL. In the absence of a will, his or her estate is distributed as laid down by statute.

intraperiod tax allocation. US term for the allocation of the annual charge for tax among the items in the profit and loss account (income statement). In the UK it is the practice to report both the profit or loss on ordinary activities and the extraordinary profit or loss gross and net of tax.

introduction. In the UK, an application for listing on The Stock Exchange, or for trading in the Unlisted Securities Market, where no marketing arrangements are required. Introductions only apply to securities which are of such amount and so widely held that adequate marketability can be assured. The main advantages to the company concerned are added marketability and more easily ascertainable market value.

inventoriable costs. Synonym for PRODUCT COSTS.

inventories. In US terminology, a general term comprising goods held for sale by a retail or wholesale business (merchandise inventory) or by a manufacturer (finished goods); goods in intermediate stages of production (work in process); and raw materials and supplies.
 See INVENTORY ACCOUNTING, INVENTORY VALUATION, STOCKS.

inventory accounting. Accounting for INVENTORIES (STOCKS). The amount of inventory significantly affects for many enterprises both the COST OF GOODS SOLD (and hence the gross and net profits) and the CURRENT ASSET total in the balance sheet. The numerous problems of inventory accounting include: (1) the choice between the PERIODIC INVENTORY METHOD and the PERPETUAL INVENTORY METHOD (if the latter is used, a debit to cost of goods sold and a credit to inventories needs to be made on the occasion of each sale); (2) the basis of INVENTORY VALUATION and the meanings to be attached to 'cost' and 'market value'; and (3) the choice among cost flow assumptions (e.g. FIRST IN FIRST OUT, LAST IN FIRST OUT).

Under all of these there are significant differences between UK and US practices.

inventory control. Discovering and maintaining the optimum level of investment in inventories (stocks). The main problem of inventory control is balancing ordering costs (which decline in total as stocks increase) against carrying costs (which increase as stocks increase), in order to calculate the economic order quantity (EOQ) which minimizes total costs. Ordering costs include clerical costs, stationery, postages, telephone, etc; carrying costs include insurance, rent and interest foregone. Using calculus, it can be shown that in a simple case

$$\text{EOQ} = \sqrt{\frac{2AP}{S}}$$

where A = annual quantity used in units, P = cost per purchase order, S = annual carrying cost p.a. of one unit. Because of the square root sign, the formula is not sensitive to minor PREDICTION ERROR. It can be adjusted to take account of quantity discounts. To motivate managers towards the EOQ, the costs charged to them should include the imputed interest as well as the outlay costs.

In the absence of uncertainty, the re-order point for inventory is simply average daily usage multiplied by the lead time (the time taken for an order to be placed and delivered). Given uncertainty, a safety stock is necessary. The optimum safety stock is at the point where the carrying costs of an extra unit equal the cost of being out of stock, having regard to the probabilities.

Not all stocks are of equal importance. The ABC method classifies items in terms of their consumption costs, with control techniques being applied to items, perhaps comprising a relatively small percentage of total stocks in volume terms, whose consumption costs are highest.

Measuring the relevant costs may not be easy. It is, for example, difficult to quantify the loss of goodwill from being out of stock.

inventory valuation. The methods of valuing inventories (STOCKS) either under historical cost accounting (HCA) or under some form of inflation accounting. Accounting standard setters in the UK (SSAP 9) and the USA (Accounting Research Bulletin No. 43) agree on the use of the lower of cost or market rule but there are significant differences of detail. Valuation at the lower of cost or market is required by UK company law.

In the UK, in the context of HCA, SSAP 9 justifies the rule on the grounds that only costs which can be recovered from future sales should be carried forward. Market is defined as NET REALIZABLE VALUE (NRV) and the comparison of cost and NRV is made in respect of each item or group of items separately. Cost is defined to comprise that expenditure which has been incurred in the normal course of business in bringing the product or service to its present location and condition, i.e. to include both variable and fixed factory overhead. Thus ABSORPTION COSTING is permitted but VARIABLE COSTING (marginal or direct costing) is not permitted for external reporting purposes; nor, in SSAP 9, are the BASE STOCK and LAST IN FIRST OUT (LIFO) methods (but company law expressly permits FIRST IN FIRST OUT, LAST IN FIRST OUT, WEIGHTED AVERAGE COST or any other similar method). The RETAIL INVENTORY METHOD is acceptable for retail stores. Stocks are not to be written down to current REPLACEMENT COST (RC) where this is lower than NRV, except where RC is the best approximation to NRV. It is argued that a write down to RC would overstate the irrecoverable costs. In a CURRENT COST ACCOUNTING (CCA) context, however, SSAP 16 requires inventory to be valued at the lower of current RC and NRV (i.e. at its VALUE TO THE BUSINESS). Company law requires the disclosure of the difference, if material, between the balance sheet valuation of stocks and their replacement cost. Under current purchasing power (CPP) accounting in the UK, stocks were valued at the lower of historical cost adjusted by a general price index and net realizable value. Different rules apply to LONG-TERM CONTRACT WORK IN PROGRESS.

In the USA, 'market' is usually defined as

replacement cost (RC) a write-down to replacement cost being justified by ARB No. 43 on the grounds of loss of utility. NRV is used instead of RC, however, where RC exceeds NRV (and both are lower than acquisition cost). Also, market value should not be less than NRV reduced by an allowance for an approximately normal profit margin. In summary, market value is defined in the USA to mean the middle value of RC, NRV and NRV less a normal profit margin. Unlike the UK, generally accepted accounting principles in the USA do not insist that the comparison of cost and market value be made in respect of each item or group of items separately. As in the UK only ABSORPTION COSTING is permitted for external reporting. It is also, unlike the UK, the only costing method accepted for tax purposes. For tax reasons also, the LAST IN FIRST OUT (LIFO) cost flow assumption is popular in the USA.

investment centre. A segment of a business that is held responsible for investments as well as revenues and costs.

investment grants. A grant of cash by a government to an enterprise in order to encourage the enterprise to purchase fixed assets of a particular kind or in a particular location.

investment income. In the UK, for tax purposes, income from dividends and interest. Some investment income is tax-free. Much of taxable investment income is taxed at source. *See also* COMPOSITE RATE.

investment period method (IPM). A method used by some lessors in the UK to allocate the total finance charges from a finance lease (*see* LEASE ACCOUNTING) over the period of the lease on an after-tax basis. The method allocates the finance charge over that part of the lease in which the lessor has a net cash investment, in proportion to the net cash investment at the end of each period.

investment properties. In UK standard accounting practice (SSAP 19), an interest in land and/or buildings in respect of which construction work and development have been completed and which is held for its investment potential, any rental income being negotiated at arm's length, but excluding properties owned and occupied by companies for their own purposes and properties let to and occupied by companies in the same group. Such properties are not depreciated but are included in the balance sheet at their OPEN MARKET VALUE (irrespective of whether HISTORICAL COST ACCOUNTING or CURRENT COST ACCOUNTING is followed). Changes in the value of investment properties are taken not to profit and loss account but to an INVESTMENT REVALUATION RESERVE; but, except in the case of investment trust companies and property unit trusts, any deficit on this reserve is written off to profit and loss account.

It is claimed in SSAP 19 that the special treatment of investment properties is justified by the overriding legal requirement in the UK to give a TRUE AND FAIR VIEW. Some writers have argued that the SSAP represents rather the result of pressure from investment companies.

investment revaluation reserve. In the UK, a reserve required to be set up under SSAP 19 where INVESTMENT PROPERTIES are included at their OPEN MARKET VALUE. Except in the case of investment trust companies and property unit trusts, any deficit on the reserve must be written off to profit and loss account.

investments. Shares, loans, bonds and debentures held either as a FIXED ASSET, i.e. to provide a continuing source of income and in some cases control or significant influence over the activities of another enterprise, or as a CURRENT ASSET, i.e. as a temporary means of earning income on funds eventually intended for other use. The distinction between fixed asset and current asset investments is primarily one of intention and may not be always easy to make in practice but it is mandatory under the UK BALANCE SHEET FORMATS. Income from fixed asset and current asset investments must be disclosed separately in the PROFIT AND

LOSS ACCOUNT FORMATS. The formats also distinguish between investments in group companies, investments in related companies, and other fixed asset investments; and between investments in shares and investments in loans. In the Notes listed investments must be distinguished from unlisted. Listed investments must be further divided into those listed in the UK and those listed overseas. Income from listed investments must be disclosed in the Notes.

In the UK a fixed asset investment is normally valued at cost but a provision for diminution in value must be made if a reduction in value is expected to be permanent. If the reduction no longer applies the provision must be written back. Under the ALTERNATIVE ACCOUNTING RULES, fixed asset investments are valued either at market or other appropriate basis, and current asset investments at current cost. In the Notes, for each item which includes listed investments disclosure is required of the aggregate market value where it differs from their balance sheet amount, and also the stock exchange value where the market value is taken as the highest of the two values.

In the USA, loan securities are valued at cost. Equity securities held as short-term investments are valued at the lower of cost or market for the entire portfolio. Equity securities held as long-term investments are also valued by this method unless they represent a majority ownership or a controlling minority ownership in which case the EQUITY METHOD is used.

investment tax credit. In the USA, a percentage of the cost of some depreciable assets used to offset income tax payable in the year the assets are purchased. In princi-ple, the credit can either be reflected in net income immediately or it can be spread over the life of the asset concerned. The latter method was supported by the ACCOUNTING PRINCIPLES BOARD (APB) in the early 1960s but it was overruled by the SEC and both methods were permitted. Later, both the APB and the SEC were overruled by Congress.

The nearest equivalent to an investment tax credit in the UK is the INVESTMENT GRANT.

investment trust. In the UK, a company whose object is investment in the securities of other companies. Unlike a UNIT TRUST, it is not in fact a trust.

issue by tender. An issue of securities in which the public is invited to apply at or above a certain minimum price. The hope is that investors will offer to buy the securities at or just below the anticipated market price.

issued share capital. In the UK, the nominal amount of the AUTHORIZED SHARE CAPITAL which has been issued. Any excess over the nominal amount is a SHARE PREMIUM.

issue price. The price at which a share, bond or debenture is issued. It is not necessarily equal to the PAR VALUE since shares can be issued at a premium and bonds and debentures at a premium or a discount.

issuing house. An institution that advises on new issues of shares or stocks for public limited companies.

J

job costing. A costing system used by organizations whose products or services are easily identified by individual units or batches, each of which receives varying inputs of direct materials, direct labour and factory overhead. In job costing, PRODUCT COSTS are accumulated on job cost sheets, which record direct material, direct labour and factory overhead absorbed. Contrast PROCESS COSTING and OPERATION COSTING.

joint costs. The costs of two or more products of relatively significant sales value that are simultaneously produced by a process or series of processes. The products are not individually identifiable until after a stage of production known as the SPLIT-OFF POINT. No one of the products may be produced without also producing the others, although the proportions in which they are produced may be variable.

The allocation of joint costs serves no useful control or decision-making purpose but is usually regarded as necessary for stock (inventory) valuation and income measurement. Allocations may be made using either physical measures or net realizable values. The former method may have no relationship to the revenue-producing powers of the individual products. It is used in the USA for amortizing costs relating to oil and gas reserves produced jointly (FASB Statement No. 19).

The latter method, based on the relative net realizable values of the joint products, is more popular. It has the effect of equalizing the gross margin percentage across the joint products. The method is more difficult to apply if the joint products are not saleable at the split-off point.

An alternative to allocation is to value stocks (inventories) of joint products at sales value at the split-off point or at net realizable values (i.e., ultimate sales values less estimated separable costs to complete and sell). To avoid the recognition of unrealiz-ed profits, a normal profit margin can be deducted from the net realizable values. *See also* JOINT PRODUCT.

joint product. A product of a relatively significant sales value that can only be produced simultaneously with other products. In deciding whether a joint product should be sold at the SPLIT-OFF POINT or processed beyond that point, regard should be had to differential income, i.e., sales less SEPARABLE COSTS. The allocation of JOINT COSTS is irrelevant in this context. It is profitable to incur extra separable costs so long as the incremental revenue exceeds the incremental costs. *See also* BYPRODUCT.

joint variance. A VARIANCE reflecting the combined effect of changes in prices and quantities as shown in the diagram.

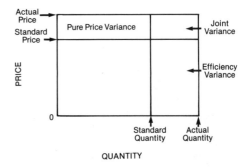

A materials joint variance is usually included in the PRICE VARIANCE on the grounds that the responsibility of the purchasing manager is to buy for all needs regardless of whether the materials are used efficiently. The same argument can be applied to labour rate variances.

joint venture. The joint prosecution of a particular transaction for mutual profit or an association of persons jointly undertaking some commercial enterprise. Unlike a partnership a joint venture does not entail a continuing relationship. Joint ventures are particularly common in mining and oil and gas exploration. In developing countries joint ventures are often established between multinational companies and government agencies. They may be operated through companies or may be unincorporated. In the UK and USA, EQUITY ACCOUNTING is usual for joint ventures but PROPORTIONAL CONSOLIDATION is also used and is common in France and the Netherlands.

journal. Any book (or other record) in which either one or both aspects of an accounting TRANSACTION or other EVENT are recorded chronologically on a day-to-day basis. More particularly, the term is applied to the book (also known as the general journal) that records those transactions which, because of their importance or rareness of occurrence, are not recorded in a specialized journal (such as a SALES JOURNAL or a PURCHASES JOURNAL). Journals are also referred to in the UK as day books and books of original or prime entry. Entries in journals are posted individually or in total to LEDGERS.

judgmental sampling. In an audit context, sampling based on the exercise of an auditor's judgment rather than on statistical techniques.

L

labour variances. Deviations from budget or standard costs in respect of direct labour. They are usually subdivided into rate or PRICE VARIANCES and EFFICIENCY VARIANCES but *see also* JOINT VARIANCE.

Laplace criterion. *See* DECISION TABLE.

lapping. The US term for TEEMING AND LADING.

last in first out. In the context of INVENTORY VALUATION, the calculation of the cost of inventories (stocks) on the basis that the quantities in hand represent the earliest units purchased or produced. Compared with the FIRST IN FIRST OUT (FIFO) method, LIFO normally results, in times of rising prices, in a higher cost of goods sold figure (and therefore a lower profit figure) and in a lower asset valuation in the balance sheet. It has been acceptable for tax purposes in the USA since 1939 but not in the UK. It is expressly permitted by UK company law but is not part of standard accounting practice (SSAP 9). In the USA, it is available to a taxpayer only if it is also used in his published financial statements.

Apart from tax considerations, LIFO may owe its popularity in the USA to the fact that its use results in an approximation to CURRENT COST OF GOODS SOLD. It does this, however, at the expense of a badly out-of-date balance sheet figure, which may distort those financial ratios that are based in part on inventory figures. In the USA, the SEC requires companies using LIFO to disclose the current value of their opening and closing inventories, and the Internal Revenue Service does not permit the lower of cost or market basis to be used with LIFO.

See also DOLLAR VALUE LIFO.

learning curve. A COST FUNCTION in which AVERAGE COSTS decline systematically as cumulative production increases. It is applicable during the learning or start-up phases of production.

lease accounting. Accounting for contracts between a lessor and a lessee for the hire of a specific asset, the lessor retaining ownership of the asset, but conveying the right to the use of the asset to the lessee for an agreed period of time in return for payment of specified rentals. Lease contracts are usually EXECUTORY CONTRACTS. A distinction can be made between 'finance leases' (or 'capital leases') that transfer substantially all the risks and rewards of ownership to the lessee and 'operating leases' (all other leases). Finance leases are usually non-cancellable. Drawing a precise distinction between a finance lease and an operating lease is difficult and has led to much complicated standard setting and interpreting in the USA. The distinction is vital, however, since the accounting treatment prescribed for finance leases by both SSAP 21 in the UK and FAS 13 in the USA differs significantly from that for operating leases. The paragraphs which follow relate more specifically to the UK but the differences between the UK and US standards relate to details rather than principle.

In the UK, a finance lease is required to be accounted for by the lessee as if it were (*see* SUBSTANCE OVER FORM) the purchase of the property rights in an asset with simultaneous recognition of the obligations to make future payments. This means that finance leases are treated for accounting purposes in the same way as assets on HIRE PURCHASE. Operating leases, on the other hand, are not shown in the balance sheet, the rental being charged to profit and loss account.

The amount at which a finance lease is shown in a balance sheet at the start of the lease is either its fair value or the present value of the minimum lease payments discounted at a commercial rate of interest, i.e., approximately the rate of interest the lessee would pay on a similar lease from another lessor. Rentals payable are apportioned between the finance charge and a reduction of the outstanding obligation for future amounts payable using either the actuarial method based on COMPOUND INTEREST and ANNUITIES or the RULE OF 78. The relevant interest rate where the lease is capitalized at its fair value is the rate implicit in the lease (akin to an INTERNAL RATE OF RETURN). The asset is depreciated, normally by the straight line method (*see* DEPRECIATION METHODS), over the shorter of the lease term or its useful life.

In the balance sheet of the lessor, a finance lease is required to be recorded in the balance sheet as a debtor at the amount of the investment in the lease net of government or other grants receivable and of finance charges allocated to future periods. The finance charges may be allocated on either a pre-tax or an after-tax basis and either actuarially or by an approximate method such as the rule of 78 or the INVESTMENT PERIOD METHOD. An operating lease, on the other hand, is required to be recorded as a fixed asset and depreciated over its useful life. Rental income is normally to be recognized on a straight line basis over the period of the lease.

Treating leases as operating rather than finance leases is preferred by many lessees for two reasons: the income reported is higher in the early years of the lease (since more finance charges are written off in earlier years than in later years); and no liability is shown in the balance sheet (i.e., there is OFF BALANCE SHEET FINANCING). Furthermore, many lessors and lessees claim that the capitalization of leases has adverse ECONOMIC CONSEQUENCES. The difficulty of precisely defining a finance (capital) lease has meant, especially in the USA, that lease agreements are drafted in such a fashion as to avoid complying with the requirement to capitalize. At the same time US standard setters have had to devote much time to leases: no less than eight of the first 30 FASB Standards and six of the first 30 FASB Interpretations are concerned with this subject.

Opponents of lease capitalization have also claimed that full disclosure in the notes would be more appropriate. The semi-strong form of the EFFICIENT MARKET HYPOTHESIS suggests that this would be as helpful to users as capitalization. On the other hand non-capitalization leads, it is argued, to the distortion of balance sheet ratios.

Tax changes brought about by the Finance Act 1984 are likely to lead to a lessening of interest in lease accounting in the UK.

least squares. Statistical techniques based on minimizing the sum of the squares of the vertical distances between observed data points and a REGRESSION line.

ledger. A book or other record containing ACCOUNTS. In practice a business of any size will subdivide its ledger into a GENERAL or NOMINAL LEDGER and several SUBSIDIARY LEDGERS (e.g., a DEBTORS LEDGER and a CREDITORS LEDGER). *See also* SELF-BALANCING LEDGERS.

legacy. A gift of PERSONALTY made by a will. Legacies are either 'general' (a gift out of the general funds of an estate), 'demonstrative' (a gift payable out of a particular fund or portion of an estate; if the fund has ceased to exist, the legacy becomes a general one), or 'specific' (a gift of some particular portion of the estate; the legacy may be lost by ADEMPTION).

legal reserve. In continental European countries a reserve required by law. A prescribed percentage of profits has to be transferred each year to an undistributable reserve until an amount equal to a prescribed percentage of share capital has been reached. The purpose of the legal reserve is to provide added protection to creditors. The option in the FOURTH DIRECTIVE to introduce legal reserves into the UK was not taken up.

lens model. A model used in HUMAN INFORMATION PROCESSING which portrays a decision maker as separated from the event of interest by time or space, faced with multiple overlapping cues (the information set available to him or her) that are imperfect predictions of the state of the environment, and combining these cues probabilistically in order to form a judgment. The model suggests that judgmental achievement is a function of both the environment and the abilities of the decision maker.

letter for underwriters. *See* COMFORT LETTER.

letter of engagement. A letter issued by a firm of accountants to a client at the time of being engaged setting out such matters as what they understand the engagement to involve, the way in which the work will be carried out, the basis on which fees are calculated, and details of other services which the firm is able to provide.

letter of representation. A letter from the directors of a company (or other entity) to an auditor placing on record the representations of management on significant matters directly affecting the accounts and financial statements.

letters of administration. The document given by the court to an ADMINISTRATOR which authorizes him or her to deal with the estate of a deceased person who has left no WILL.

leverage. *See* GEARING (LEVERAGE).

leveraged lease. In general terms, a finance lease (*see* LEASE ACCOUNTING) to which there are three parties: a lessee, a lessor and a lender who provides financing to the lessor. The lender has no right to the lessor's assets other than the leased asset and the lessee's payments; the lessor's investment during some periods of the lease increases because of net cash outflows.

liability. An obligation, arising from a transaction or other event that has already occurred and that involves an enterprise in a probable future transfer of cash, goods or services, or the foregoing of a future cash receipt, the amount of which and the date of settlement of which are measurable with reasonable accuracy. A liability need not be a legally enforceable claim. Liabilities may thus be classified as follows: those with fixed payment dates and amounts; those with fixed payment amounts but estimated payment dates; those for which both payment dates and amounts must be estimated; and those arising from advances from customers on unexecuted contracts and agreements. Not generally recognized as liabilities to be shown in a balance sheet are EXECUTORY CONTRACTS, i.e., obligations under mutual unexecuted contracts (e.g., long term contracts for the supply of goods) and CONTINGENT LIABILITIES.

In principle, liabilities can be stated at either the amount of cash (or its equivalent) ultimately payable or the PRESENT VALUE of that cash, discounting at either the interest rate appropriate when the liability was first incurred or the interest rate appropriate at the date of the balance sheet.

life-renter. The Scottish equivalent of the English LIFE-TENANT.

life-tenant. In England and Wales and the USA the person who enjoys, during his or her lifetime, the income from real estate. The Scottish term is LIFE-RENTER. On the death of the life-tenant the estate goes to the REMAINDERMAN.

limited liability company. A company the liability of whose shareholders is limited. Limited liability was first made generally available in the UK in 1855. Most limited liability companies are COMPANIES LIMITED BY SHARES but some are COMPANIES LIMITED BY GUARANTEE. There are also UNLIMITED COMPANIES. The vast majority of UK companies are PRIVATE COMPANIES (whose names end with the word 'Limited' or 'Ltd.') but the economically significant ones are PUBLIC COMPANIES (whose names end with the words 'public limited company' or 'plc'). LISTED COMPANIES are those public companies which are listed on a recognized stock exchange.

limiting factor. Synonym for CONSTRAINT.

Limperg, Th., Jr. (1879-1961). Dutch accountant responsible for the introduction of CURRENT VALUE ACCOUNTING into the Netherlands and with a great influence on commercial education (especially at the University of Amsterdam, at which he held a chair from 1922 to 1949), and the development of auditing and public accountancy. Limperg was one of the founders of the largest Dutch audit firm. His name is also commemorated in the Limperg Institute, an inter-university accounting and auditing research and development institute in which the Dutch accountancy body (NIVRA) also participates. Limperg published little in his lifetime but his collected works, based on his lecture notes to students, were edited and published after his death. A translation into English of some of his articles on auditing is to be published by the Limperg Institute.

linear cost function. A COST FUNCTION which can be represented by a straight line. Accountants usually assume that cost functions are linear over a RELEVANT RANGE.

linear depreciation. Synonym for straight-line depreciation. *See* DEPRECIATION METHODS.

linear function. A mathematical relationship that when graphed is a straight line.

linear programming. A formal DECISION MODEL for deciding how to make the best use of a given set of scarce resources. A linear programming problem can be formulated as a series of simultaneous linear equations and inequalities in the following form:

$$\text{maximize } z = x_1a + x_2b$$
$$\text{subject to} \quad x_3a + x_4b \leq 24$$
$$x_5a + x_6b \leq 40$$
$$a, b \geq 0$$

where z = contribution and a and b are units of products A and B respectively. The first line is the objective function (which can be expressed in terms of minimization as well as maximization), and the other lines represent constraints including, in the last line, the constraint that negative production of A and B is not possible. The second and third lines may refer to constraints such as those on the availability of machine capacity.

LP models assume that all relationships are linear, that constraints and coefficients can be stated and are known, and that the production of fractional units is possible (*see* INTEGER PROGRAMMING).

If there are only two products a graphical solution is often possible. This will lie at one of the corners of the feasible area (see diagram) — which corner depends on the slope of the (dashed) lines representing the objective function that is furthest from the origin but still has a feasible point on it.

A graphical solution is not possible in most cases and it is necessary to use the SIMPLEX METHOD and to make use of a computer.

The solution to a linear programming problem obviously depends upon the accuracy of the data used. SENSITIVITY ANALYSIS can be used to discover the cost of PREDICTION ERROR and whether it is worth devoting resources to improve the accuracy of the predictions.

See also SHADOW PRICE, GOAL PROGRAMMING, DYNAMIC PROGRAMMING, TRANSPORTATION METHOD.

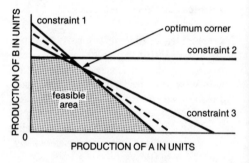

line manager. A manager who is directly responsible for the efficient attainment of the objectives of an enterprise.

liquid assets. Current assets other than stocks and work in progress (inventories). They are also referred to as QUICK ASSETS.

liquidator. In the UK, a person appointed to conduct the winding up of a company. His functions are to realize the company's assets in the most advantageous manner, and to distribute the proceeds, first to creditors, and then, if there is any money left, to shareholders in order of priority. In a WINDING UP BY THE COURT his or her remuneration is fixed by the court. In a MEMBERS' VOLUNTARY WINDING UP it is fixed by the company in general meeting; in a CREDITORS' VOLUNTARY WINDING UP by the COMMITTEE OF INSPECTION, or, if there is no committee, by the general body of creditors.

In a winding up by the court in England and Wales a liquidator must keep proper books, and in particular a record book and a cash book, which are audited by the committee of inspection. These rules do not apply to a voluntary winding up. A liquidator must send to the Department of Trade and Industry, at least twice a year, an account of receipts and payments.

liquidity crisis. For an individual enterprise, a shortage of LIQUID ASSETS leading to a danger of INSOLVENCY.

liquid ratio. Synonym for QUICK RATIO.

listed company. A COMPANY LIMITED BY SHARES and listed upon a recognized stock exchange. In the UK companies are 'listed' on The Stock Exchange but 'traded' on the Unlisted Securities Market.

listed securities. Any securities of a company listed on a recognized stock exchange.

Littleton, Ananias Charles (1886-1974). One of the most influential of American academic accountants; on the staff of the University of Illinois from 1915 to 1952. Littleton was a prolific writer and a pioneer of postgraduate courses in accounting. He was president of the American Accounting Association in 1943 and editor of *The Accounting Review* from 1943 to 1947. His most important books were *Accounting Evolution to 1900* (1933), *An Introduction to Corporate Accounting Standards* (1940, with W.A. Paton) and *Structure of Accounting Theory* (1953). Many of his articles are reprinted in his *Essays on Accountancy* (1961). Littleton was an 'accounting Darwinist', who sought to generalize principles from practice. He was a strong supporter of historical cost accounting.

loan capital. A company's long-term

sources of funds raised from creditors rather than shareholders.

long range planning. Planning the direction and control of the future operations of an enterprise for periods extending beyond one year. It can be subdivided into STRATEGIC PLANNING, which is concerned with deciding on objectives and the obtaining and use of resources to achieve them, and OPERATIONS PLANNING, concerned with detailed programmes for achieving the desired objectives.

long-term contract work in progress. Work in progress arising from long-term contracts. In the UK, SSAP 9 requires that the gross amount of long-term contract work in progress should be stated at cost plus attributable profits less foreseeable losses and progress payments received and receivable. There is no attributable profit until the outcome of a contract can be assessed with reasonable certainty. If anticipated losses on individual contracts exceed cost incurred to date less progress payments received and receivable, the excess should be shown separately as a provision.

loss contingencies. In the USA, those CONTINGENT LIABILITIES that are recognized in the balance sheet. The conditions of recognition are that information available before the issue of the financial statements indicates that it is probable that an asset has been impaired or that a liability has been incurred and the amount of the loss can be reasonably estimated.

loss on holding money. A loss of purchasing power that arises through holding MONETARY ASSETS through a rise in a price level. *See* PURCHASING POWER LOSS OR GAIN.

loss reliefs. Reliefs from tax granted in respect of losses. Such reliefs may be available against any income or may be restricted in some way. Tax rules may allow losses to be carried forward or back or both.

lower of cost or market. *See* INVENTORY VALUATION.

M

macroaccounting. By analogy with the term macroeconomics, NATIONAL ACCOUNTING, i.e., those aspects of accounting concerned with nations rather than individuals or organizations. Macroaccounting has been developed by economists and statisticians rather than accountants. *See* NATIONAL IN-COME AND EXPENDITURE ACCOUNTS, INPUT-OUTPUT TABLES, FLOW OF FUNDS ACCOUNTS, NATIONAL BALANCE SHEET, NATIONAL WEALTH STATEMENTS.

mainstream corporation tax (MCT). The difference between a UK company's total corporation tax liability and advance corporation tax paid and recoverable.

managed costs. Synonym for DISCRETIONARY COSTS.

management accounting. That part of accounting which is concerned mainly with internal reporting to the managers of an enterprise. It emphasizes the control and decision-making rather than the stewardship aspects of accounting. It is relatively free of constraints imposed by legal regulation and accounting standards. It may be contrasted with FINANCIAL ACCOUNTING.

management audit. An independent review and investigation of the performance of an enterprise's management with a view to recommending improvements in established policies and procedures. In the public sector a management audit may be concerned with EFFECTIVENESS as well as EFFICIENCY.

management buy-out. A transaction by means of which a team of managers acquires a substantial holding in a company. The managers are usually, but not necessarily, those already employed by the company. Buy-outs may occur where a conglomerate group wishes to dispense with subsidiaries or divisions; where assets are realized by a liquidator or a receiver; or where private company shareholders wish to realize their investment. Buy-outs have been encouraged in the UK by the relaxation in the Companies Act 1981 of prohibitions on financial assistance for the acquisition of a company's shares.

management by exception. Concentrating on those areas that are not going according to plan, i.e., on VARIANCES from BUDGET, rather than on areas of operation which are running smoothly. Management by exception is related to the attention-directing aspect of management accounting.

management by objectives (MBO). A procedure whereby a subordinate and his or her superior jointly formulate the subordinate's objectives (goals) and the plans for attaining them in a subsequent period. The plans are quantified in a BUDGET and the subordinate's performance is evaluated in relation to the budgeted goals agreed upon.

management control. The plans, policies, procedures and practices used by an enterprise in an attempt to make sure that the objectives of the enterprise are achieved. INTERNAL CONTROL can be regarded as that part of management control internal to the enterprise. In designing a management control system regard must be had to the establishment of RESPONSIBILITY CENTRES, PERFORMANCE EVALUATION and rewards and punishments. It is important that performance should be measurable as objectively as possible and should influence the rewards. The formal management control system may not be the same as that which operates informally. A successful system will achieve GOAL CONGRUENCE and provide MOTIVATION.

management information systems (MIS). Systems which provide information to managers in the areas of STRATEGIC PLANNING, OPERATIONS PLANNING and MANAGEMENT CONTROL.

management style. The way in which a

manager (superior) characteristically deals with his subordinates.

manufacturing expenses. Synonym for FACTORY OVERHEAD.

manufacturing overhead. Synonym for FACTORY OVERHEAD.

marginal cost. The extra cost of an extra unit of production. Marginal cost is thus dependent upon VARIABLE COSTS not FIXED COSTS. Accountants usually assume that over a RELEVANT RANGE of production marginal cost and variable cost are equal.

marginal costing. UK term for what is usually referred to in the USA as DIRECT COSTING. A more precise term is VARIABLE COSTING. Marginal costing can be contrasted with ABSORPTION COSTING.

marginal pricing. Basing prices on the marginal costs of products, i.e. (if marginal costs are constant over the relevant range), on product costs based on marginal costing (VARIABLE COSTING). Marginal pricing is less common in practice than FULL COST PRICING but has the advantage that it is based on costs that will change in the future and does not attempt to spread fixed costs over a NORMAL VOLUME that may not represent actual or potential sales. It is generally accepted that marginal pricing is superior for special, as distinct from routine, pricing decisions.

marginal rate of tax. The rate of tax applicable to a small increase in a taxpayer's income. It is above the AVERAGE RATE OF TAX for a PROGRESSIVE TAX; equal to the average rate for a PROPORTIONAL TAX; and below the average rate for a REGRESSIVE TAX.

marginal utility. The extra utility obtained from an extra unit of any good or service.

margin of safety. The excess of budgeted or actual sales over the breakeven sales volume. It shows the amount (if the assumed cost relationships are valid) by which sales may decrease before losses occur.

marketable securities. US term for INVESTMENTS held as CURRENT ASSETS.

market beta. *See* BETA.

market capitalization. The total value of all a listed company's shares on the stock market.

market failure. The failure of the market system to provide the optimal level of production of a good or service. Such failure is most likely with PUBLIC GOODS of which it can be claimed accounting information is one. The existence of market failure is one of the arguments for the REGULATION OF CORPORATE FINANCIAL REPORTING.

market portfolio. A PORTFOLIO of all securities available in the securities market, weighted by their respective total market values.

market price. In a stock exchange context, the price at which a listed company's securities can be bought and sold. It is not necessarily equal to the PAR VALUE or the ISSUE PRICE.

market raid. *See* DAWN RAID.

market risk. Synonym for SYSTEMATIC RISK.

Markov analysis. A method for forecasting the future movement of a variable based on an analysis of the present movement of the variable and using TRANSITION PROBABILITY matrices.

martingale process. A statistical time series of a variable in which the expected value of the variable changes randomly from period to period. The best estimate of the expected value is thus the actually realized value in the most recent period. Empirical research on the statistical properties of earnings makes use of the martingale process.

master budget. A BUDGET which summarizes the objectives of all the sub-units of an organization. Details vary in practice but within the master budget there is likely to be an OPERATING BUDGET (subdivided into, say, sales, production, selling expenses, administrative expenses and income statement) and a FINANCIAL BUDGET (subdivided into, say, cash, capital, balance sheet and funds statement).

matching. The allocation of the financial effect of TRANSACTIONS and other EVENTS into appropriate accounting periods so that relevant income and expenditure is matched. The matching concept is thus an essential part of ACCRUAL ACCOUNTING. The allocations made are, however, sometimes arbitrary and hard to defend (*see* ALLOCATION PROBLEM).

materiality. The threshold for recognition of an accounting item in a financial statement. The materiality of an item depends upon its degree of importance to users in terms of its relevance to evaluation or decision making. Materiality is thus an expression in accounting terms of the legal maxim 'de minimis non curat lex'. *See also* PRECISION.

materials control account. *See* STORES LEDGER CONTROL ACCOUNT.

materials requisition. A document recording materials issued to a job or process and used both as a means of recording materials issued and of fixing responsibility.

materials variances. Deviations from budgeted or standard cost in respect of direct materials. They are usually subdivided into PRICE VARIANCES and usage or EFFICIENCY VARIANCES, but *see also* JOINT VARIANCE.

mathematical programming. A mathematical model containing one or more functions to be optimized subject to constraints. LINEAR PROGRAMMING is a form of mathematical programming in which the functions and constraints are linear.

Mathews Report. A report on inflation and taxation published in Australia in 1975. It recommended, *inter alia*, that business taxation should be adjusted for specific price changes.

matrix. A rectangular array of numbers ('elements') arranged in rows and columns and enclosed in brackets. Within the rules of matrix algebra, matrices can be added, subtracted, multiplied and inverted.

matrix organization. An ORGANIZATIONAL STRUCTURE in which one manager is given responsibility for a project or products that uses services from several functional RESPONSIBILITY CENTRES.

maximax criterion. *See* DECISION TABLE.

maximin criterion. *See* DECISION TABLE.

maximum basis. Method of calculating EARNINGS PER SHARE (EPS) in the UK which assumes that a company has distributed all its earnings and is liable to pay ADVANCE CORPORATION TAX (ACT) on them. Its use is not standard accounting practice but it is used by the London *Financial Times* in its calculation of DIVIDEND COVER.

May, George Oliver (1875-1961). An influential English-born American practitioner who was also a prolific writer on accounting theory and practice. After serving articles in Exeter (Devon), May qualified as an English chartered accountant in 1897 and joined Price Waterhouse, moving almost immediately to the USA. He succeeded Sir Arthur Lowes Dickinson as senior partner of the US firm in 1911, retiring from this post in 1926. In 1930 he was appointed chairman of a joint committee of the New York Stock Exchange and the American Institute of Accountants investigating the need for greater uniformity in accounting principles. The system of accounting regulation as it developed in the USA in the 1930s and from which the present US system descends owes much to May's influence. His most influential book was *Financial Accounting: A Distillation of Experience* (1943). Most of his articles written before 1936 were reprinted in *Twenty-Five Years of Accounting Responsibility: 1911-1936* (1936, ed. B.C. Hunt). A full bibliography is given in *Memoirs and Accounting Thought of George*

O. May (1962, ed. P. Grady). May's writings deal with the practical problems of his times and reflect the views of a practitioner who gave much thought to the profession he practised.

Meade Committee Report (1978). Report of a committee on *The Structure and Reform of Direct Taxation* set up by the UK Institute for Fiscal Studies under the chairmanship of J.E. Meade. The report concluded that comprehensive and radical reforms were necessary. It recommended *inter alia* a shift to a progressive expenditure tax system, together with progressive taxation of wealth and discrimination against inherited wealth; a reform of the social security system; self-assessment for direct taxation; the movement of corporation tax towards a flow-of-funds basis; and an accessions tax. The report provides an authoritative review of the British tax system but there have been few signs of its recommendations being implemented.

mean variance rule. A decision rule for evaluating capital investments on the basis of their expected returns and standard deviations (used as a measure of risk). Project A is preferred to project B if *either* the expected return of A exceeds (or is equal to) the expected return of B and the standard deviation of A is less than the standard deviation of B *or* the expected return of A exceeds that of B and the standard deviation of A is less than (or equal to) that of B.

measurement scales. Ways of quantifying. Four measurement scales can be distinguished: nominal, ordinal, interval and ratio. A nominal scale simply uses a numeral as a label. An ordinal scale ranks properties in accordance with a number system, permitting the use of comparisons such as 'greater than', 'equal to' and 'less than'. An interval scale has steps such that properties so measured can be added, subtracted, multiplied, divided, etc., but the starting point of the scale is arbitrary. A ratio scale is one whose starting point is not arbitrary. All four scales enable an equality to be determined; all but the nominal scale allow

determination of a rank order; only the interval and the ratio scales allow determination of the equality of intervals; only the ratio scale allows determination of equality of ratios.

The temperature of water may be used as an example. Assigning the numeral 2 to 'hot' and the numeral 0 to 'cold' is to use a nominal scale. Adding 1 for 'warm' produces an ordinal scale. The Fahrenheit and Celsius (centigrade) scales are interval scales since they have class intervals of regular size but have arbitrary starting points. The Kelvin scale is a ratio scale because its starting point is set non-arbitrarily at absolute zero.

In the context of accounting, charts of accounts provide examples of the use of a nominal scale (if the account numbers have no place value) and an ordinal scale (if the chart uses, for example, a decimalized place system, e.g., 1.00 cash 1.01 debtors).

median. A measure of the central tendency of a group of numerical data obtained by selecting the value of the middle amount when the amounts are ordered by size.

medium companies. *See* SMALL AND MEDIUM COMPANIES.

members' voluntary winding up. In the UK, a VOLUNTARY WINDING UP in which a DECLARATION OF SOLVENCY has been made.

memorandum of association. In the UK, a document required to be filed with the Registrar of Companies when a company is incorporated. It states the name of the company, that the company is a public company (if such is the case), the situation of the registered office, the objects of the company, that the liability of the members (shareholders) is limited (unless the company is an unlimited one), the authorized share capital and how it is divided (or, if the company is limited by guarantee, the maximum amount to be contributed by members on a winding up), and details of the subscribers (the persons 'desirous of being formed into a company').

merchant bank. In the UK, banks which act

as ACCEPTING HOUSES, ISSUING HOUSES, company financial advisers, managers of TAKE-OVER BIDS, unit trust managers, etc.

merger. In general, a situation in which two or more enterprises cease to be distinct enterprises. In the UK, mergers are regulated under the Fair Trading Act, 1973 and may also be subject to European Community law. Proposed mergers may be referred by the government to the Monopolies and Mergers Commission.

merger accounting. The preparation of CONSOLIDATED FINANCIAL STATEMENTS on the assumption that one company has merged with another rather than acquired another. In the UK, ACQUISITION ACCOUNTING, not merger accounting, is the norm. In the USA, the terms used are respectively purchase accounting and pooling of interests and the latter is more common than in the UK.

Merger accounting applies only when the purchase consideration is wholly or mainly in the form of shares rather than cash. If the purchase consideration is shares, the previous shareholders of the acquiree become shareholders of the acquirer, which is not the case where the purchase consideration is cash.

Merger accounting differs from acquisition accounting in that the shares are deemed to be issued at par rather than at a current market value; assets are not revalued at the date of acquisition; no goodwill arises; and the pre-acquisition profits of the acquired company are not eliminated from the distributable profits of the group.

It follows from the above that not only will the consolidated financial statements differ, depending upon whether or not merger accounting is used, but so also will the financial statements of the acquiring company.

Merger accounting usually leads to higher reported retained earnings, net profits and earnings per share. This is because no pre-acquisition profits are eliminated, depreciation charges are lower (since fixed assets are not revalued) and there is no goodwill to be amortized. These factors are less important in the UK than in the USA since in the latter fixed assets are not normally revalued

and the amortization of goodwill cannot be avoided. This no doubt explains in part why pooling of interests has become so popular in the USA.

In the UK, merger accounting was used during the merger wave of the 1960s but its legal status was always in some doubt. The *Shearer v Bercain* case (1980) confirmed this and it was necessary for the Companies Act 1981 to make it retrospectively legal and to define the restricted circumstances in which it can be used in future. The Accounting Standards Committee failed to achieve a standard on the subject in the 1970s but issued a further exposure draft in 1982. It is proposed that merger accounting should be applied when a business combination is brought about by an exchange of shares and no significant resources leave the combining companies.

In the USA, Opinion No. 16 of the Accounting Principles Board was promulgated in 1970, after considerable controversy. It requires that a business combination be treated as either a purchase or a pooling of interests. Only if the combination meets 12 conditions can it be treated as a pooling. The general philosophy is that there should be a mutual sharing of risks and benefits. The complexity of the conditions demonstrates how difficult it is in practice to distinguish a merger from an acquisition.

Metcalf report. A report on the US 'accounting establishment' prepared on behalf of a senate sub-committee chaired by Senator Metcalf and published in 1976. The report severely criticized the US accountancy profession and recommended, *inter alia*, that accounting and auditing standards should be set by the federal government.

microaccounting. By analogy with the term microeconomics, those aspects of accounting concerned with individuals and organizations rather than nations.

minority interest. That part of the net profit or loss, or of the net assets, of a subsidiary attributable to shares owned other than by the parent company or other group company. A minority interest only arises if

100% of each of the subsidiary's assets and liabilities is taken into the consolidated balance sheet, i.e., it is not applicable if EQUITY ACCOUNTING or PROPORTIONAL CONSOLIDATION is used. Under the parent company concept of consolidation (*see* CONSOLIDATED FINANCIAL STATEMENTS) the minority interest is not credited with a share of GOODWILL ON CONSOLIDATION. If the entity concept of consolidation were adopted it would be so credited.

The minority interest is a difficult item to classify in a balance sheet. Under the generally accepted parent company concept it is neither part of shareholders' funds (as it would be under the entity concept) nor a liability. It is usually shown as a separate item between them, although sometimes it is deducted from the net assets.

The existence of a minority interest complicates the adjustments necessary for the elimination of INTER-COMPANY PROFITS.

mixed cost. Synonym for SEMIVARIABLE COST.

mix variances. VARIANCES which arise when the interaction of the costs of products are analyzed. They act as supplements to the basic PRICE VARIANCES, EFFICIENCY VARIANCES and VOLUME VARIANCES.

mode. A measure of the central tendency of a group of numerical data obtained by selecting the value that occurs most frequently.

model. A simplified representation of reality, e.g., the ACCOUNTING IDENTITY is a model of the financial state of a business. Models can be classified as iconic (e.g., a statue), analogue or symbolic (usually mathematical symbols).

modern equivalent asset. In CURRENT COST ACCOUNTING (CCA) systems, the asset which would be bought now if one were not already held. It may differ from the existing asset in respect of initial capital cost, operating costs, life or output.

modified accounts. In the UK, financial statements filed with the Registrar of Companies in which advantage has been taken of the exemptions available to SMALL AND MEDIUM COMPANIES.

monetary assets. Those ASSETS which have a fixed monetary exchange value which is not affected by a change in the price level although it may be affected by INDEXATION. Examples are cash at bank and in hand and debtors (accounts receivable). Investments with fluctuating market values are usually regarded as non-monetary assets. In the absence of INDEXATION (the normal situation in the UK and the USA) there is no legal requirement for a greater or lesser number of dollars to be tendered to compensate for a changing price level. The distinction between monetary and non-monetary assets is useful in INFLATION ACCOUNTING and FOREIGN CURRENCY TRANSLATION.

monetary/non-monetary method. *See* FOREIGN CURRENCY TRANSLATION.

monetary unit sampling (MUS). In an audit context, a sampling plan in which the monetary unit is the sample item and is then subjected to RANDOM SAMPLING or SYSTEMATIC RANDOM SAMPLING. The auditor performs his test not on the individual monetary unit but on the account balance which includes the monetary unit selected. MUS is most suitable for SUBSTANTIVE TESTS where the distribution of the population being tested is significantly skewed and the amount of misstatement is expected to be very low. It is designed to control beta risk not ALPHA RISK.

monetary working capital adjustment (MWCA). An adjustment made in some CURRENT COST ACCOUNTING systems (e.g., in SSAP 16 in the UK) in order to take account of the effect of changing prices on monetary working capital. It is argued that increased prices tie up in money terms not only more stocks (inventory) but also more trade debtors and creditors. As with the COST OF SALES ADJUSTMENT (COSA), the MWCA can be calculated in practice in a number of ways, e.g., by the averaging method. The adjustment is made with reference to changes in the SPECIFIC PRICES of stocks, not to changes in the GENERAL PRICE LEVEL. Difficulties may arise in defining monetary working capital in this context. The definition in SSAP 16 includes (a) trade debtors, prepayments and trade bills receivable, plus (b) stocks not subject to a COSA, less (c) trade creditors, accruals and trade bills payable, plus (d) that part of bank balances or overdrafts arising from fluctuations in the volume of stock or the items in (a), (b) and (c) together with any cash floats required to support day-to-day operations of the business.

In principle a separate monetary working capital adjustment can also be made in CURRENT PURCHASING POWER (CPP) ACCOUNTING, in which case general price indexes are appropriate.

See also PURCHASING POWER LOSS OR GAIN.

money capital. The value of the net assets of an enterprise in nominal monetary units, as in HISTORICAL COST ACCOUNTING. *See* CAPITAL MAINTENANCE CONCEPT.

money market. The market for short-term finance operated by the central bank, the commercial banks and financial institutions. *See* CAPITAL MARKET.

monitoring costs. *See* AGENCY COSTS.

Monte Carlo method. A form of SIMULATION, in which random numbers are used to generate a set of values that has the same distributional characteristics as the process being simulated.

moral hazard. A divergence between the private MARGINAL COST of an action and its marginal SOCIAL COST which results in a less than optimal allocation of resources. In accounting a moral hazard problem arises because of INFORMATIONAL ASYMMETRY. An agent (*see* AGENCY COSTS) may have access to superior information which he may use to maximize his own self-interest at the expense of his principal.

moratorium. A procedure whereby major creditors individually agree not to press for payment of debts owing, on the grounds that their interests will be better served by continued trading.

motivation. The desire for a selected goal together with a drive towards that goal. Motivation may be extrinsic (e.g., salary increases) or intrinsic (e.g., greater self-satisfaction). The former depends upon a clear connection between performance and rewards.

The motivation theories of Maslow, Herzberg and McClellan are generally regarded as relevant to management accounting. Maslow argued that each person has a hierarchical set of needs to be satisfied, i.e., in descending order, physiological needs, safety, love and belongingness, esteem and self-actualization. If this is accepted, the prospect of additional economic rewards is not sufficient to motivate organizationally desirable behaviour on the part of many individuals who are already well paid. Herzberg distinguished between motivators (sources of satisfaction, mainly related to job content) and hygiene factors (sources of dissatisfaction, mainly related to job context). The absence of hygiene factors can adversely affect performance, but their presence will not necessarily improve it. McClellan distinguished between high achievers and low achievers and found the former less concerned about monetary rewards.

See also GOAL CONGRUENCE, ASPIRATION LEVEL.

moving average. An average calculated from a group comprising a fixed number of terms within a series, each group, except the first, being equal to the immediately preceding group less the first term of that group plus the immediately following term. See TIME SERIES.

multi-column reporting. The side-by-side presentation of financial data drawn up on several different measurement bases (e.g., historical cost, replacement cost, net realizable value and each of these adjusted for changes in the general price level) with equal importance attached to each. It is argued that in the context of general-purpose financial statements this would better meet the needs of the various user groups, since each measurement base has both advantages and disadvantages.

Arguments against multi-column reporting are that the publication of several different but equally 'true and fair' profit figures would diminish public credibility in company financial reporting and also lead to INFORMATION OVERLOAD.

Multi-column reporting has not been adopted in any legislation or accounting standard, although the US FAS 33 (1979) requires items of both general price level and current cost financial information to be published by certain enterprises. These, however, are published in a supplementary statement. Such SUPPLEMENTARY FINANCIAL STATEMENTS are to be distinguished from multi-column reporting in that they are subsidiary to the primary historical cost statement.

mutually exclusive projects. Capital investment projects of which for technical reasons only one can be selected, e.g., projects to build houses or factories on the same block of land.

N

naamlose venootschap (NV). The approximate Dutch equivalent of a UK public company.

naive investor. An investor who lacks a good knowledge and understanding of the accounting practices and theories relevant to published financial statements and does not have ready access to a person who has such knowledge and understanding. Private shareholders rather than institutional shareholders are likely to be naive as opposed to SOPHISTICATED INVESTORS.

national accounting. Recording the transactions, both current and capital, of a national economy, as distinct from those of entities in sectors of the economy such as public authorities and business enterprises. In principle the whole of the national accounts could be derived by consolidating and reclassifying transactions already recorded by other entities. In practice this is not possible and some data (especially those relating to consumers or households) must be collected from non-accounting sources. It is also necessary to record current rather than historical costs and valuations in national accounts (*see* STOCK APPRECIATION and CAPITAL CONSUMPTION).

The transactions recorded in national income accounts relate to production, distribution, CAPITAL FORMATION, saving, and borrowing and lending, as explained in the entries on NATIONAL INCOME AND EXPENDITURE ACCOUNTS, FLOW OF FUNDS ACCOUNTS, INPUT-OUTPUT TABLES, NATIONAL BALANCE SHEET and NATIONAL WEALTH STATEMENT.

National Audit Office (NAO). A body established by the British National Audit Act of 1983. It is headed by the COMPTROLLER AND AUDITOR GENERAL (C & AG). The annual budget of the NAO is examined and presented for parliamentary approval by the PUBLIC ACCOUNTS COMMISSION which also appoints the auditor of the NAO. The NAO reports, however, to the COMMITTEE OF PUBLIC ACCOUNTS.

national balance sheet. A statement recording the assets and financial obligations of an economy and its sectors at a point of time. In a national balance sheet, unlike a NATIONAL WEALTH STATEMENT, sector balance sheets are combined rather than consolidated and inter-sector financial claims are not eliminated. In principle, a national balance sheet should be drawn up in current rather than historical terms. Serious problems may arise in obtaining the necessary data.

national income and expenditure accounts. Accounts that show how the goods and services of a national economy are produced, distributed and either consumed or added to wealth during an accounting period. National income and expenditure accounts do not include financial flows. These are recorded in FLOW OF FUNDS ACCOUNTS.

National Loans Fund. In the UK, a fund, maintained by the Treasury at the Bank of England, from which loans are made to the nationalized industries, other public corporations, certain other agencies and local authorities.

national wealth statement. A statement recording the fixed assets, stocks (inventories) and net foreign claims (positive or negative) of a national economy. *See also* NATIONAL BALANCE SHEET.

negative goodwill. A credit balance on GOODWILL account representing an excess of the sum of the values of the enterprise's net assets taken individually over the value of the business as a whole. In the UK, the Accounting Standards Committee recommends that negative goodwill be credited to reserve and in certain circumstances released later to profit and loss account. *See also* GOODWILL ON CONSOLIDATION, RESERVE ON CONSOLIDATION.

negative income tax. A scheme under which, if taxable income exceeds a certain amount, tax is payable whereas if it falls short of that amount a cash sum is received by the 'taxpayer' as a supplement. Such a scheme (also known as a tax credit system) is intended to combine income tax and social security into a single co-ordinated system.

negotiable instruments. Documents, such as BILLS OF EXCHANGE, with the characteristics that the property in them passes by delivery, the holder in due course is not prejudiced by any defects of title on the part of the transferor or any previous holder, and the holder can sue upon them in his own name.

negotiated static budget. A STATIC BUDGET arrived at after negotiation. Such budgets are normal for discretionary costs.

netback. Synonym for RECOVERABLE AMOUNT.

net basis. Method of calculating EARNINGS PER SHARE (EPS) in the UK which takes account of all the components, both constant and variable, in a company's tax charge. It has the advantage that all the relevant facts are taken into account, but unlike the NIL BASIS and the MAXIMUM BASIS it is not independent of the level of dividend distribution.

net current assets. CURRENT ASSETS less CURRENT LIABILITIES.

net investment concept. See FOREIGN CURRENCY TRANSLATION.

net liquid funds. Defined by SSAP 10 (Statements of Source and Application of Funds) in the UK as cash at bank and in hand and cash equivalents (e.g., investments held as current assets) less bank overdrafts and other borrowings repayable within one year of the date of the balance sheet.

net national product. GROSS NATIONAL PRODUCT less CAPITAL CONSUMPTION (depreciation).

net present value (NPV). The discounted value of the future incremental cash receipts expected from the use of an asset less the discounted value of the incremental cash outlays. The NPV of the cash flows is

$$\sum_{t=0}^{n} \frac{A_t}{(1+i)^t}$$

where A_t is the cash flow (in or out) for period t, n is the number of periods and i is the required rate of return.

NPV is one of the DISCOUNTED CASH FLOW methods of CAPITAL INVESTMENT APPRAISAL. It also, in an INFLATION ACCOUNTING context, represents the VALUE TO THE BUSINESS of an asset where it is greater than NET REALIZABLE VALUE and less than current REPLACEMENT COST.

net profit. The excess of revenues over expenses. It may be calculated before or after extraordinary items and before or after tax depending upon the context. *See also* EARNINGS PER SHARE, PROFIT.

net profit ratio. The ratio of net profit to sales.

net realizable value. The amount of money for which an asset can be exchanged in a market, i.e., selling price less selling costs. A distinction can be made between realization in the ordinary course of business and a forced sale on, e.g., a liquidation. The use of NRV as an asset valuation base is advocated by exponents of CONTINUOUSLY CONTEMPORARY ACCOUNTING (CoCoA). It is one possible measure of the VALUE TO THE BUSINESS of an asset. NRV provides a measure of what an enterprise is foregoing by not selling an asset. It can be argued, however, that it is not a relevant measure for a GOING CONCERN in that it ignores value in exchange and that it contravenes the REALIZATION CONVENTION. NRV is less objective than historical cost but usually more objective than REPLACEMENT COST.

In the UK, stock and work and work in progress is valued at the lower of cost and NRV (*see* INVENTORY VALUATION) and SSAP 9 sets out the principal situations where stocks (inventories) are likely to have a NRV less than cost. They are where there has been: (a) an increase in costs or a fall in selling price; (b) physical deterioration; (c) obsolescence; (d) a decision as part of a company's marketing strategy to manufacture and sell products at a loss; (e) errors in production or purchasing.

See also CURRENT CASH EQUIVALENT.

network analysis. A general term for the analysis of projects by drawing networks showing the sequence of activities and their activity times and costs. *See* CRITICAL PATH METHOD (CPM) and PROGRAMME EVALUATION AND REVIEW TECHNIQUE (PERT).

neutrality. In an accounting context, the absence in reported information of bias intended to attain a predetermined result or to induce a particular mode of behaviour. Neutrality is included among the QUALITATIVE CHARACTERISTICS OF ACCOUNTING INFORMATION set out in the FASB's STATEMENT OF FINANCIAL ACCOUNTING CONCEPTS No. 2. It is argued by some writers that neutrality can only be assured by the adoption of an explicit CONCEPTUAL FRAMEWORK.

nil basis. Method of calculating EARNINGS PER SHARE (EPS) in the UK which takes account only of the constant components in a company's tax charge. Like the MAXIMUM BASIS, but not the NET BASIS, it has the advantage that it is independent of the level of dividend distribution.

no credit interval. See DEFENSIVE INTERVAL.

nominal accounts. Those accounts in a LEDGER that deal with revenues and expenses.

nominal ledger. Strictly, a ledger containing only NOMINAL ACCOUNTS, but used in the UK as a synonym for GENERAL LEDGER which usually contains REAL ACCOUNTS also.

nominal share capital. In the UK, a synonym for AUTHORIZED SHARE CAPITAL.

nominee shareholder. A shareholder who holds shares on behalf of another person or firm who is the beneficial holder. The use of nominee shareholders may make it difficult to discover the real owner of a company's shares. In the UK, significant INTERESTS IN SHARES must be disclosed to the company.

non-adjusting events. *See* POST BALANCE SHEET EVENTS.

non-market risk. Synonym for NON-SYSTEMATIC RISK.

non-monetary assets. Assets other than monetary assets. Examples are land and buildings, plant and machinery, stock-in-trade (inventory) and investments with fluctuating market values. The distinction between monetary and non-monetary assets is useful for INFLATION ACCOUNTING and FOREIGN CURRENCY TRANSLATION.

non-renewable assets. Synonym for WASTING ASSETS.

non-systematic risk. That part of the risk of a security which cannot be eliminated by combining it in a diversified portfolio. It is also known as specific or non-market risk. Non-systematic risk is measured as a percentage return per annum. The higher the percentage the greater the risk.

non-vendible durable. A highly specialized fixed asset which cannot be sold to another business. Such an asset has a NET PRESENT VALUE (NPV) in excess of its NET REALIZABLE VALUE (NRV). Its current REPLACEMENT COST (RC) may be greater or less than its NPV. Chambers, the originator of this term, argues that non-vendible durables should be valued at their NRV even if it is zero. Accountants who support the VALUE TO THE BUSINESS concept argue that it should be valued at either RC or NPV, whichever is the lower. Both of these figures are likely to be more subjective than either NRV or the depreciated historical cost of conventional accounting.

non-zero sum game. A game in which the sum of the rewards to the players does not total to zero. A well-known example of a non-zero sum game is the 'prisoner's dilemma' which shows that rational behaviour by each player may lead to an apparently irrational outcome. Each prisoner is interrogated separately and knows that if no one confesses, all will go free. If one prisoner confesses, and the others do not, he will go free and the others will receive severe sentences. If all confess, all will be sentenced, but less severely. A rational prisoner may well confess and intend to let the others suffer the consequences. If, however, all prisoners act in this way, all will be sentenced and no one will go free.

no par value shares/stock. Shares or stock without a par value. They are fairly usual in the USA but illegal in the UK despite the recommendation in their favour of the Gedge Committee (1954) endorsed by the Jenkins Committee (1962). In the USA it is customary, and in some states obligatory, to assign a 'stated value' to no par value shares.

normal spoilage. SPOILAGE which arises under efficient operations and is uncontrollable in the short run.

normal volume. That level of utilization of capacity that will satisfy average consumer demand over a period of time, allowing for seasonal, cyclical and trend factors. It is not necessarily equal to the budgeted volume for the coming year.

notes to financial statements. US term for NOTES TO THE ACCOUNTS.

notes to the accounts. Information relating to the financial statements not given on the face of the statements. In both the UK and the USA, notes to the accounts have become very voluminous and detailed. In the UK, information supplementing the balance sheet must by law cover such matters as share capital, debentures, fixed assets, investments, reserves and provisions, indebtedness, and guarantees and other financial commitments; and that supplementing the profit and loss account, separate disclosure of certain items of income and expenditure, taxation, turnover, staff and staff costs, and extraordinary and prior year items. Information must also be given on the translation of foreign currencies, significant shareholdings, and subsidiaries and related companies. This information must be given by all companies to their shareholders but exemptions are granted to SMALL AND MEDIUM COMPANIES in relation to financial statements required to be filed with the Registrar of Companies. Medium companies are exempt from filing analyses of turnover and profit and small companies are required to file only a limited amount of information.

null hypothesis. In general, the particular hypothesis under test, as distinct from the alternative hypotheses under consideration. *See* TYPE I ERROR and TYPE II ERROR.

numerosity. Defined by the Oxford English Dictionary as the state of being numerous, but used by some accounting theorists to mean the quality of being stated in terms of a unit of account. It is close in meaning to the economists' term numéraire, an expression of a standard of value, money being a numéraire by which different commodities can have units compared.

nuncupative will. A will made by a valid oral declaration, rather than in writing.

O

objective function. A function relating the objective to the variables in an OPTIMIZATION problem. The objective may be the maximization of CONTRIBUTION or the minimization of cost.

objectives of financial statements. *See* TRUEBLOOD REPORT.

objectivity. An accounting concept which stresses the need to establish rules for recording financial transactions which as far as possible do not depend upon the personal judgment of the measurer. Emphasis can be placed either upon the inherent quality of the financial information based upon the availability of evidence, or upon establishing a degree of consensus among measurers.

obsolescence. The decline in value of a fixed asset through external causes such as technological change or changes in demand.

off balance sheet financing. Financing assets by 'borrowing' in such a fashion (e.g., by means of leasing: *see* LEASE ACCOUNTING) that the debt does not appear as a balance sheet item.

offer for sale. An offer to the public, either by an issuing house or by a stockbroker, of securities already in issue or for which the issuing house or the broker has agreed to subscribe.

Official Receiver (OR). In England and Wales, an officer of the Department of Trade and Industry having the status of an officer of the court. The OR conducts a WINDING UP BY THE COURT until the meeting of the creditors of the company at which a LIQUIDATOR other than the OR may be nominated. The OR acts in a similar way in a BANKRUPTCY. There is no OR in Scotland.

oil and gas accounting. Accounting for the acquisition, exploration, development and production phases of the exploitation of oil and gas deposits and for proved oil and gas reserves. Over the whole life of an oil field all the expenses arising are eventually written off against revenue, but no general agreement has been reached as to the way in which this should be done. Three possibilities are the writing off of all expenditures as they are incurred, the full-costing method and the successful efforts method.

The first of these methods relies entirely upon PRUDENCE and ignores ACCRUALS completely; it has not been adopted to any great extent. The full-costing method involves the capitalization of all pre-production costs, including those on areas which are subsequently abandoned. The rationale of this method is that it is necessary to undertake both successful and unsuccessful expenditures in order to find a commercial deposit. Under the successful efforts method all expenditure is capitalized until an area is either abandoned or a commercial deposit is found. If an area is abandoned the expenditures that have been carried forward are written off as losses; if an area is not abandoned they are carried forward further to be matched with the related revenue when production commences. Which expenditures are regarded as successful and which unsuccessful depends crucially on the COST CENTRE employed for accounting purposes. The larger the cost centre the closer the successful efforts method approaches the full-costing method. In the USA, the SEC requires cost centres to be established on a country-by-country basis.

Production costs are treated as a PRODUCT COST under the successful efforts method but as a PERIOD COST under the full-costing method. Stocks (inventories) are, however, usually larger under full costing, because the latter method capitalizes acquisition and exploration costs. Income under full costing tends to be significantly higher in the early years than under the successful efforts method. The former method tends to be supported by the smaller oil companies.

As a WASTING ASSET, capitalized oil and gas expenditures are subject to DEPLETION, usually by the units of production method (*see* DEPRECIATION METHODS).

A different method is reserve recognition accounting. The rationale of this method is that the most significant event affecting the economic value of an oil and gas company is the discovery of new natural resources. The method assumes that at the time of discovery the costs associated with each of the phases have either been incurred or can be estimated and that the marketability of the resources at prices at or above current levels is reasonably assured. The criteria for REVENUE RECOGNITION are thus deemed to be satisfied at the time of the discovery.

Oil and gas accounting has received much attention from standard setters in the USA. In 1977 the FASB attempted to establish successful efforts as the only acceptable method but it was overruled by the SEC, which permitted either successful efforts or full cost and championed the use of reserve recognition accounting (ignoring future price or cost changes and discounting at a fixed rate of 10% p.a.) in supplementary statements. The current position in the USA is set out in FAS 69 (1982) which requires disclosure of the method of accounting adopted and the manner of disposing of associated capitalized costs. Supplementary information to be disclosed includes: proved oil and gas reserves; capitalized costs relating to oil and gas producing activities; costs incurred in oil and gas property acquisition and development activities; results of operations for oil and gas producing activities; and a STANDARDIZED MEASURE OF DISCOUNTED FUTURE NET CASH FLOWS (SMDCF) relating to proved oil and gas reserve quantities.

By contrast UK standard setters have been almost silent despite the importance of oil and gas to the UK economy. There has been no attempt to rule on full cost, successful efforts or reserve recognition accounting but an exposure draft on PETROLEUM REVENUE TAX was issued in 1981 and draft guidance notes on the application of SSAP 16 to the oil and gas industries in 1980.

oncost. Synonym for OVERHEAD.

one-line consolidation. *See* EQUITY ACCOUNTING.

open market value. The value on the open market of non-specialized buildings and land. Open market value is recommended as the valuation method for such assets in the UK when CURRENT COST ACCOUNTING (CCA) is used (SSAP 16), and also for INVESTMENT PROPERTIES irrespective of whether CCA or HISTORICAL COST ACCOUNTING (HCA) is used (SSAP 19).

operating budget. That part of the MASTER BUDGET of an organization that deals with operations. Practice varies, but it may be subdivided into sales, production, selling expenses and administrative expenses.

operating lease. *See* LEASE ACCOUNTING.

operating leverage. The GEARING (LEVERAGE) which results from an enterprise's asset structure as distinct from its CAPITAL STRUCTURE. A high operating leverage suggests the desirability of a relatively low financial leverage.

operational audit. That branch of INTERNAL AUDIT concerned with non-financial as well as financial performance and with evaluating efficiency and effectiveness. The scope of an operational audit includes the minimization of waste; ensuring and improving the quality of information available to management; and the review of decision models and techniques.

operation costing. A hybrid of PROCESS COSTING and JOB COSTING, used in the manufacture of goods that are produced in batches. Direct materials are charged to each batch whereas direct labour and factory overhead are charged to each operation through which the batches pass.

operations planning. That part of LONG RANGE PLANNING concerned with the detailed plans required to meet an enterprise's objectives as specified in its STRATEGIC PLANNING. It involves the planning of production, marketing, research and development, and personnel and also FINANCIAL PLANNING.

opinion. A reference either to an AUDIT OPINION or to the Opinions of the ACCOUNTING PRINCIPLES BOARD which, to the extent that they have not been superseded, form part of generally accepted accounting principles in the USA.

opportunity cost. The maximum contribution that is foregone by using scarce resources for a particular purpose. Opportunity costs cannot be routinely recorded in an accounting system.

opportunity value. Synonym for VALUE TO THE BUSINESS.

optimal capital structure. *See* CAPITAL STRUCTURE.

optimization. The use of procedures or models to produce a best possible result.

option. A contract giving the right to buy or sell securities or commodities within or at the end of a given time period at an agreed price. A contract to buy is a call option; a contract to sell is a put option; the two may be combined. Convertible securities and warrants are forms of option. A European option is one that can be exercised only at its expiration date; an American option can be exercised at any time up to and including the expiration date. *See* BLACK-SCHOLES OPTION MODEL.

ordinal number. A number designating order in a series, e.g., 1st, 2nd, 3rd. *See* CARDINAL NUMBER.

ordinary shares. In the UK, those shares on the holders of which are normally conferred the residue of rights which have not been conferred on other classes of shares. Ordinary shareholders have both higher expected returns and higher expected risks than other shareholders. On a winding up the ordinary shares rank behind all creditors and, normally, behind all other classes of shares. Ordinary shares normally, but not always, carry voting rights.

organizational goals. The goals assumed to be adopted by an organization. Organizational goals are often treated as if they were independent of the members of an organization, but strictly they are the goals of the organization's dominant members. The goals may be imperfectly defined and continually changing. The achievement of such goals underlies the rationale for BUDGETARY CONTROL.

organizational slack. The difference between the total resources available to an organization and the total resources necessary for efficient and effective performance. Managers can create it by underestimating revenues and overestimating costs. It can be argued that a limited amount of organizational slack is desirable because it permits a blending of personal and organizational goals.

organizational structure. The way in which lines of responsibility within an enterprise are arranged, e.g., by functions or by divisions.

outlay cost. A cost arising from a disbursement of cash.

out-of-pocket costs. Those costs that entail outlays immediately or in the near future in relation to a given decision.

outstanding capital stock. The capital stock of a corporation in the hands of the public. It is equal to the issued capital stock less treasury stock. This US term is not used in the UK.

outturn. In UK public sector accounting, actual expenditure incurred, normally in a financial year.

overabsorbed overhead. A credit balance resulting from the use of PREDETERMINED OVERHEAD RATES. More overhead is charged to production than is actually incurred. In practice overabsorbed overhead is usually written off to cost of goods sold rather than prorated over cost of goods sold, finished goods and work in progress.

overhead. Expenses other than the costs of direct material and direct labour. Overhead may be classified into FACTORY OVERHEAD, distribution overhead and administrative overhead. In accounting terminology overhead may be fixed or variable but as used by economists it usually refers only to FIXED COSTS.

overhead variances. Deviations from budgeted or standard costs in respect of overheads. Overhead variances are more complicated than those for direct materials and direct labour; a distinction has to be made between fixed and variable overhead and the latter at least has to be assumed to vary directly with some measure of activity (assumed below to be direct labour hours). The variable overhead variance can be subdivided into an EFFICIENCY VARIANCE, calculated by multiplying the difference between actual hours used and standard allowed hours by the standard price per hour, and a PRICE VARIANCE (often called a spending variance), calculated by deducting the efficiency variance from the total variance.

If fixed and variable overheads are separated and absorption costing is used, a predetermined fixed factory overhead rate is calculated based on a normal volume level. Such a rate has no value for control purposes. The fixed factory overhead variance can be subdivided into a spending or price variance and a VOLUME VARIANCE, the latter being calculated by multiplying the difference between the actual volume and the normal volume by the fixed overhead rate.

If absorption costing is used but a single predetermined overhead rate only is calculated, either two variances (budget and volume) or three variances (spending, efficiency and volume) can be calculated. The budget variance is the difference between actual costs and the budget allowance based on standard hours allowed; in the three-way analysis it is divided into spending and efficiency variances.

overtime. Wages paid, usually at a premium rate, for work beyond normal hours. It may be classified as either a direct labour cost or an indirect labour cost, depending on the circumstances.

overtrading. A situation in which a business expands its sales and may appear to be highly profitable but does not have the resources available to finance the expansion and runs out of cash, most of its assets being tied up in debtors and stocks (inventories) which cannot be converted rapidly enough into cash to pay its liabilities.

owners' equity. That part of the finance of an enterprise provided by its owners. In BALANCE SHEET terms it is equal in total to the ASSETS less the LIABILITIES, but it is more appropriately measured in some contexts by the market value of the ORDINARY SHARES (common stock).

own shares. In the UK, a company's own shares acquired by purchase, redemption, gift, surrender or forfeiture. If such shares are shown as an asset in the company's balance sheet a transfer must be paid to a RESERVE FUND from profits otherwise available for dividend. In the UK, companies are allowed to purchase their own shares subject to certain prescribed procedures. Such a purchase may be either on the market or off-market. The approximate US equivalent is TREASURY STOCK.

P

Pacioli, Luca (c.1445-c.1517). Mathematician and author of the first printed work on accounting. Born in Borgo San Sepolcro in Tuscany, Pacioli became a Franciscan friar, the friend of many of the leading men of the Italian Renaissance and taught mathematics at several Italian universities. His *Summa de Arithmetica, Geometria, Proportioni et Proportionalità* was published in Venice in 1494, the section on DOUBLE ENTRY bookkeeping being entitled *Particularis de computis et scripturis*. Pacioli was not the inventor of double entry, which had been in use in the Italian city states for about two centuries, but his book, written in Italian, not Latin, greatly helped its diffusion, not only in Italy but also throughout Europe. It was plagiarized, translated and adapted into many languages.

paid-up share capital. In the UK, the ISSUED SHARE CAPITAL to the extent that it has been called up from the shareholders and cash or other consideration has been received from them.

Panel on Take-overs and Mergers. *See* CITY CODE ON TAKE-OVERS AND MERGERS.

paper profits. A rather vague term referring to profits that cannot be or have not been realized in cash or that result from using HISTORICAL COST ACCOUNTING rather than some form of INFLATION ACCOUNTING.

parameter. A quantity which remains constant in a given context. Contrast VARIABLE.

parent company. A company which controls another company. The term parent company is often used as a synonym for HOLDING COMPANY a term which, in the UK, is legally defined. It would be useful, but not in accordance with the Companies Acts, to restrict the latter term to parent companies whose sole function is to hold the shares of other companies. The SEVENTH DIRECTIVE uses the term parent undertaking.

partial tax allocation. *See* DEFERRED TAXATION.

participative budgeting. Allowing persons who will be responsible for performance under a BUDGET to participate in the decisions by which the budget is established. Participative budgeting is thought to provide a sense of responsibility and to have the effect of persuading employees to adopt ORGANIZATIONAL GOALS as their own. On the other hand, it may encourage managers to build ORGANIZATIONAL SLACK into their budgets and to set themselves unduly low ASPIRATION LEVELS.

partnership accounts. The accounts and financial statements of an unincorporated business or professional enterprise owned by two or more persons. In the UK, partnerships are found mainly among small businesses, farming, merchant banking and the professions. They are governed by the Partnership Act 1890, which defines partnership as 'the relation which subsists between persons carrying on business in common with a view to profit.'

The proprietorship section of a partnership balance sheet contains CAPITAL ACCOUNTS and CURRENT ACCOUNTS for each partner, the former recording each partner's fixed stake in the partnership and the latter his or her fluctuating stake (share of profit less drawings). A separate drawings account may also be kept. A PROFIT AND LOSS APPROPRIATION ACCOUNT is an essential part of partnership accounts. The items recorded in it depend upon the partnership agreement or the Partnership Act. They will always include the net profit or loss for the period and the division of the balance according to the profit-sharing ratios (the Act provides for equal profit shares in the absence of agreement). They may also include partners' salaries, interest on capital and interest on drawings. If the partnership agreement is silent on these matters, the Act provides that no salaries are to be paid and no interest on capital or drawings is to be allowed, but interest on advances (loans by partners to the partnership) is to be allowed at 5% p.a.

Although a partnership as such does not pay tax, it acts as a collector of tax from the partners on behalf of the Inland Revenue. Thus, the partnership profits are assessed (under Schedule D, Case I or Case II) and apportioned to each partner (after making allowance for any reliefs), the partnership pays the tax due, and each partner's current account is debited for his or her appropriate share. No taxation is debited to the profit and loss appropriation account.

Special entries are necessary on the admission, retirement and death of partners, and on the dissolution of a partnership. A partnership may be converted into a limited company by the partners forming a company and then selling the assets of the partnership to it. The rationale behind the entries made is that although partnership assets are usually recorded in the books at historical cost and GOODWILL is unrecorded, all assets need to be revalued on a change of ownership. A REVALUATION ACCOUNT is used if the assets are retained in the partnership; a REALIZATION ACCOUNT is used if they are to be sold.

On the bankruptcy of a partnership, all partners are made bankrupt simultaneously and one trustee in bankruptcy is appointed for them all, and for the firm. A deficiency on the partnership estate must be made up by the partners out of the surpluses, if any, on their separate estates. Difficulties arise if one partner has a final debit balance on his capital account and a deficiency on his separate estate, whilst other partners are solvent (*see* GARNER V. MURRAY, RULE IN).

par value. The face value or nominal value of a share or a debenture. It is not necessarily equal to ISSUE PRICE (since shares can be issued at a premium and debentures at a premium or a discount) or to the current market price. Dividend and interest percentages are calculated with reference to par value.

patents. Grants (by the Crown in the UK, by the Federal Government in the USA) to authors of new inventions giving them the sole and exclusive right to use, exercise and sell their inventions and to secure the profits arising therefrom for a limited period (17 years in the USA; a maximum of 16 in the UK). The economic life of a patent may be less than this period. Patents are intangible assets and, in the UK, company law permits their capitalization and subsequent amortization if they are acquired for valuable consideration or created by the company itself. In the USA only the cost of patents purchased may be capitalized and amortized.

Paton, William Andrew (1889-). One of the most influential of American academic accountants; on the staff of the University of Michigan 1914 to 1959 except for a short break during World War I. He was president in 1922 of the predecessor body of the American Accounting Association; first editor of *The Accounting Review* (1926-1929); and the first research director of the American Accounting Association. A prolific author, his most influential books are *Accounting Theory* (1922) and *An Introduction to Corporate Accounting Standards* (1940, with A.C. Littleton). Many of his articles are reprinted in *Paton on Accounting* (edited H.F. Taggart, 1964). A full bibliography (to 1976) is included in *Essays in Honor of William A. Paton. Pioneer Accounting Theorist* (edited Zeff, Demski and Dopuch, 1979). Paton is a stimulating writer who during a long and productive career has not hesitated to change and develop his ideas.

pay as you earn (PAYE). The mechanism used in the UK for withholding tax from wages and salaries. Unlike similar systems used elsewhere it is operated on a cumulative basis, i.e., a taxpayer's pay and allowances are accumulated throughout the tax year so that the amount withheld in any one period is dependent on the income received throughout the year up to and including the current period. It is thus possible for rebates of tax to be made during the fiscal year, as well as after its end. Tax is withheld extremely accurately but the administrative and compliance costs of the system are high. The system depends on the marginal rate of tax being constant over a long range of incomes.

payback period. A method of CAPITAL IN-VESTMENT APPRAISAL, which measures the expected length of time over which the undiscounted cash receipts of a capital project equal the undiscounted outlays. The shorter the payback period the better the project is assumed to be. The method ignores cash flows after the payback period and the TIME VALUE OF MONEY but is a very popular method in practice, especially in conjunction with other methods.

payoff matrix. Synonym for DECISION TABLE.

payoff table. Synonym for DECISION TABLE.

payroll accounting. Accounting for wages and salaries. The objectives of payroll accounting are: to calculate accurately each employee's earnings and to pay them promptly; to make such deductions or withholdings, e.g. for income tax, social security and pensions, as are required and to pay over the sums deducted to the appropriate authorities; and to allocate labour costs to functions, departments and products. Payroll accounting affects every employee in an organization and may be the one part of the ACCOUNTING SYSTEM which is carefully monitored by all of them. The volume of repetitive transactions is such that payroll is often the first part of the accounting system to be computerized.

peer review. In the USA, the review by one firm of auditors of the procedures of another audit firm for organizing and supervising its planning and execution of audit work. Peer reviews are not carried out in the UK.

pension costs. The costs to an employer of providing pension benefits to employees. UK company law requires the disclosure of pension costs recognized in the profit and loss account during the year and also disclosure in the notes to the accounts of any financial commitments (including pension commitments) not included in the balance sheet. An exposure draft was issued in 1983 on the disclosure of pension information in company accounts but the Accounting Standards Committee has as yet made no attempt to standardize the calculation of pension costs. The usual practice in the UK is to charge against revenue each year the actual amounts contributed to a pension scheme plus the amount of any benefit paid directly by the employer. In the USA, Opinion No. 8 of the Accounting Principles Board requires accrual accounting in the income statement. Suggestions that actuarial liabilities and assets should be recognized in the balance sheet are under discussion.

pension scheme accounts. The financial statements and other information published by pension schemes (US: pension plans). In the UK, these usually comprise a net assets statement showing the investment assets, long-term borrowings and net current assets; a revenue account showing, *inter alia*, contributions receivable, investment income, benefits payable and administrative expenses; a movement of funds statement (the fund being the accumulation of assets held by the pension scheme for the purpose of meeting benefits as they become due); and an investment report containing a detailed analysis of the investment portfolio of the scheme. Investments are usually valued at their open market value. It is also normal to include a report by the actuary on the adequacy of the funding arrangements to meet expected pensions and other benefits.

P/E ratio. *See* PRICE-EARNINGS RATIO.

perfect market. In an accounting and financial context, a market in which there are no transactions costs, no firm or individual has any special advantage or opportunity to earn abnormal returns on investments, and prices are not affected by the actions of any individual or firm.

performance evaluation. The assessment by a superior of a subordinate and an important part of any MANAGEMENT CONTROL system. To evaluate performance it is necessary to decide which measures are to be used to represent organizational goals, how these measures are to be defined and quantified, what standards are to be used, and what form FEEDBACK is to take.

performance report. A report comparing actual with budgeted performance.

period costs. Costs that cannot be identified with goods acquired or produced for sale. They are non-inventoriable costs, i.e., they are written off as expenses during the period in which they are incurred without having been previously classified as part of the costs of producing the goods manufactured (i.e., as assets).

periodic inventory method. A method under which the amount of inventory (stock) on hand and hence the cost of goods sold is determined by means of physical counts at periodic intervals.

permanent differences. Differences, not reversible in future periods, between profits as computed for taxation purposes and profits as stated in financial statements. They result from the inclusion of items of income and expenditure in taxation computations different from those in the financial statements. Examples of permanent differences in the UK are entertaining UK customers (which is not allowed as a tax deduction) and interest on tax repayments (which is tax free). *See also* TIMING DIFFERENCES and DEFERRED TAXATION.

perpetual inventory method. A method of accounting for inventories (stocks) which involves the continual recording of additions to and issues or sales of materials on a daily basis.

perpetuity. An ANNUITY which lasts for ever. The present value of a perpetuity is equal to the annual receipt or payment divided by the rate of interest.

personal accounts. Those accounts in a ledger which record transactions with persons, e.g., debtors and creditors.

personal ledger. A LEDGER containing PERSONAL ACCOUNTS. The most common examples are the DEBTORS LEDGER and the CREDITORS LEDGER.

personal representative. A general term covering EXECUTOR and ADMINISTRATOR. A person who interferes with the property of a deceased person by acting as personal representative while not so appointed may become an 'executor de son tort', i.e., an executor by his or her own wrong doing.

personalty. Movable property such as cash and shares, in contradistinction to REALTY or immovable property.

petroleum revenue tax (PRT). A tax on profits arising from the extraction of oil and gas in British territory (both land and sea). The tax is chargeable on each field separately, and the liability apportioned among the participating companies. PRT is deductible in the calculation of profit for corporation tax purposes. The Accounting Standards Committee issued an exposure draft in 1981 dealing with the treatment of PRT in published financial statements.

petty cash. Cash balances held in the form of notes and coins rather than bank deposits and used in payment of minor expenditures. For control purposes all receipts of notes and coins should be paid into the bank and petty cash receipts limited to periodic transfers out of cash at bank.

petty cash book. A book recording PETTY CASH transactions. It is usually kept by the imprest system, in which a fixed sum or 'float' is allocated as sufficient to meet petty cash expenditure for an agreed period of time. At the end of the agreed period, usually a week or a month, the sum expended by the petty cashier is reimbursed, thus making up the balance to the original sum. Control of petty cash is facilitated under this system since at any time the cash in hand plus the amount expended from the last reimbursement should equal the cash float.

The receipts side of the petty cash book records the periodic reimbursements; the payments side the expenditure, analysed over columns, on such items as postages, stationery and travelling expenses.

physical capital maintenance. *See* CAPITAL MAINTENANCE CONCEPT.

pie chart. A graphical representation of data in which percentages or other proportions are displayed by the segments of a circle. Pie charts are common in EMPLOYEE REPORTS.

placing. The sale of, or the obtaining of subscriptions for, securities by either an issuing house or a stockbroker through the stock market and to or by its own clients. Placings are only allowed by the Stock Exchange where there is not likely to be a significant public demand for the securities. The advantage of placings is their relative cheapness.

plan comptable. French term for ACCOUNTING PLAN.

planning, programming, budgeting system (PPBS). A system of governmental budgeting which involves the identification of goals and objectives in each major area of governmental activity; analysis of a given programme in terms of its objectives; measurement of total programme cost for several years ahead; the formulation of objectives and programmes extending beyond the single year of the annual budget; analysis of alternatives to find the most effective means of reaching basic programme objectives; and establishment of the above analytical procedures as a systematic part of budget review.

ploughed back profit. Profit retained for reinvestment instead of being distributed to owners.

politicization of accounting. The settlement of accounting questions and the determination of accounting standards by 'political' pressures (in the widest sense) rather than by reference to an implicit or explicit CONCEPTUAL FRAMEWORK. Political pressures can come from governments (which have, for example, tended to prefer current cost accounting to current purchasing power accounting) or from companies (as in the case of INVESTMENT PROPERTIES in the UK). Well-known instances of political 'interference' in standard setting in the USA relate to the INVESTMENT TAX CREDIT and OIL AND GAS ACCOUNTING.

In favour of politicization it can be argued that accounting standards ought to represent the views of the preparers and users of accounts. Against it is the argument that accounting will lose credibility if it loses its NEUTRALITY.

The issue is complicated by the difficulty of distinguishing between bringing pressure to bear on a standard-setting body and the submission to it of a reasonable and conceptually sustainable point of view.

poll. A method of voting whereby each member of a company can vote for or against a resolution according to the number of shares that he or she owns.

poll tax. A tax whose size bears no relationship to any TAX BASE except the existence of the taxpayer.

pooling of interests. US term for MERGER ACCOUNTING.

portfolio. In a financial context, a collection of different securities or other assets held by an individual or an institution which can be evaluated in terms of their combined risks and returns. The risk of a portfolio depends not only on the riskiness of each security but also on the relationship among the securities.

portfolio risk. A risk that depends not only on the riskiness of the individual securities or other assets of a portfolio but also on the relationship among those securities. The contribution of a security to the risk of a portfolio is usually defined as the COVARIANCE of returns on the security and returns on the portfolio. MARKET RISK is a special case in which the portfolio consists of the whole market.

post balance sheet events. Events, both favourable and unfavourable, which occur between the date of a balance sheet and the date on which the financial statements are approved by the board of directors. In the UK, SSAP 17 distinguishes between 'adjusting events' (those which provide additional evidence of conditions existing at the balance sheet date, e.g., the insolvency of a debtor) and 'non-adjusting events' (those which concern events that did not exist at the balance sheet date, e.g., loss of stocks as the result of a flood) and requires that changes be made in the financial statements if a post balance sheet event is material and is either an adjusting event or one which indicates that application of the GOING CONCERN concept to the whole or a material part of the company is not appropriate. Disclosure is required of non-adjusting events which are of such materiality that their non-disclosure would affect the ability of users of the financial statements to reach a proper understanding of the financial position and also of material events representing the reversal or maturity after the year end of a transaction entered into before the year end, the substance of which was primarily to alter the appearance of the company's balance sheet (*see* WINDOW DRESSING).

post balance sheet events review. Auditing procedures applied to the period between completing the basic audit fieldwork and the audit approval of the financial statements.

post-completion audit. An audit of a capital project after its completion, comparing budget estimates with actual results and enquiring into the reasons for any variances.

posting. The transferring of an amount and its description from a JOURNAL to a LEDGER.

postponable costs. Costs that may be shifted into the future with little or no effect on the efficiency of current operations.

postulate. An AXIOM or ASSUMPTION constituting the basis of a theory. The truth of a postulate is taken for granted or accepted as self-evident. *See* ACCOUNTING ASSUMPTIONS, AXIOMS, CONCEPTS, CONVENTIONS, POSTULATES AND PRINCIPLES.

pre-acquisition profits. The retained profits as at the date of acquisition of a company acquired by another company. Pre-acquisition profits are eliminated during the process of consolidation if ACQUISITION ACCOUNTING (purchase accounting) is used but not if MERGER ACCOUNTING (pooling of interests) is adopted.

precept. In the UK, a levy on a rate-collecting local authority by a non-rate-collecting local authority.

precision. The degree of certainty that the error rate in a sample applies to the population. Precision is determined by the choice of CONFIDENCE LEVEL and the statistical nature of the sample and may be expressed as a sample estimate plus or minus some deviation. It is related to the concept of MATERIALITY in accounting. An auditor may, for example, wish to achieve a 95% CONFIDENCE LEVEL that a reported account balance is not materially different (say, $\pm$ £5,000) from the audited amount. The range of values in this case is a measure of precision.

predetermined overhead rate. An overhead rate estimated in advance in order that jobs and processes may be charged with a share of factory overhead without having to wait for details of overhead actually incurred. It can be calculated as total budgeted overhead divided by total budgeted volume but it may be preferable to calculate different overhead rates for different departments rather than a single plant-wide rate. If VARIABLE COSTING is used, only a variable overhead rate is used; if ABSORPTION COSTING is used, it may be preferable to calculate separate rates for variable and fixed overheads. Annualized rates are usually preferred to those set on a basis of weekly or monthly activity.

The use of predetermined overhead rates results in the use of normal PRODUCT COSTS based on annual averages, rather than actual product costs affected by month-to-month fluctuations in volume and by seasonal differences.

prediction error. Failure to forecast

accurately a critical parameter. The cost of prediction error is a key concept in SEN- SITIVITY ANALYSIS.

predictive ability. The ability of an accounting number to provide information that is useful in predicting future accounting numbers. For example, studies have been made to see whether historical cost, current purchasing power or current cost income is the best predictor of itself or of future cash flows. Other studies have looked at the ability of financial ratios to predict bankruptcy (*see* Z-SCORES).

pre-emption right. The entitlement of an existing shareholder to have allotted to him or her a proportionate part of a new issue of shares. The pre-emption right is intended to protect the shareholder against a DILUTION of his or her present holding in the company. *See* RIGHTS ISSUE.

preference shares. In the UK, SHARES which carry preferential rights in relation to other shares but which often do not carry voting rights. The rights depend upon the terms of issue but most preference shareholders have a right to receive, before any dividend is paid on the ORDINARY SHARES, a fixed dividend and also a right to repayment prior to the ordinary shares in the event of a winding up. Dividends are not deductible for tax purposes which makes preference shares a costly source of capital compared to debt. Preference shares may be cumulative or non-cumulative. If they are cumulative, shareholders have the right to claim a missed dividend in subsequent years and before payment of a dividend to the ordinary shareholders. Arrears of cumulative dividends must be shown in the Notes. If the dividends are non-cumulative there is no subsequent entitlement to a missed dividend. Participating preference shares carry a right to a share in profits beyond a fixed dividend and are regarded by law as part of the EQUITY SHARE CAPITAL.

preferential creditors. In the UK, creditors whose claims rank ahead of all others, except for secured creditors (other than those secured by a floating charge). All preferential debts rank equally among themselves and, if the assets are insufficient to pay them in full, are proportionately abated. Preferential creditors include the following (all with time limits and some with maximum amounts): local rates; corporation tax; value added tax; wages, salaries and commissions of employees; accrued holiday remuneration; national insurance contributions.

preferred stock. US term for PREFERENCE SHARES.

preliminary expenses. The expenses of forming a company, such as legal costs, registration fees, stamp duty and printing charges. UK company law forbids their capitalization.

prepaid expenses. *See* PREPAYMENTS.

prepayments. Expenses (e.g. insurance) which have been paid for but the benefits of which have not been received at the balance sheet date. In accordance with the ACCRUALS convention the charge to profit and loss account is decreased accordingly and a CURRENT ASSET established (in the UK BALANCE SHEET FORMATS it is also permissible to show prepayments as a separate item). *See also* ACCRUED EXPENSES.

present value. *See* NET PRESENT VALUE.

price-earnings ratio (P/E ratio). The multiple of last reported EARNINGS PER SHARE (EPS) that the stock market is willing to pay per ordinary share. It is the reciprocal of the EARNINGS YIELD multiplied by 100. The higher the P/E ratio (the lower the earnings yield), the more the market thinks of the company and the cheaper the cost of equity capital to the company. The London *Financial Times* calculates P/E ratios on a net basis (see EARNINGS PER SHARE) but indicates whether calculation on a nil basis would result in a difference of 10% or more.

price variance. A variance arising as the result of actual unit prices differing from budgeted or standard unit prices. The variance is usually calculated by multiplying the price difference by the actual quantity of units. Price variances may be calculated for direct materials, direct labour (where the term rate variance is more common), variable overhead and fixed overhead.

For control purposes a materials price variance should be calculated at the point of purchase of materials rather than at the point of usage. Labour price (rate) variances are often more influenced by national wage awards than by factors controllable by a particular company.

See also EFFICIENCY VARIANCE, JOINT VARIANCE.

prime cost. The sum of DIRECT MATERIALS and DIRECT LABOUR.

principle. In an accounting context, a general term including ASSUMPTIONS, AXIOMS, CONCEPTS, CONVENTIONS and POSTULATES. *See* ACCOUNTING ASSUMPTIONS, AXIOMS, CONCEPTS, CONVENTIONS, POSTULATES AND PRINCIPLES; ACCOUNTING PRINCIPLES; GENERALLY ACCEPTED ACCOUNTING PRINCIPLES.

prior charges. Claims on a company's assets and profits that rank ahead of those of the ordinary shareholders.

priority budget. An INCREMENTAL BUDGET in which budget requests must be accompanied by a statement of what changes would occur if last year's budget amount were increased or decreased by a certain percentage. The rationale of such a budget is that it makes possible a comparison of the priorities of subordinates and superiors. See also ZERO-BASE BUDGETING.

priority percentages. A method of calculating GEARING (LEVERAGE) by computing the percentage of earnings that is required to service each category of loan and share capital. The method ignores the existence of distributable profits retained from previous years.

prior year adjustments. As defined by SSAP 6 in the UK, these are material adjustments applicable to prior years arising from changes in ACCOUNTING POLICIES and from the correction of FUNDAMENTAL ERRORS. In the USA (FAS No. 16) they are restricted to accounting errors and adjustments resulting from the realization of income tax benefits from pre-acquisition losses brought forward by a purchased subsidiary.

private company. In the UK, a company which is not a PUBLIC COMPANY. A private company is not permitted to issue shares or debentures to the public.

private ledger. A ledger containing confidential accounts. It can be linked to the GENERAL LEDGER through a CONTROL ACCOUNT.

probability proportional to size (PPS) sampling. In an audit context, a method of drawing a sample in which the probability of each sample unit being selected is not random but proportional to its size. PPS sampling may be regarded as an alternative to STRATIFIED SAMPLING.

probate. The official proof of a WILL by the court.

process costing. A costing system used by organizations whose products or services are mass produced in continuous fashion through a series of processes, each of which receives varying inputs of direct materials, direct labour and factory overhead, which are charged to each process rather than to individual jobs or batches. Contrast JOB COSTING and OPERATION COSTING.

process tracing. *See* HUMAN INFORMATION PROCESSING (HIP).

product costs. Costs identified with goods acquired or produced for sale. In relation to a manufactured product, product costs comprise DIRECT MATERIALS, DIRECT LABOUR and FACTORY OVERHEAD. They are also known as inventoriable costs. Product costs become expenses rather than assets when they form part of COST OF GOODS SOLD on the sale of the goods manufactured.

production overhead. Synonym for FACTORY OVERHEAD.

profession. An occupational group possessing certain attributes or functions. The 'trait' approach to professionalism concentrates on the specification of key attributes; the 'functionalist' approach on the functions of a profession within a social system and on relationships between a professional person and the client. There is no clear-cut distinction between a profession and a nonprofession or agreement on the list of attributes, but those usually mentioned include: a basis of systematic theory; authority recognised by the clientele of the professional group; sanction and approval of this authority by the community and by the state; a code of ETHICS; and a professional culture sustained by formal professional associations.

An alternative way of looking at a profession is to concentrate on the supply and demand for professional services. A profession is regarded as a means of controlling an occupation, and professions are classified according to the extent to which the professional body can control the nature of the services it renders without intervention either by the client (patronage) or by the state. Professionalization is seen as an attempt to derive economic and social rewards from the possession of special knowledge and skills.

professional ethics. The rules of conduct of a PROFESSION. ACCOUNTANCY BODIES may impose such rules on their members or may issue guidelines. The ethical rules of accountants in public practice are mainly concerned with the preservation of INDEPENDENCE.

profit. A general term for the excess of revenues over expenses. See GROSS PROFIT, NET PROFIT. Profit may be calculated in various ways depending upon whether HISTORICAL COST ACCOUNTING or some form of INFLATION ACCOUNTING is adopted.

profitability index. A variant of the NET PRESENT VALUE method of CAPITAL INVESTMENT APPRAISAL. The index is derived by dividing the present value of the expected

cash receipts by the expected cash payments at the commencement of the project. It is appropriate for independent projects, where it gives the same indication as the net present value and INTERNAL RATE OF RETURN methods, but not for mutually exclusive projects, where it fails to distinguish between projects of different sizes.

profit and loss account formats. Methods of presenting the items in a PROFIT AND LOSS ACCOUNT. As a result of the Companies Act 1981, passed in implementation of the FOURTH DIRECTIVE, UK companies have a choice of four formats, i.e., two formats (vertical or horizontal) based on the type of expenditure (e.g., raw materials, staff costs) and two formats (vertical or horizontal) based on expenditure classified by function (e.g., distribution costs, administrative expenses). The format nearest to previous British practice is format 1, which is as follows:

1. Turnover
2. Cost of sales
3. Gross profit or loss
4. Distribution costs
5. Administrative expenses
6. Other operating income
7. Income from shares in group companies
8. Income from shares in related companies
9. Income from other fixed asset investments
10. Other interest receivable and similar income
11. Amounts written off investments
12. Interest payable and similar charges
13. Tax on profit or loss on ordinary activities
14. Profit or loss on ordinary activities after taxation
15. Extraordinary income
16. Extraordinary charges
17. Extraordinary profit or loss
18. Tax on extraordinary profit or loss
19. Other taxes not shown under the above items
20. Profit or loss for the financial year

Profit and loss accounts must also show profit or loss on ordinary activities before taxation, transfers to and withdrawals from reserves and dividends paid and proposed.

There are no prescribed formats for income statements in the USA.

profit and loss account/statement. In the UK, a financial statement of an enterprise's revenues, expenses and profit. The format of the profit and loss accounts of companies is regulated by law and includes a profit appropriation section. The usual US term is income statement. The equivalent statement for an accounting entity such as a club is an INCOME AND EXPENDITURE ACCOUNT/STATEMENT. In bookkeeping terms, a profit and loss account, unlike a balance sheet, is an account in the ledger, but the details of the ledger account may be rearranged for publication.

profit and loss appropriation account/statement. An account or statement prepared by partnerships and companies that discloses how the net profit or loss for the year (augmented in the case of companies but not partnerships by previously accumulated profits or losses) has been or is intended to be dealt with. The entries in a partnership's profit and loss appropriation account depend upon the partnership agreement. They will always include the net profit or loss for the year and a division of the balance between the partners in their profit-sharing ratios. They may include interest on capital, interest on drawings and partners' salaries. A company's profit and loss appropriation account contains entries for retained profits (losses) brought forward from previous years, the net profit (loss) for the year, taxation, dividends paid and proposed, and transfers to and from reserves.

profit centre. A segment of a business which is held responsible for both revenues and costs.

profit maximization. The assumption that the objective of a firm (company) is to maximize profits. It is rejected in modern finance theory in favour of WEALTH MAXIMIZATION, in which it is assumed that the objective of the firm is to maximize its value to the shareholders.

pro forma financial statements. Financial statements prepared for future periods on the basis of assumptions contained in BUDGETS.

program(me). In public sector and non-business accounting an identifiable segment of activities whose output (goal) is in the form of services rather than goods. The costs of a programme can be measured without much difficulty, but, in the absence of market prices, the benefits may be hard to quantify.

programme evaluation and review technique (PERT). A form of NETWORK ANALYSIS suited to projects where there are uncertainties. Probability estimates are used for activity times and costs. Unlike the CRITICAL PATH METHOD (CPM) which is deterministic, PERT is a stochastic model from which can be derived statements about the probability of completing a project within a certain time.

progressive tax. A tax that takes an increasing proportion of a taxpayer's income (or other tax base) as his or her income rises. The marginal rate of such a tax will always be above the average rate.

proportional consolidation. A method of consolidation in which a proportion, instead of 100%, of each item of assets, liabilities, revenues and expense is brought into the CONSOLIDATED FINANCIAL STATEMENTS. It is rarely used in the UK and USA but is regarded by some accountants as more appropriate than EQUITY ACCOUNTING for JOINT VENTURES. No MINORITY INTEREST arises under this method.

proportional tax. A tax that takes a constant proportion of a taxpayer's income (or other tax base) as his income rises. For such a tax the marginal rate of tax is equal to the average rate.

proprietary view. A view of an enterprise or group of enterprises which stresses the importance of the proprietors (owners) of an enterprise rather than the enterprise itself, i.e., in terms of the ACCOUNTING IDENTITY, assets less liabilities equals proprietorship. The distinction between the proprietary view and the ENTITY VIEW is of great importance in such areas as INFLATION ACCOUNTING (where it favours CURRENT PURCHASING POWER ACCOUNTING rather than CURRENT COST ACCOUNTING) and consolidated financial statements. A proprietary view of enterprise appeals more to owners than to managers and employees.

pro rata consolidation. *See* PROPORTIONAL CONSOLIDATION.

prospectus. In the UK, defined by the Companies Acts as any prospectus, notice, circular, advertisement or other invitation, offering to the public for subscription or purchase any share or debentures of a company. The Stock Exchange considers as a prospectus any offer for sale, advertisement, circular, scheme of arrangement or other equivalent document published or circulated, or proposed to be published or circulated.

The contents of a prospectus are determined by company and investor protection law and the requirements of The Stock Exchange's YELLOW BOOK. The five main parts of a UK prospectus are: preliminary information; the company's history, present business and future prospects; a number of statutory reports (including those by the auditors and the reporting accountants); other financial information (including COMFORT LETTERS); and statutory and general information.

In the USA, prospectuses are issued under the rules of the federal SECURITIES AND EXCHANGE COMMISSION or state BLUE-SKY LAWS.

protocol analysis. Recording the steps involved in making a decision and analysing them in order, for example, to discover which decision rules are used and/or to develop a predictive computer model.

provision for depreciation. In the UK, an amount written off a fixed asset and ac-

cumulated over the life of the asset. A charge (debit) is made periodically against income; the credit balance is accumulated and deducted from the cost or other gross amount of the asset. *See* DEPRECIATION, DEPRECIATION METHODS, PROVISIONS.

provision for doubtful debts. *See* DOUBTFUL DEBTS.

provisions. In the UK, either PROVISIONS FOR LIABILITIES AND CHARGES or valuation adjustments, i.e. amounts written off fixed assets (by way of depreciation or amortization) or current assets (e.g., a provision for DOUBTFUL DEBTS). In both cases a charge (debit) is made to profit and loss account. The credit side of a provision for liabilities and charges is shown in the balance sheet as part of the capital and liabilities, however, whereas that for a valuation adjustment is deducted from the asset concerned.

provisions for liabilities and charges. In the UK, amounts retained as reasonably necessary for the purpose of providing for any liability or loss which is either likely to be incurred, or certain to be incurred, but uncertain as to amount or as to the date on which it will arise. The BALANCE SHEET FORMATS of the Companies Act 1981 subdivide this category, which did not exist in British practice before the Act, into pensions and similar obligations, taxation including DEFERRED TAXATION, and other provisions.

proxy. A person authorized to attend and vote at a company meeting on behalf of a shareholder or stockholder, or the form, signed by the latter, which grants that authority.

prudence. One of the accounting principles included in the EEC FOURTH DIRECTIVE and the British Companies Act 1981. The Act requires that the amount of any item shall be determined on a prudent basis, and in particular (a) only profits realized at the balance sheet date shall be included in the profit and loss account and (b) all liabilities and losses which have arisen or are likely to arise in respect of the financial year or a previous financial year shall be taken into account, including those that only become apparent between the date of the balance sheet and the date on which it is signed on behalf of the board of directors.

Prudence is one of the four FUNDAMENTAL ACCOUNTING CONCEPTS of Statement of Standard Accounting Practice No. 2 but it is not one of the FUNDAMENTAL ACCOUNTING ASSUMPTIONS of International Accounting Standard No. 1, where it is regarded instead as one of the considerations governing the selection of ACCOUNTING POLICIES.

According to SSAP 2, where there is a conflict between prudence and ACCRUALS, the former should prevail.

Public Accounts Commission. A body set up by the British National Audit Act of 1983; all of its members are Members of the House of Commons. It examines the annual budget of the NATIONAL AUDIT OFFICE (NAO) and presents it for parliamentary approval. The Commission also appoints the external auditor of the NAO.

Public Accounts Committee. *See* COMMITTEE OF PUBLIC ACCOUNTS.

public company. In the UK, a company whose MEMORANDUM OF ASSOCIATION states that it is a public company, whose name ends with the words 'public limited company' ('plc'; 'ccc' for Welsh companies) and which has a minimum (currently £50,000) authorized and allotted share capital at least one quarter paid up. A public company, unlike a PRIVATE COMPANY, has the right to make public issues of shares and debentures.

public dividend capital. In the UK, capital provided as permanent finance to nationalized industries and on which a dividend is expected to be paid to the Exchequer. The annual dividend is normally related to the industry's profitability in that year, although on average dividends are expected to be not less than the interest which would be payable on government loans. Not all nationalized industries have public dividend capital.

Public Expenditure Survey Committee

(PESC). In the UK, a group of senior officials from all major central government departments responsible for making an annual survey of public expenditure plans as the basis for ministerial decisions on their total and composition.

public good. A good with the characteristics that (a) individuals cannot be excluded from consuming it, even if they do not pay for it; (b) consumption by one individual does not prevent anyone else from consuming it. The market left to itself will tend to underproduce such goods, which may therefore need to be paid for by the government out of taxation.

It can be argued that published financial statements have some of the characteristics of public goods and that therefore ACCOUNTING STANDARDS are necessary.

Public Works Loans Board (PWLB). A UK central government agency responsible for making loans to public authorities. The interest rate charged is slightly higher than that at which the government itself can borrow. Local authorities finance part of their capital expenditure from this source.

purchase accounting. US term for ACQUISITION ACCOUNTING.

purchase discount. US term for CASH DISCOUNT.

purchases day book. *See* PURCHASES JOURNAL.

purchases journal. A book or other record containing a chronological list of credit purchases. Each entry in the journal is credited to an account in the CREDITORS LEDGER. Totals are posted periodically to the debit of purchases account in the GENERAL LEDGER and the credit of creditors ledger control account.

purchases ledger. Synonym for CREDITORS LEDGER.

purchasing power loss or gain. A HOLDING GAIN or loss arising from holding net

MONETARY ASSETS through a period of change in the general price level. In the simplest case, the loss or gain may be calculated as below.

Let M = net monetary assets,
N = an historical cost measure of the non-monetary assets,
R = owner's equity and
p = $[(p_1 - p_o)/p_o]$, the proportionate change in the general price level during an accounting period in which there are no transactions. Then the balance sheet at the beginning of the accounting period can be expressed as $M + N = R$ and at the end of the period as

$$M(1+p) + N(1+p) = R(1+p)$$

which can be rearranged as

$$M + N(1+p) = R(1+p) - Mp$$

where Mp is the purchasing power loss or gain. Where there are transactions during the period it is usual to use average price changes as a simplification.

The concept of a purchasing power loss or gain is unfortunately more complicated than the above suggests. Net monetary assets may be divided into monetary assets and liabilities, with a LOSS ON HOLDING MONEY arising on the former and a GAIN ON BORROW-ING arising on the latter. Liabilities can be further divided into current liabilities regarded as a component of monetary working capital (see MONETARY WORKING CAPITAL ADJUSTMENT), and long-term debt. Highly geared companies are likely to show very large gains on borrowing. The ENTITY VIEW, as distinct from the PROPRIETARY VIEW, suggests that such gains are gains of the owners' equity at the expense of the long-term debt holders, not the distributable gains of the company itself. Concern with this problem has led in the UK to the notion of a GEAR-ING ADJUSTMENT.

A different approach has been taken in the USA, where FAS 33 makes no references to a gearing adjustment or a monetary working capital adjustment but requires disclosure of the gain (loss) from decline (increase) in purchasing power of net amounts owed.

purchasing power parity (PPP) theorem. The theorem that, between two countries, changes in the exchange rate are proportional to changes in the relative price levels. The empirical evidence supports the theorem in the long run but not in the short run. It is thus of limited use to accountants and financial managers. Some accounting theorists have argued that purchasing power parities and not exchange rates should be used for currency translation purposes.

P/V chart. A chart which measures profit on the vertical axis and volume in physical or monetary units on the horizontal. In essence it is a simplified form of the BREAKEVEN CHART and is based on the same assumptions.

Q

qualified audit report. *See* AUDIT OPINION.

qualitative characteristics of accounting information. Those characteristics that accounting information should have in order to be of maximum usefulness to readers of accounting reports. The FASB's STATEMENT OF FINANCIAL ACCOUNTING CONCEPTS (SFAC) No. 2 distinguishes the user-specific qualities of understandability and decision usefulness; the primary decision-specific qualities of relevance and reliability; and the ingredients of the primary qualities, i.e., predictive value, feedback value, timeliness, COMPARABILITY and CONSISTENCY, verifiability, NEUTRALITY and representational faithfulness. It will often be necessary for there to be trade-offs between the various characteristics.

quality control. Policies and procedures used to determine and maintain a desired quality of goods and services. Quality control has traditionally been applied to manufacturing operations but may also be applied to the services (especially audit) provided by public accountants.

questionable payments. Bribes and other payments made to foreign governments or persons in order to obtain contracts. Such payments are forbidden to US companies by the FOREIGN CORRUPT PRACTICES ACT.

queueing theory. The mathematical analysis of problems in which items requiring or providing service are occasionally idle, and it is necessary to discover a solution which minimizes costs. Solutions can be arrived at analytically or by SIMULATION.

quick assets. Current assets less stocks (inventories) i.e. mainly bank balances, debtors and readily realizable investments. They are also referred to as liquid assets.

quick ratio. The relationship between quick assets and current liabilities. Also known as the acid test, or liquid ratio, it is widely regarded as the most useful single test of liquidity. It differs from the current ratio in the exclusion of stocks (inventories), which may not be readily realizable and which may be valued in different ways by different companies.

R

random sampling. In an audit context, a method of drawing a sample in which each item in the population, e.g., the purchase invoices for May, has an equal chance of being selected. Random sampling is commonly implemented through the use of random number tables and may be with replacement or (as is usual in auditing applications) without replacement. *See* SYSTEMATIC RANDOM SAMPLING.

random walk hypothesis. The hypothesis that share prices move independently of previous movements. This is equivalent to the weak form of the EFFICIENT MARKET HYPOTHESIS.

range. A measure of DISPERSION calculated by obtaining the difference between the largest and smallest items in a group of numerical data.

rateable value. In the UK, a value placed on all properties subject to RATES. The value is based on a notional rent that the property could be expected to yield after deducting the cost of repairs.

rate of return pricing. Basing prices on a planned rate of return on capital employed. It is a variant of FULL COST PRICING and is probably most suitable when prices need to be established on a basis acceptable to a powerful customer (e.g., a government agency).

rates. In the UK, a local property tax levied by certain local authorities. Rates are calculated by multiplying a property's 'rateable value' (i.e., its notional annual market rent less cost of upkeep) by a 'rate poundage' (percentage in the £) fixed by each rating authority. Rate poundages vary considerably as between authorities and types of property.

Rates are generally regarded as being regressive and not taking into account ABILITY TO PAY. The Layfield Report (1976) recommended their replacement by a local INCOME TAX.

rate support grant (RSG). The main source of local government finance in UK. It is divided into a domestic rate relief grant (used to reduce domestic rate bills) and a block grant. The main objective of the RSG is to subsidize local services by redistributing central taxation to compensate local authorities for differences in spending needs and differences in their ability to raise local revenue from their taxable resources.

rate variance. See PRICE VARIANCE.

RAWP. In the UK, the acronym of Resource Allocation Working Party. The abbreviation is commonly used to signify the philosophy and process of allocating financial resources in the National Health Service so as in time to raise all regional health authorities to an equal standard of resources as determined on a weighted-population basis.

real accounts. Those accounts in a ledger which record transactions involving NON-MONETARY ASSETS, e.g., plant and machinery.

realization account. An account used on the dissolution of a partnership. The book value of assets to be sold is transferred to the debit of realization account and the proceeds of sale are placed to its credit. Any balance is divided amongst the partners.

realization convention. The convention that increases or decreases in the market values of assets and liabilities are not recognized as gains or losses until the assets are sold or the liabilities paid. The lower of cost or market rule of stock (inventory) valuation may be regarded as an exception to the convention based on PRUDENCE.

UK company law requires that only profits realized at the balance sheet date may be included in the profit and loss account, but realization is defined in accordance with accounting principles that are generally accepted at the time of preparation of the accounts.

See also REVENUE RECOGNITION.

realized profit. The sum of CURRENT OPERATING PROFIT and realized HOLDING GAINS. It is equal in total to conventional accounting profit, but the latter does not recognize the dichotomy between operating and holding activities.

real proprietary capital. The value of the net assets of an enterprise in units of general purchasing power, as in CURRENT PURCHASING POWER (CPP) ACCOUNTING and RELATIVE PRICE CHANGE ACCOUNTING. *See* CAPITAL MAINTENANCE CONCEPT.

real terms accounting. *See* RELATIVE PRICE CHANGE ACCOUNTING.

realty. Immovable property such as land, in contradistinction to PERSONALTY or movable property.

receiver. In the UK, a person appointed, usually by a bank or the trustees for debenture-holders, to take possession of those assets of a company covered by a FLOATING CHARGE and to realize sufficient of them to repay the principal and accrued interest, and to pay all liabilities ranking before the debentures, plus the costs of the receivership and the receiver's remuneration. A receiver is often granted the power to manage the company's business to help his realization of the assets. He or she then becomes a receiver and manager. A receiver may subsequently be appointed as LIQUIDATOR. In the USA, a receiver is appointed by a court.

A STATEMENT OF AFFAIRS is prepared in a receivership as in a winding up. The receiver must also prepare an abstract of his receipts and payments in a prescribed form. The receiver's remuneration usually takes the form of a percentage on amounts realized.

receiving order. In the UK, an order by which the court declares a debtor or debtors

bankrupt and vests the assets in the OFFICIAL RECEIVER.

reciprocal. The quotient obtained by dividing any number into 1.

Recommendations on Accounting Principles. Recommendations issued by the Institute of Chartered Accountants in England and Wales from 1942 to 1969. They were not mandatory but had persuasive force. Twenty nine recommendations were issued before they were superseded from the 1970s onwards by Statements of Standard Accounting Practice (SSAPs).

reconstruction. A change in the CAPITAL STRUCTURE of a company, including schemes for the AMALGAMATION of two or more companies.

recoverable amount. The greater of the NET REALIZABLE VALUE (NRV) and NET PRESENT VALUE (NPV) of an asset. The VALUE TO THE BUSINESS of an asset is the lower of recoverable amount and current REPLACEMENT COST (RC).

redeemable preference shares. *See* REDEEMABLE SHARES.

redeemable shares. In the UK, shares, whether preference or ordinary, which are specifically redeemable under their terms of issue. Redeemable shares may only be redeemed out of distributable profits or the proceeds of a fresh issue of shares made for the purposes of redemption. In the former case a CAPITAL REDEMPTION RESERVE must be established on redemption.

redemption. The repayment of shares and debentures (stocks and bonds), usually at prearranged amounts and times.

redemption yield. A YIELD which takes account not only of periodical returns on an investment but also of the amount receivable on redemption. *See* FLAT YIELD.

reducing balance depreciation. *See* DEPRECIATION METHODS.

registered office. In Britain, the official address of a company. The MEMORANDUM OF ASSOCIATION must state whether it is in England, Wales or Scotland.

register of charges In the UK, a STATUTORY BOOK kept by companies. It contains details of all charges created by the company upon its assets (including fixed and floating charges to secure debentures) and required to be registered with the REGISTRAR OF COMPANIES.

register of members. In the UK, a STATUTORY BOOK required to be kept by companies limited by shares, containing the members' (i.e., shareholders') names and addresses, numbers of shares held, with serial numbers if any, amounts paid or deemed to be paid, and dates of entry on the register and of ceasing to be a member. The register of members is usually combined in practice with a SHARE LEDGER.

Registrar of Companies. In Britain, the government officer with whom ANNUAL REPORTS (including financial statements) and other documents must be filed: in Cardiff for companies registered in England and Wales; in Edinburgh for companies registered in Scotland.

registration statement. In the USA, a formal statement, required to be filed with the SECURITIES AND EXCHANGE COMMISSION or other body. It contains financial and other information relating to a proposed sale of securities.

regression. An analysis involving the fitting of an equation to a set of data points, usually by the method of ordinary LEAST SQUARES. Simple linear regression, as used by accountants to determine COST FUNCTIONS, involves the fitting of a linear function between two variables. Multiple regression involves the fitting of a linear function containing two or more variables.

regressive tax. A tax that takes a decreasing proportion of a taxpayer's income (or other tax base) as his income rises. The marginal rate of such a tax will always be below the average rate. The most regressive form of taxation in the UK is local authority rates.

regulation of corporate financial reporting. The establishment and enforcement of the rules to be followed by companies in their published financial statements. The rules may relate to conventions of measurement and valuation, to disclosure or to both. It is possible to have no regulations at all, i.e., each preparer of financial statements makes his own rules. In practice, a combination of public sector and private sector regulation is usually found. This is true of both the UK and the USA, whose systems of regulation show significant differences as well as similarities.

In the UK, public sector regulation is carried out through the Companies Acts, which lay down accounting rules and formats. These are by no means comprehensive, however, and they are supplemented by the private sector regulation of the ACCOUNTING STANDARDS COMMITTEE (ASC), which is controlled by the UK ACCOUNTANCY BODIES. The STATEMENTS OF STANDARD ACCOUNTING PRACTICE (SSAPS) that it issues are very influential but they do not have statutory authority and they are not backed by any government department or agency. The Companies Acts and most accounting standards cover all companies (although with modifications) but are supplemented for listed companies by the requirements of the Stock Exchange.

In the USA, by contrast, company law is unimportant and the accounting standards-setting body acts under the delegated authority of a federal government agency. Listed companies and many others come under the jurisdiction of the SECURITIES AND EXCHANGE COMMISSION, which has statutory power to determine GENERALLY ACCEPTED ACCOUNTING PRINCIPLES. It has delegated this power to the FINANCIAL ACCOUNTING STANDARDS BOARD (FASB), a body which, unlike its predecessors, the COMMITTEE ON ACCOUNTING PROCEDURE (CAP) and the ACCOUNTING PRINCIPLES BOARD (APB), is not under the control of the US accountancy profession as represented by the American Institute of Certified Public Accountants. The listing requirements of the New York Stock Exchange are also important.

See also ACCOUNTING STANDARDS, STANDARD SETTING.

related company. A company, other than a GROUP COMPANY, in which an investing company holds, on a long-term basis, a qualifying capital interest (usually 20% or more of equity share capital carrying voting rights) for the purpose of securing a contribution to the investing company's own activities by the exercise of any control or influence arising from that interest. Related companies, defined as above in the British Companies Act 1981, are usually also associated companies as defined in SSAP 1.

In the USA the term related company is used as a synonym for AFFILIATED COMPANY.

related party transactions. Transactions between related enterprises, especially those in which the terms and conditions are, or appear to be, unduly favourable to one of the parties.

relative price change accounting. Forms of INFLATION ACCOUNTING that take account of changes in both the GENERAL PRICE LEVEL and in SPECIFIC PRICES. An example can be found in FAS 33 in the USA where, after calculation of income (loss) from continuing operations in current cost terms (but without a monetary working capital adjustment or a gearing adjustment), adjustments are made for the gain from the decline in purchasing power of net amounts owed and the excess of the increase in specific prices of non-monetary assets held during the year over the increase in the general price level. Another example is CONTINUOUSLY CONTEMPORARY ACCOUNTING (CoCoA) as adapted to take account of movements in the general price level.

Relative price change accounting is based on a financial CAPITAL MAINTENANCE CONCEPT (units of purchasing power).

relative price changes. Changes in the prices of specific goods and services relative to each other, independent of changes in the GENERAL PRICE LEVEL.

relevance. A desirable qualitative characteristic of accounting information. Relevant information is information that is capable of making a difference to a decision by a user. To be relevant, information must be timely and must have either predictive value (*see* PREDICTIVE ABILITY) or feedback value (i.e. be capable of confirming or correcting earlier expectations).

relevant range. That range of activity over which budgeted sales and expense relationships (frequently assumed to be linear) remain valid. The presumption is that the enterprise will not operate outside this range.

reliability. A desirable qualitative characteristic of accounting information. According to STATEMENT OF FINANCIAL ACCOUNTING CONCEPTS No. 2, reliability has three components: verifiability, representational faithfulness and NEUTRALITY. There may be conflicts between verifiability and representational faithfulness and also between reliability and RELEVANCE.

remainderman. In England and Wales and in the USA, the person entitled to real estate on the death of a life-tenant. The Scottish term is FIAR.

renewals basis. *See* DEPRECIATION METHODS.

replacement cost. The cost of replacing an asset. Replacement cost can be interpreted as either the cost of reproduction (i.e., replacement of the physical object) or the cost of equivalent services (*see* MODERN EQUIVALENT ASSET). If these are not identical, the implication is that the assets currently used by the firm are not those it would currently buy in the market. Replacement cost as a method of ASSET VALUATION takes account of changes in SPECIFIC PRICES, produces up-to-date balance sheet figures and matches current revenues with current costs, but is less objective than historical cost.

required rate of return. The rate of return required by an enterprise on its capital investment projects. *See* COST OF CAPITAL.

research and development costs. Expenditure on pure research, applied research and development. In UK standard accounting practice (SSAP 13), pure research is defined as original investigation undertaken in order to gain new scientific or technical knowledge and understanding but without any specific practical aims or application; applied research as original investigation undertaken in order to gain new scientific or technical knowledge and directed towards a specific practical aim or objective; and development as the use of scientific or technical knowledge in order to produce new or substantially improved materials, devices, products, processes, systems or services prior to the commencement of commercial production.

SSAP 13 requires that expenditure on pure and applied research (other than that on fixed assets) be written off in the year of expenditure. Development expenditure, as a result of representations made especially by the aerospace industry, is treated more permissively. If it is separately identifiable; represented by a clearly defined project which is technically feasible and commercially viable; the future revenue is expected to outweigh its future costs; and adequate resources for completion exist, it may either be written off immediately or be capitalized and amortized against future benefits. Movements on deferred development expenditure and amounts brought and carried forward must be disclosed. The Companies Act 1981 prohibits the capitalization of research costs but allows the capitalization and amortization of development costs in undefined special circumstances. The Act also requires that an indication of research and development activities be given in the DIRECTORS' REPORT.

In the USA, FAS No. 2 differs in three important respects from SSAP 13: it requires the immediate write-off of both research and development costs and disclosure of the amount; it provides a detailed analysis of the costs that are to be regarded as research and development costs; and it makes no distinction between pure and applied research in its definitions.

The accounting treatment in the UK of research and development expenditure costs provides an interesting case study of the conflict between the concepts of PRUDENCE and ACCRUALS and of how the statement in SSAP 2 that prudence should prevail over accruals can be overridden by the POLITICIZATION OF ACCOUNTING standards setting.

reservation of title. *See* ROMALPA CLAUSE.

reserve accounting. The practice of passing extraordinary and prior year items through reserves rather than through the profit and loss account. Reserve accounting has diminished in the UK in recent years, a trend reinforced by SSAP 6.

reserve fund. In UK company accounting, a RESERVE represented by an earmarked asset (usually cash or investments).

reserve liability. In the UK, an amount outstanding on a partly paid share that by special resolution of the company cannot be called up except on a winding-up.

reserve on consolidation. In the UK, NEGATIVE GOODWILL transferred to reserve.

reserve recognition accounting. *See* OIL AND GAS ACCOUNTING.

reserves. In UK company accounting, those items of OWNERS' EQUITY that arise from SHARE PREMIUMS, the retention of profits and the upward revaluation of assets. Reserves should not be confused with PROVISIONS. Reserves are not usually represented by earmarked assets. If they are they are known as RESERVE FUNDS. The Companies Act 1948, but not subsequent Acts, divided reserves into CAPITAL RESERVES and REVENUE RESERVES and these terms are still sometimes used. The Companies Act 1980 distinguishes between DISTRIBUTABLE RESERVES and UNDISTRIBUTABLE RESERVES. The BALANCE SHEET FORMATS require the separate disclosure of share premium account, REVALUATION RESERVE, other reserves (including CAPITAL REDEMPTION RESERVE, reserve for OWN SHARES, and reserves provided for by the articles of association) and the balance on PROFIT AND LOSS ACCOUNT. Reserves of whatever type can be converted into share capital by means of a BONUS ISSUE.

In public sector accounting, a reserve is a fraction of a cash funding allocation held back to meet inflation or the cash needs of a future commitment. Thus public sector reserves unlike those of companies are usually represented by cash.

See also SECRET RESERVES.

residual equity. That group of claimants in a company whose rights are superseded by all other claimants (normally the ordinary shareholders or common stockholders).

residual income. The net income of an IN-VESTMENT CENTRE, less the imputed interest on the net assets invested in the centre. It can be used as an alternative measure of the performance of the centre to RETURN ON IN-VESTMENT (ROI). Use of residual income implies that the goal is not the maximization of ROI but the maximization of return in excess of minimum desired ROI (i.e., residual income has much the same relationship to ROI as NET PRESENT VALUE has to INTERNAL RATE OF RETURN).

residual value. The value, actual or estimated, of a fixed asset at the end of its economic life. In practice it is often assumed to be zero.

responsibility accounting. A system of accounting in which RESPONSIBILITY CENTRES are established throughout an organization and individual managers are held responsible for costs (COST CENTRES), revenues and costs (PROFIT CENTRES) or revenues, costs and investments (INVESTMENT CENTRES).

responsibility centre. An organizational unit accountable for its performance (e.g., for costs, revenues, investment) to a higher authority. See COST CENTRE, PROFIT CENTRE, INVESTMENT CENTRE.

retail inventory method. A method of IN-VENTORY VALUATION used by retail stores in which stock is taken at retail price and then reduced to cost price by the use of mark-up percentages.

retained profits. Profits not distributed to shareholders but reinvested in a company. *See* COST OF CAPITAL.

retention of title. *See* ROMALPA CLAUSE.

return on investment (ROI). The relationship between profit and investment, used as a measure of performance of an INVESTMENT CENTRE (which may be a division, a company or a group of companies). Return on investment can be analysed as follows:

$$\frac{\text{sales}}{\text{investment}} \times \frac{\text{profit}}{\text{sales}} = \frac{\text{profit}}{\text{investment}}.$$

Such a breakdown is of great use for internal performance measurement but runs into difficulties for a group of companies with many ASSOCIATED COMPANIES, since their sales are not included in group turnover.

Both 'profit' and 'investment' need to be defined carefully and consistently. A number of investment bases are possible, e.g., total assets available or employed; total assets net of current liabilities; shareholders' funds (i.e., total assets less total liabilities). The last is of interest to owners but is not a measure of managerial performance. Profit should be measured in a manner consistent with the investment base. In particular, it is usual to take a profit figure before interest and tax in order to separate managerial performance from the effects of different capital structures and tax rates. Exceptional, extraordinary and prior year items are also excluded.

The assets included in the investment base may be valued at depreciated historical cost (the most common practice), gross historical cost, net replacement cost, gross replacement cost, net realizable value, or net present value. If net rather than gross assets are used conventional DEPRECIATION METHODS can give misleading results which, it is argued, can be avoided by the use of compound interest depreciation methods. (But they are not used in practice.)

In order to distinguish good managers

from good divisions, a manager should be judged against a budget target rather than against other investment centres.

An alternative measure of the performance of an investment centre is RESIDUAL INCOME.

returns inwards. Sales returns, i.e. goods sold but then returned by one enterprise to another.

returns outwards. Purchases returns, i.e. goods purchased but then returned by one enterprise to another.

revaluation. The writing-up of a fixed asset to its current market value. Revaluations are not permitted under US generally accepted accounting principles but have always been a part of UK accounting practice and are expressly permitted under the ALTERNATIVE ACCOUNTING RULES of the Companies Acts.

revaluation account. An account used in PARTNERSHIP ACCOUNTS when assets are revalued on the admission, death or retirement of a partner. The purpose of the account is to recognize these events on a current value rather than an historical cost basis.

revenue account. The equivalent of a profit and loss account or income and expenditure account in public sector accounting.

revenue expenditure. Expenditure that is written off completely in the profit and loss account in the accounting period in which it is made. The dividing line between revenue expenditure and CAPITAL EXPENDITURE is not always easy to draw.

revenue recognition. Recognizing and recording revenue in the accounts. It is necessary to decide when revenue arises and how much of it is to be recognized. In principle revenue can be recognized at the point of purchase of a good, at the point of sale, at the point when cash is collected, or at any intermediate point. In practice, recognition depends upon the extent to which the services to be provided by the good have been performed and whether cash or a claim to cash susceptible to objective measurement has been received. In most cases this means recognition of revenue at the point of sale. Examples of exceptions are LONG-TERM CONTRACT WORK IN PROGRESS (where revenue may be recognized during production) and where debt collection is doubtful (in which case revenue may be recognized on collection in cash).

Unrealized HOLDING GAINS and losses may occur between the point of purchase and the point of sale. Because of PRUDENCE, conventional accounting recognizes unrealized holding losses (as in the lower of cost or market rule) but not unrealized holding gains.

See also REALIZATION CONVENTION.

revenue reserve. In UK company accounting, any RESERVE that is not a CAPITAL RESERVE.

reverse yield gap. *See* YIELD GAP.

reversion. A right to property that will fall into the possession of some person after the expiration of a grant of that property for a limited period to another person, or on the occurrence of some particular event.

Richardson Report. A report on inflation accounting issued in New Zealand in 1976. Its recommendations were similar to those of the UK Report of the SANDILANDS COMMITTEE and the Australian MATHEWS REPORT but it recommended a different approach on monetary items.

rights issue. An issue of shares in which the existing shareholders have a pre-emptive right to subscribe for the new shares. The offer price is usually fixed a little below the current market price. The rights can be sold if the shareholder does not wish to subscribe. If the shareholder fails to do so it is normal for the company to sell the rights on the shareholder's behalf. A shareholder should in principle be equally well off whether or not he or she decides to subscribe.

risk. A situation in which future events are not known with certainty but an array of alternative outcomes and their probabilities can be estimated. It can be distinguished from UNCERTAINTY where no such probabilities can be estimated. *See also* BUSINESS RISK, FINANCIAL RISK, NON-SYSTEMATIC RISK, SYSTEMATIC RISK.

risk aversion. A tendency to avoid risk. A risk averter is a person with a diminishing MARGINAL UTILITY of money who requires a higher expected return as compensation for an increase in risk. It is generally thought that most people are risk averse rather than 'risk lovers' or 'risk neutral'.

risk congruence. Sharing of the same attitudes towards risk on the part of superiors and their subordinates.

roll over relief. A tax relief that allows a capital gain realized on the sale of a fixed asset to be deducted for tax purposes from the cost of the replacement asset. The effect is to postpone, sometimes indefinitely, the payment of capital gains tax. If assets are always replaced, the tax on capital gains (part of corporation tax in the case of UK companies) will never be paid, especially in times of rising prices.

Romalpa clause. In the UK, any clause in a contract for the sale or supply of goods whereby the supplier seeks to obtain priority over other creditors of the purchase by retaining, or purporting to retain, the title or other interest to the goods supplied until the debt has been paid. The legal effects of such a clause are uncertain but of great importance to, among others, accountants and auditors since they affect the ownership of stock-in-trade (inventories). Problems of SUBSTANCE OVER FORM arise if it is thought that the commercial substance is that stocks subject to such a clause are the assets of the purchaser (if the latter is a going concern).

Rooker-Wise amendment. A resolution of the British Parliament in 1977 that income tax allowances should be automatically indexed unless Parliament decides otherwise.

Royal Mail case. English legal case (1931) which ended the respectability of SECRET RESERVES and drew attention to the need for CONSOLIDATED FINANCIAL STATEMENTS.

rule of 78. A method of allocating finance charges sometimes used in HIRE PURCHASE AND INSTALMENT SALE ACCOUNTING and in LEASE ACCOUNTING. It is based on the sum of the digits 1 to 12 and provides an approximation to the figures provided by the use of actuarial or COMPOUND INTEREST methods.

S

sale and leaseback. A transaction in which an owner sells an asset and immediately re-acquires the right to use the asset by entering into a lease with the purchaser. The lease may be either a finance (capital) lease or an operating lease (*see* LEASE ACCOUNTING).

sales day book. *See* SALES JOURNAL.

sales forecast. A forecast of future sales based on consideration of such factors as past sales volumes, general economic and industry conditions, relationship of the organization's sales to macroeconomic indicators, relative product profitability, market research studies, pricing policies, advertising, quality of the sales force, competition, seasonal variations and productive capacity. The sales forecast is the usual starting point of the budgeting process.

sales journal. A book or other record containing a chronological list of credit sales. Each entry in the journal is debited to an account in the DEBTORS LEDGER. Totals are posted periodically to the debit of debtors ledger control account and the credit of sales account.

sales ledger. Synonym for DEBTORS LEDGER.

sales mix. The relative combination of quantities of the variety of products that comprise total sales.

salvage value. Synonym for the RESIDUAL VALUE of a fixed asset.

sampling frame. A list of the units in a population which is to be sampled.

Sandilands Committee. A UK committee on inflation accounting which reported in 1975 ('The Report of the Inflation Accounting Committee', Cmnd. 6445). The report rejected the system of CURRENT PURCHASING POWER (CPP) ACCOUNTING proposed by the UK accountancy bodies and favoured CURRENT COST ACCOUNTING (CCA) instead. Through the work of the Inflation Accounting Steering Group and the Accounting Standards Committee, the report was eventually translated into SSAP 16, but only after many problems had been surmounted. The findings of the Committee have not, however, been fully accepted by all British accountants or by British business.

satisficing. Achieving a satisfactory level of, say, wealth or profits, instead of maximizing. Satisficing is often regarded as a more realistic description of managerial behaviour than maximizing but it is less suitable as a normative goal.

SATTA. Acronym for *Statement on Accounting Theory and Theory Acceptance* published by the AMERICAN ACCOUNTING ASSOCIATION in 1977. It differs from its predecessor ASOBAT (1966) in that it is a statement about accounting theory rather than of accounting theory. SATTA surveys a number of theoretical approaches to accounting (the so-called classical approaches divided into a normative deductive school and an inductive school; the decision-usefulness approach based on DECISION MODELS; and the INFORMATION ECONOMICS APPROACH) and seeks to explain the development of accounting theory in terms of the paradigms of Thomas Kuhn's *The Structure of Scientific Revolutions* (2nd ed., 1970).

scatter diagram. A graphical representation of data in which the observed values of one variable are plotted against those of another as an aid to determining whether any mathematical relationship exists between them.

scheme of arrangement. In the UK, a compromise or arrangement between a company and its creditors or between a company and its shareholders. Because they require the support of a substantial number of creditors, are cumbersome to operate and difficult to monitor, and usually offer little financial advantage compared with liquidation, schemes of arrangement are rare in practice.

Schmalenbach, E. (1873-1955). A leading German business economist and accountant long associated with the University of Cologne. Schmalenbach exercised a great influence in Germany and in other European countries on accounting theory, charts of accounts (accounting plans), commercial education, public sector accounting and cost accounting. He founded a research journal in 1906 and edited it until 1933. Of his many books only *Dynamic Accounting* (first published 1919) is available in English in a translation by G.W. Murphy and Kenneth S. Most of the 12th edition. An account of Schmalenbach's life and work is given in David A.R. Forrester, *Schmalenbach and After* (Glasgow, 1977).

scientific management. An approach to management associated with the name of Frederick W. Taylor (1856-1915) and others and concerned largely with procedures for the efficient organization and conduct of routine work.

scorekeeping. The accounting function of accumulating data and reporting to all levels of management. It may be contrasted with attention directing and problem solving. Scorekeeping is essential but limiting, as illustrated by the story of the would-be management accountant admonished by the Yorkshire businessman: 'Be silent, lad. Thou art nowt but scorekeeper.'

scrap. Residue from a manufacturing process which can be either sold or re-used. It has a small but measurable value.

scrap value. Synonym for the RESIDUAL VALUE of a fixed asset.

scrip. In the UK, a popular term for share and bond certificates.

scripophily. The collection and study of SHARE CERTIFICATES and bond certificates.

secret reserves. Undisclosed understatement of net worth resulting from, e.g., the excessive writing down of assets, overstatement of provisions and liabilities, and the writing off of additions to fixed assets as expenses. In the UK, secret reserves were accepted as representing prudent accounting and sound finance until the ROYAL MAIL CASE of 1931, after which they ceased to be respectable. The Companies Act 1948 made their creation more difficult by distinguishing more carefully between PROVISIONS and RESERVES. It can be argued that the valuation of fixed assets at historical cost during periods of inflation should also be regarded as creating secret reserves.

Securities and Exchange Commission (SEC). A US federal government regulatory agency established under the Securities Exchange Act 1934. The SEC has the duty of ensuring full and fair disclosure of all material facts concerning securities offered for public investment. It is also concerned with initiating litigation against fraud and providing for the registration of securities. The SEC administers the Securities Act 1933, the Securities Foreign Exchange Act 1934 and a number of secondary acts, including the FOREIGN CORRUPT PRACTICES ACT 1977. About 10,000 corporations are subject to its jurisdiction.

Companies subject to SEC jurisdiction must file a number of forms, notably FORM 10-K annually and FORM 10-Q quarterly. The former includes consolidated and unconsolidated balance sheets, income statements and statements of changes in financial position and much other detailed information.

The SEC has a legal power to determine accounting principles in the USA. In exercising this power, it has relied heavily upon the FINANCIAL ACCOUNTING STANDARDS BOARD and its predecessor bodies to help establish GENERALLY ACCEPTED ACCOUNTING PRINCIPLES. The SEC itself issues Regulation S-X (which prescribes the form and context of financial statements to be filed), ACCOUNTING SERIES RELEASES and Staff Accounting Bulletins. It has not hesitated to intervene directly on a number of issues, e.g., the INVESTMENT TAX CREDIT, INFLATION ACCOUNTING and OIL AND GAS ACCOUNTING.

See also REGULATION OF CORPORATE FINANCIAL REPORTING.

security. Either the backing for a loan or a generic name for stocks, shares, debentures etc.

security market line. The linear relationship between the expected return of a security and its SYSTEMATIC RISK, the expected return comprising a risk-free return plus a risk premium.

segment reporting. The reporting to outsiders of the results of a diversified group of companies by major class of business and geographical area. The main argument in favour of segment reporting is that the highly aggregated data contained in the consolidated financial statements of diversified groups leads to a loss of information unless the data are disaggregated into segments. The disclosure of segment differences in profitability, risk and growth prospects may enable investors to make a better allocation of resources and may also be of use to employees and trade unions in wage bargaining; to consumers in helping to restrain price discrimination and the reduction of competition; and to governments in formulating industrial policy. It is also sometimes claimed that segment reports facilitate comparability between companies or groups that have segments in the same industry, or between such segments and single industry companies.

The arguments against segment reporting are that it gives an undue advantage to competitors; that it is inequitable between groups (e.g., the operations of a segment in a small group may be deemed significant and require reporting while operations of similar size in a larger group may be deemed insignificant and not require reporting); that the costs of data preparation and audit may be too high (this is unlikely where the data are already collected for internal use); and that there may be undesirable regulatory or tax consequences.

Segment reporting (by both class of business and geographical area) is required by company law in the UK (although much is left to the discretion of directors) but plans for an accounting standard have been dropped. US reporting is regulated by SEC re-quirements and FASB Statement No. 14 (1976). An international accounting standard (IAS 14) was issued in 1981.

Identifying a business segment is difficult and to some extent arbitrary. Possible criteria include: legal entities, organizational divisions, customers, products and industries. Use of either of the first two would mean that the information should be readily available. FAS 14 requires segmentation by industry; a segment must be reported if it contributes 10% or more of sales, of operating profit (loss) or of identifiable assets.

The argument for segmentation on a geographical basis is that risks and returns may differ significantly from country to country. Such segmentation is required by law in the UK and by standard in the USA but the classification of countries, beyond domestic and foreign, is left to each company to decide for itself.

The reporting of segment data is likely to involve arbitrary cost allocations. FAS 14 requires the disclosure for industry segments of operating profits, defined as sales revenues less operating costs, including those indirect costs that can be 'allocated on a reasonable basis'. For geographical segments, other measures of profit are permissible. The FASB, unlike the British Companies Act 1981, also requires the reporting of identifiable assets. Both require that segment data be audited. FAS 14 and IAS 14, but not British company law, require information about inter-segment transfers.

self-assessment. A system under which the taxpayer rather than the tax authority is primarily responsible for calculating tax liability and ensuring that payment is made. It is not used in the UK for income tax (although it is an essential part of the income tax systems of such countries as the USA and Australia) but there are elements of self-assessment in the administration in the UK of value added tax and capital transfer tax. When used for income tax purposes it requires all taxpayers to complete a return annually (unlike most British taxpayers at present). It is common for too much tax to be withheld during the tax year, thus providing an incentive for taxpayers to complete their returns promptly and accurately in order to speed up their rebates. Self-assessment tends to reduce administrative costs but may increase compliance costs. It would make unnecessary the long basic rate band of the present British income tax system and could lead to greater understanding by the taxpayer of how the system works.

self-balancing ledgers. Ledgers that contain an equal amount of debits and credits. This should always be true of the GENERAL LEDGER and is also true of those SUBSIDIARY LEDGERS that contain general ledger control accounts.

semivariable cost. A cost that has both fixed and variable elements. Some services, for example, are paid for by a minimum charge plus a variable cost based on use.

sensitivity analysis. Varying the data in a calculation so as to ascertain which variables have a material effect on the results. For example, several cash budgets may be constructed to determine whether or not the results are materially changed by differences in, say, sales forecasts or in the assumed collection period for debtors. Sensitivity analysis is also used in CAPITAL INVESTMENT APPRAISAL. A best estimate is made of the expected cash receipts and payments and the sensitivity of the NPV, IRR or other criteria of investment worth to possible errors of estimation is checked. Sensitivity analysis has been made easier by the increased use of computers.

separable costs. Costs incurred beyond the SPLIT-OFF POINT for JOINT PRODUCTS. They are not part of the joint production process and can be identified with individual products.

sequestration. A legal process by virtue of which an officer of the court is empowered to hold goods or property belonging to a person or body pending the settlement of a dispute or payment of a debt. In Scotland, sequestration is a procedure involving the realization of assets under the supervision of the court and is instituted by a petition made to the court either by the debtor or by one or more creditors.

settlement day. In the UK, a synonym for ACCOUNT DAY.

Seventh Directive. A DIRECTIVE on company law approved by the EEC in 1983 but not yet implemented in any member state. The directive represents a compromise between different national rules, practices and attitudes. It changes the law relating to CONSOLIDATED FINANCIAL STATEMENTS (including techniques of preparation as well as publication) in all member states but will lead to relatively few changes in the UK.

shadow price. The OPPORTUNITY COST of a scarce resource, i.e., a shadow price is a measure of the CONTRIBUTION foregone by failing to have one more unit of scarce capacity in a particular situation. Resources in excess supply have a shadow price of zero. Shadow prices usually form part of the information provided by optimal solutions to LINEAR PROGRAMMING problems. They are valid only over certain ranges.

share. In the UK, an expression of a proprietary relationship in a company. Shareholders are proportionate owners of a company but the company's net assets belong not to them but to the company as a separate and independent legal entity. The most common types of shares are ORDINARY SHARES and PREFERENCE SHARES.

share capital. Part of the OWNERS' EQUITY section of a UK balance sheet. It does not include the share premium and other CAPITAL RESERVES. *See also* AUTHORIZED SHARE CAPITAL, ISSUED SHARE CAPITAL, CALLED-UP SHARE CAPITAL, PAID-UP SHARE CAPITAL, SHARE.

share certificate. A certificate giving documentary evidence of title to a share.

shareholder surveys. EMPIRICAL RESEARCH into the use made of company ANNUAL

REPORTS by shareholders. A listing and analysis of shareholder surveys carried out in the UK, USA, Australia and New Zealand is given in R.D. Hines, 'The Usefulness of Annual Reports: the Anomaly between the Efficient Markets Hypothesis and Shareholder Surveys', *Accounting and Business Research*, Autumn 1982. In general, the surveys show that annual reports are regarded as important sources of information although the financial statements they contain are not well understood, especially by private as distinct from institutional shareholders. The CHAIRMAN'S STATEMENT (REVIEW) is the most popular section, perhaps because it is in narrative form and often deals with future prospects.

share ledger. A book or other record showing in debit and credit form changes in the shareholding of each member (shareholder) of a company listed by shares. It is usually combined with the REGISTER OF MEMBERS.

share option. *See* OPTION.

share premium account. In the UK, an account to which is credited the premium on shares issued at a premium. A share premium is treated almost but not quite as if it were share capital. It may only be used for the issue of BONUS SHARES; in writing off PRELIMINARY EXPENSES; in writing off UNDERWRITING COMMISSIONS; or in providing a premium payable on the redemption of debentures. *See also* MERGER ACCOUNTING.

SIFT. In the UK, the acronym of Special Increment for Teaching. It is an increment to the funding allocation regional health authorities receive on RAWP target criteria.

simple discount. The deduction from the maturity value (S) of an obligation that is sold or settled for an amount P before its maturity date. The amount of the simple discount is $S - P$, where

$$S = P(1 + ni) \text{ and } P = S(1 - nd),$$

n being the number of periods, i the simple interest rate and d the simple discount rate $(d = Pi/S)$.

simple interest. Interest calculated on the original sum (principal) invested and not also on interest reinvested. It can be calculated from the formula $I = Pni$, where I = the amount of simple interest, P = the principal, n = the number of periods, and i = the simple rate of interest per period. Simple interest is normally only used when the interval of time involved is short. *See also* SIMPLE DISCOUNT, COMPOUND INTEREST.

simplex method. A general technique for solving LINEAR PROGRAMMING problems by an iterative process. The method tests feasible solutions to see whether they can be improved and continues until an optimum solution is found. For all but very simple problems a computer is necessary in order to use this method.

simplified financial statements. Financial statements with a reduced information content prepared so that those unskilled in accounting (e.g., NAIVE INVESTORS) may more readily understand a company's financial position and performance. Surveys of lay shareholders show that much of what is published in full company annual reports is neither read nor understood. Surveys of sophisticated shareholders and the semi-strong form of the EFFICIENT MARKET HYPOTHESIS, however, suggest that accounting information is well understood by SOPHISTICATED INVESTORS in listed companies and by analysts and advisers. It has been suggested that two reports be prepared for shareholders in listed companies: a market report for the experts and a stewardship report for the non-expert.

The failure of the non-expert to understand arises because he or she understands neither accounting terminology (the semantic problem) nor accounting conventions of income and wealth measurement (the syntactic problem).

It has been suggested, although empirical research backing is lacking, that simplified statements might best take the form of a narrative explanatory statement followed by summaries of the balance sheet and profit and loss account. Some EMPLOYEE REPORTS are of this nature, except that a VALUE ADDED STATEMENT rather than a profit and loss account is provided. It has alternatively been suggested that CASH FLOW ACCOUNTING would be more comprehensible to lay investors.

Two problems that arise in the preparation of simplified statements are how to ensure that companies are not misleadingly selective in the choice of information presented and how to prevent additional information being given that is not in the full report. To avoid these problems the minimum contents of simplified statements could be laid down by statute or standard and these contents could be a sub-set of the full report.

In neither the UK nor the USA has much progress been made in the production of simplified financial statements, although a research study has been published by the ICAEW (1979). This concluded, *inter alia*, that it was not possible for an auditor to express an opinion on the truth and fairness of such statements. The auditor could, however, be asked to confirm that the data in the simplified statements were drawn from the full report.

simulation. The representation of one system by another especially with the use of a computer. Simulation can be used, for example, in CAPITAL INVESTMENT APPRAISAL and in QUEUEING THEORY. *See also* MONTE CARLO METHOD.

single entry bookkeeping. A system of bookkeeping which records one aspect only of each transaction. For example, accounts may be kept recording transactions affecting PERSONAL ACCOUNTS but not REAL ACCOUNTS or NOMINAL ACCOUNTS. In practice

cash transactions are also likely to be recorded in such a system, i.e., there will be a CASH BOOK as well as a PERSONAL LEDGER. These strictly constitute INCOMPLETE RECORDS rather than single entry accounting.

sinking fund. A fund established to accumulate the amount of money required to pay off a debt at a set date in the future. The constant amount to be invested periodically can be shown to be equal to

$$\frac{D}{Sn\rceil i}$$

where D is the amount to be repaid and

$$Sn\rceil i = \frac{(1+i)^n - 1}{i},$$

where i is the rate of interest to be earned and n the number of periods. *See also* ANNUITY.

sinking fund method. *See* DEPRECIATION METHODS.

skewness. A measure of the lack of symmetry of a statistical distribution. Distributions skewed to the right are positively skewed; distributions skewed to the left are negatively skewed.

small and medium companies. In the UK, companies with the privilege of filing modified accounts with the Registrar of Companies. A company qualifies as small or medium if, for the financial year in question and the immediately preceding financial year, it is, on its own (i.e., excluding any other members of a group), within the limits of at least two of the following criteria below. Where a company is a HOLDING COMPANY required to prepare GROUP ACCOUNTS it is entitled to prepare modified individual accounts only if the group (the

	Small	Medium
Balance sheet total (i.e., total assets)	£700,000	£2,800,000
Turnover	£1,400,000	£5,750,000
Average number of employees	50	250

Small and medium companies

	Small	*Medium*
Balance sheet	Main headings and	No modifications
	amounts only	
Profit and loss account	Not required	May commence with
		gross profit or loss
Notes to the accounts	Only limited information	Analyses of turnover and
	required	profit not required
Directors' report	Not required	No modifications

company plus its subsidiaries) taken as a whole is small or medium on the above criteria.

The moderifications allowed are as above.

The modifications do not apply to the financial statements sent to shareholders. The modified accounts must be accompanied by a special AUDIT REPORT.

small companies relief. In the UK, a reduced rate of corporation tax designed for small companies but, to avoid problems of definition, applied to companies with small taxable incomes. There is a tapering relief between the lower rate and the full rate. In 1980-81 an estimated 95% of all UK companies either took advantage of small companies relief or paid no tax at all.

social accounting. A synonym for either SOCIAL RESPONSIBILITY REPORTING or for NATIONAL ACCOUNTING.

social audit. An examination of the extent to which the operations of an organization, public or private, have contributed to social goals. Social audits can be seen as a means of giving some control to groups such as employees, consumers and the local community. They are concerned more with EFFECTIVENESS than with EFFICIENCY. Such audits are difficult to perform, compared with statutory audits, for a number of reasons: the persons being reported to are likely to have multiple objectives; there is no generally accepted measure of social performance; and the necessary audit techniques are not well developed.

Social audits may be government-sponsored, voluntary or done without the approval of the organization being audited. In the UK, for example, compliance with the Health and Safety at Work Act 1974,

which requires, *inter alia*, that employees provide information about their health and safety records and policies, is monitored by the Factory Inspectorate; in the USA, the Environmental Protection Agency monitors the efforts of organizations to comply with anti-pollution legislation. Voluntary social audits have been carried out by a number of organizations in North America, possibly in order to forestall regulation and to improve the public image of corporate business.

Social audits carried out without the consent of the organization being audited include those carried out by the Project on Corporate Responsibility on General Motors in the USA and by the Public Interest Research Centre on Tube Investments in the UK.

social balance sheet (bilan social). *See* EMPLOYMENT REPORT.

social benefits. Benefits, not recorded in the accounts of business enterprises, which arise from the existence of EXTERNALITIES.

social costs. Costs, not recorded in the accounts of business enterprises, which arise from the existence of EXTERNALITIES.

social responsibility reporting. Reporting the costs and benefits relating to socially responsible actions by business enterprises. This may be done in a number of ways, e.g., publication in the annual report of a list of socially responsible actions (a popular method in the USA); publication of a list together with disclosure of the cost to the enterprise of each activity; publication of a list together with disclosure of the extent to which the objectives of the actions have been achieved; publication of a list together with the costs and benefits of each activity. The costs disclosed will be those of the enterprise and are not difficult to measure, although allocations may be necessary. The benefits disclosed will be SOCIAL BENEFITS (or reductions in SOCIAL COSTS) and their definition and quantification may be extremely difficult.

There is no consensus as to what constitute socially responsible actions but they probably include at least the following: control of pollution, energy conservation, health and safety measures, employment of disadvantaged persons, product safety, community involvement, and donations to educational institutions and charities. Some at least of these actions are likely to benefit the enterprise itself, if only in terms of good publicity or the avoidance of legislation. Definitions of corporate responsibility are not static over time or from country to country.

See also EMPLOYMENT REPORT, VALUE ADDED STATEMENTS.

Societas Europea (SE). The name given (in Latin) to the proposed European company, as distinct from companies formed under the national laws of the EEC member states.

Société Anonyme (SA). The approximate French equivalent of the British public company. Not all SAs are listed on a stock exchange.

Société à Responsabilité Limitée (SARL). The approximate French equivalent of the British private company.

sold ledger. Synonym for DEBTORS LEDGER.

sole trader's accounts. The accounts and financial statements of an unincorporated enterprise owned by a single person. The proprietorship section of the balance sheet contains a CAPITAL ACCOUNT and, usually, a CURRENT ACCOUNT, the former recording the owner's fixed stake in the enterprise and the latter his or her fluctuating stake (net profit less drawings). The profits of a sole trader are taxed as part of his or her personal income and for this reason income tax is not recorded in the enterprise's accounts. In practice the distinction between the owner and the business may not be clearly made and, in particular, the expenses in the profit and loss account are likely to be influenced by taxation considerations. A PROFIT AND LOSS APPROPRIATION ACCOUNT is not usually regarded as necessary in a sole trader's accounts.

solvency. The ability of a debtor (whether an individual or a corporate body) to pay debts as they fall due. *See also* INSOLVENCY, TECHNICAL INSOLVENCY.

sophisticated investor. An investor with a good knowledge and understanding of the accounting practices and theories relevant to published financial statements or with access to the advice of a person with such knowledge and understanding. Most INSTITUTIONAL INVESTORS are likely to be sophisticated investors whereas private shareholders are more likely to be NAIVE INVESTORS.

source and application of funds. *See* FUNDS STATEMENTS.

special legacy. *See* LEGACY.

specific prices. The prices, observable in a market, of specific goods and services (commodities). A change in a specific price can be divided into two components: that part which is due to a change in the GENERAL PRICE LEVEL; and that part which is due to a change in the price of specific commodities relative to other commodities. The latter can be regarded as the 'real' increase in the price of the specific commodity. In the UK the government provides specific price indexes periodically in its publication *Price Index Numbers for Current Cost Accounting*.

specific risk. Synonym for NON-SYSTEMATIC RISK.

split-off point. That stage of production where JOINT PRODUCTS become individually identifiable.

split-rate system. A system of taxation in which a lower rate of tax is charged on distributed income than on undistributed income.

spoilage. Goods that are not up to standard and are sold for disposal value. The objectives of accounting for spoilage are to measure its magnitude and to draw it to the attention of management, distinguishing between NORMAL SPOILAGE and ABNORMAL SPOILAGE.

spread sheet. A two-dimensional table or matrix in which the rows may represent accounting items such as revenues and costs and the columns time periods. It is used extensively in FINANCIAL MODELLING and may be regarded as an electronic WORKSHEET.

stabilized accounting. The stabilization of financial statements drawn up in nominal monetary units by the substitution as the unit of account of gold (as in the German hyperinflation of the 1920s) or a measure of general purchasing power. *See also* CURRENT PURCHASING POWER (CPP) ACCOUNTING.

staff manager. A manager (for example, a chief accountant or a financial controller) whose primary task is the provision of advice and services to LINE MANAGERS.

stag. An investor who makes an application for a new security in the hope that on ALLOTMENT it can be sold at a premium over the issue price.

stakeholders. Individual interests associated with an accounting entity and in some degree dependent upon its financial performance. Stakeholders may include shareholders and other proprietors, employees, suppliers, customers, lenders, managers and even central and local government and local communities. All stakeholders are likely to be users of accounting reports but not all users (as listed, for example, in THE CORPORATE REPORT) are necessarily stakeholders.

standard costing. A system of costing using STANDARD COSTS. The major purpose of a standard costing system is improved control over operations but it may also be used to save record-keeping costs. Standard costing can be used in conjunction with JOB COSTING, PROCESS COSTING or OPERATION COSTING and with either ABSORPTION COSTING or VARIABLE COSTING. An essential element of standard costing is the analysis of VARIANCES, on which *see* EFFICIENCY VARIANCES, JOINT VARIANCE, LABOUR VARIANCES, MATERIALS VARIANCES, MIX VARIANCES, OVERHEAD VARIANCES, PRICE VARIANCES, VOLUME VARIANCE.

standard costs. Predetermined measures of what costs should be under specified conditions. Ideal standard costs are the absolute minimum costs possible under the best conceivable operating conditions. Currently attainable standard costs are the costs that should be attained under very efficient operating conditions, allowance being made for normal spoilage, ordinary machine breakdowns and lost time. They are more widely used than ideal standards because they can be used simultaneously for product costing, budgeting and motivation.

standard deviation. The most usual measure of DISPERSION. It represents the square root of the VARIANCE of a group of numbers, i.e., the square root of the sum of the squared differences between a group of numbers and their ARITHMETIC MEAN. It is denoted by a lower case Greek sigma (s). It takes account of not only the spread between the lowest and highest numbers but also the intermediate values.

standardization. The result of a process of STANDARD SETTING. The distinction between standardization and HARMONIZATION is not very clear. Both aim to increase the compatability of accounting practices by setting bounds to their degree of variation but harmonization is used only in an international context, although, in a confusion of terminology, international harmonization can lead to INTERNATIONAL ACCOUNTING STANDARDS.

standardized measure of discounted future net cash flows (SMDCF). In the

USA, a measure of the present value of proved reserves in OIL AND GAS ACCOUNTING. Disclosure of SMDCF and its method of calculation are laid down in FAS 69.

standard setting. Setting the rules to be followed in the preparation of corporate financial statements. There is no generally agreed model of the standard-setting process. One approach (positive rather than normative) is to regard it as a mechanism for resolving the conflicts of interest among the various preparers and users of accounts, the standard setting body (e.g., the ACCOUNTING STANDARDS COMMITTEE in the UK, the FINANCIAL ACCOUNTING STANDARDS BOARD in the USA) acting as an arbitrator. An alternative normative model is that standard setting should serve the public interest and be based on an explicit CONCEPTUAL FRAMEWORK developed from A PRIORI THEORIES OF ACCOUNTING. Supporters of this approach consider it important to avoid the POLITICIZATION OF ACCOUNTING. Those preferring the other approach regard politicization as inevitable. There is no general agreement as to what should be the membership, functions and powers of standard-setting bodies.

See also ACCOUNTING STANDARDS, REGULATION OF CORPORATE FINANCIAL REPORTING.

standard stream concepts of income. Concepts of income based on the maintenance intact of a stream of future receipts (e.g., dividends to shareholders) in real or money terms. Such concepts are thus based on CONSUMPTION MAINTENANCE rather than CAPITAL MAINTENANCE. *See* HICKSIAN INCOME CONCEPTS.

statement of affairs. In the UK, a statement as to the affairs of a company required in windings up and in receiverships. In effect, it is a break-up balance sheet with assets valued at estimated realizable amounts and full particulars of all creditors and their securities if any. The form of the statement is prescribed.

statement of basic accounting theory. *See* ASOBAT.

statement of changes in financial position. *See* FUNDS STATEMENTS.

statement of source and application of funds. *See* FUNDS STATEMENTS.

statement on accounting theory and theory acceptance. *See* SATTA.

Statements of Auditing Standards. Statements on external audit issued by the American Institute of Certified Public Accountants. They comprise ten generally accepted auditing standards and additional pronouncements and interpretations.

Statements of Financial Accounting Concepts (SFACs). Statements issued by the Financial Accounting Standards Board as part of its CONCEPTUAL FRAMEWORK project. They do not form part of US GENERALLY ACCEPTED ACCOUNTING PRINCIPLES. SFAC 1 is concerned with the objectives of financial reporting by business enterprises; SFAC 2 with the QUALITATIVE CHARACTERISTICS OF ACCOUNTING INFORMATION; SFAC 3 with definitions of ten elements of financial statements; and SFAC 4 with the objectives of financial reporting by non-business organizations.

Statements of Recommended Practice (SORPs). Non-mandatory statements issued by the UK Accounting Standards Committee. A company need not disclose that it has not followed a SORP, or give reasons or state its effect.

Statements of Standard Accounting Practice (SSAPs). Accounting standards prepared in the UK and Ireland by the ACCOUNTING STANDARDS COMMITTEE and issued by the six members of the Consultative Committee of Accountancy Bodies and applicable to all accounts intended to give a true and fair view. The first SSAP was issued in 1971. Each SSAP is preceded by one or more exposure drafts (EDs). Some but not all SSAPs apply to UK local authority accounts. As at 30 June 1984, 20 SSAPs had been issued, of which two were no longer operative. Interpretations of standards are not issued.

The SSAPs issued up to 30 June 1984 were as follows:

1. Accounting for the Results of Associated Companies.
2. Disclosure of Accounting Policies.
3. Earnings per Share.
4. The Accounting Treatment of Government Grants.
5. Accounting for Value Added Tax.
6. Extraordinary Items and Prior Year Adjustments.
7. Acccounting for Changes in the Purchasing Power of Money (provisional only, replaced by SSAP 16).
8. The Treatment of Taxation under the Imputation System.
9. Stocks and Work in Progress.
10. Statements of Source and Application of Funds.
11. Accounting for Deferred Taxation (replaced by SSAP 15).
12. Accounting for Depreciation.
13. Accounting for Research and Development.
14. Group Accounts.
15. Accounting for Deferred Taxation.
16. Current Cost Accounting.
17. Accounting for Post Balance Sheet Events.
18. Accounting for Contingencies.
19. Accounting for Investment Properties.
20. Foreign Currency Translation.

Two SSAPs on Accounting for Leases and Hire Purchase Contracts and Accounting for Goodwill were on the point of issue.

Statements on Auditing. Statements issued from 1961 onwards for the guidance of members of the Institute of Chartered Accountants in England and Wales. The statements tended to reflect the current practice of leading auditing firms. Statements are withdrawn when superseded by definitive AUDITING STANDARDS issued since 1980 by the AUDITING PRACTICES COMMITTEE of the CONSULTATIVE COMMITTEE OF ACCOUNTANCY BODIES.

Statements on Internal Auditing Standards (SIAs). Statements issued from 1983 onwards by the Internal Responsibilities

Committee of the US-based Institute of Internal Auditors.

states (of nature). The set of mutually exclusive and collectively exhaustive possible occurrences of an uncertain future. *See* INFORMATION ECONOMICS APPROACH TO ACCOUNTING.

static budget. A BUDGET based on a single planned volume level. See FLEXIBLE BUDGET.

stationary state. A state of nature in which all prices are constant through time and are expected to remain so, and in which each asset has a single price (i.e., replacement cost, net realizable and net present value are all equal to each other). In a stationary state, HISTORICAL COST ACCOUNTING (HCA) would not give results different from any form of INFLATION ACCOUNTING.

statutory audit. An AUDIT required by statute of the financial statements of limited companies and other organizations. It has developed as an expert and objective examination of management-prepared statements by an independent and impartial third party who expresses an opinion on the statements so as to enhance their credibility in the eyes of investors and other interested parties. In the UK the auditor of a company reports in writing on the truth and fairness of financial statements; in the USA on their fairness and accordance with generally accepted accounting principles.

There was no general legal requirement for a statutory audit in the UK until 1900. Under the Companies Acts 1948-1981 an audit is required of all companies, both public and private, except that the shareholders of a DORMANT COMPANY may choose not to appoint an auditor. The auditor must be a chartered or a certified accountant. There are no general legal requirements for the audit of partnerships and sole traders.

statutory books. In the UK, books required by the Companies Acts to be kept outside the accounting system. They include the REGISTER OF MEMBERS, the REGISTER OF CHARGES, minute books, the register of directors and secretaries, the register of directors' interests and (in the case of public companies) the register of interests in shares.

step-function cost. A cost which is constant over various small ranges of output, but which increases in step fashion from one range to the next. If the steps are sufficiently small, linear approximations may be used. If the steps are wide enough, one step may represent the RELEVANT RANGE, so that the cost may be assumed to be fixed.

stock appreciation. That part of the increase in the monetary value of stock-in-trade (inventories) which is due to changes in prices rather than changes in physical quantities. It is eliminated on an aggregate basis in NATIONAL INCOME AND EXPENDITURE ACCOUNTS and by individual companies that publish current cost (CCA) information. *See also* STOCK APPRECIATION RELIEF and COST OF SALES ADJUSTMENT (COSA).

stock appreciation relief. In the UK, a tax relief that aimed to alleviate the taxation of unrealized gains on stocks (inventories) during periods of rising prices. Introduced in 1973 and abolished in 1984, the rules relating to the relief (including carry forwards of unused relief and claw-backs) changed frequently. The Finance Act 1981 introduced a system whereby an 'all stocks index', published by the government, applied to a company's opening stock. The relief may be regarded as having been, along with generous CAPITAL ALLOWANCES, a way of indirectly, and rather crudely, taxing current cost income rather than historical cost income.

stock control. *See* INVENTORY CONTROL.

stock dividend. *See* BONUS ISSUE.

stocks. In the terminology of SSAP 9 in the UK, a general term comprising goods or other assets purchased for resale; consumable stores; raw materials and components purchased for incorporation into products for sale; products and services in

intermediate stages of completion; and finished goods. The balance sheet format on UK company law suggests an analysis of stocks into raw materials and consumables; work in progress; finished goods and goods for resale; and payments on account. SSAP 9 requires that the ACCOUNTING POLICIES relating to stocks and works in progress be disclosed.

See also INVENTORIES, INVENTORY ACCOUNTING, INVENTORY VALUATION, LONG-TERM CONTRACT WORK IN PROGRESS.

stock split. US term for SUBDIVISION OF SHARES.

stock turnover. The ratio of cost of sales or sales to stock-in-trade (inventory) i.e., sales/stocks or (cost of sales)/stocks. It measures the number of times a business's stock turns over during a year. It is likely to differ substantially from one industry to another. Since stocks are usually valued at an entry price, cost of sales is preferable as the numerator but it may not be available to an external analyst.

stores card. *See* BIN CARD.

stores ledger control account. An account recording in total materials purchased and issued to production and the balance which should be on hand at any given moment. On the issue of direct materials, the WORK IN PROGRESS CONTROL ACCOUNT is debited; on the issue of indirect materials, the factory overhead absorbed account is debited.

stores requisition. *See* MATERIALS REQUISITION.

straight-line depreciation. *See* DEPRECIATION METHODS.

strategic planning. That part of LONG RANGE PLANNING that concerns deciding upon the objectives of an enterprise (e.g., the kinds of business to be in, the goods and services to be sold, the markets to be served, the share of a market to be aimed at, required rates of sales and profit growth, desired size of the company) and how to achieve them. It usually involves also a forecast of the enterprise's environment, an analysis of the enterprise's strengths and weaknesses, an appraisal of the company both internally and externally, formulation of a strategy, and a development plan relating to acquisition, mergers, diversification and divestment.

stratified sampling. In an audit context, a method of sampling in which the population is divided into strata, each stratum being subject to a separate test. It is appropriate to an audit where parts of the total population are subject to different degrees of risk (e.g., domestic debtor balances vs. foreign debtor balances) or the population is significantly skewed (e.g., a small number of high value debtors' balances and a large number of low value debtors' balances).

subdivision of shares. The division of shares of one nominal value into a larger number of shares of a smaller nominal value, e.g., the division of a £1 share into four 25p shares.

subjective goodwill. The excess of the NET PRESENT VALUE of the prospective cash receipts of an enterprise over the current value of its net tangible assets.

subjective probabilities. Probabilities based on individual assessment rather than on experience or mathematical calculation.

'subject to' opinion. *See* AUDIT OPINION.

subsidiary. In the UK, a company controlled by a HOLDING COMPANY. A company is a subsidiary of another company if that other company is a member of it and controls the composition of its board of directors, *or* if the other company holds more than half the nominal value of its EQUITY SHARE CAPITAL.

subsidiary ledger. A ledger in which a special class of ACCOUNTS (e.g., debtors) is kept so as not to overburden the GENERAL LEDGER and to allow separate usage. What is recorded in detail in the subsidiary ledger

is recorded in a CONTROL ACCOUNT (e.g., a debtors ledger control account) in the general ledger; the balance on the control account should agree with the total of the schedule of balances from the subsidiary ledger. If it is desired to make the subsidiary ledger self-balancing, this can be achieved by the use in the subsidiary ledger of a general ledger control account which is a mirror image of the subsidiary ledger control account in the general ledger.

substance over form. An accounting concept whereby transactions or other events are accounted for and presented in accordance with their economic reality rather than their legal form. It is included, along with PRUDENCE and MATERIALITY, in International Accounting Standard No. 1 as a consideration that should govern the selection and application by management of appropriate ACCOUNTING POLICIES. The case for the capitalization of leases (*see* LEASE ACCOUNTING) rests mainly on the substance over form concept.

In the USA, substance over form is the right of the Internal Revenue Service to look through the form of a transaction to its substance. In the UK, the Ramsay (1981) and Furniss v. Dawson (1984) decisions suggest that the courts in the UK are increasingly drawing a distinction between the substance and the form of transactions when contemplating their tax consequences.

substantive tests. Auditing tests the purpose of which is to obtain evidence as to the completeness, accuracy and validity of information in accounting records or in financial statements. They are contrasted with COMPLIANCE TESTS. Substantive tests include procedures such as VOUCHING, VERIFICATION, DEPTH TESTING and ANALYTICAL REVIEW.

successful efforts method. *See* OIL AND GAS ACCOUNTING.

Sudreau report. French report on company law amendment (1975). Its most notable recommendation concerned the publication of a social balance sheet (*bilan social*). *See* EMPLOYMENT REPORT.

sum of the years digits method. *See* DEPRECIATION METHODS.

sunk costs. Costs incurred in the past and unaffected by any future action and thus irrelevant to decision making. The English economist Jevons expressed this irrelevance as follows: 'In commerce, bygones are for ever bygones; and we are always starting clear at each moment, judging the values of things with a view to future utility' (*The Theory of Political Economy*, 1871, p. 159).

supplementary financial statements. Statements presented as additional to primary financial statements and explicitly or implicitly of less importance. British companies may, for example, publish historical cost statements supplemented by, e.g., current cost statements. The EFFICIENT MARKET HYPOTHESIS suggests that all publicly available information is rapidly impounded into share prices but surveys of financial analysts suggest that they pay less attention to information presented as supplementary. Supplementary statements are to be distinguished from MULTI-COLUMN REPORTING.

supply estimate. In the UK, a statement presented to the House of Commons of the estimated expenditure of a central government department during a financial year (1 April to 31 March) asking for the necessary funds to be voted. An individual supply estimate is known as a Vote. Expenditure within a Vote that is separately identified in an Appropriation Account is known as a subhead.

synergy. A relationship in which the whole is greater than the sum of the parts ('2 + 2 = 5'). Synergy is often hoped for in BUSINESS COMBINATIONS but by no means always achieved.

system. A group of related elements organized for a purpose.

systematic (market) risk. The non-diversifiable component of the risk of a security, i.e. that part of the risk of its returns which cannot be eliminated by including it in a diversified portfolio. It is also known as market risk. Systematic risk is quantified as the BETA of a security.

systematic random sampling. In an audit context, a method of drawing a sample in which the first item is chosen at random and then every k^{th} item thereafter is chosen, where k is the number of items in the population divided by the required sample size, until the full sample has been drawn. *See* RANDOM SAMPLING.

systems-based audit. An audit in which the nature and depth of audit tests depends upon the auditor's evaluation of the internal control system and in which that evaluation forms a major part of the audit.

T

Table A. In the UK, a model set of AR-TICLES OF ASSOCIATION which can be adopted by a company in full or modified form.

T account. An ACCOUNT with a left-hand side recording DEBIT ENTRIES and a right-hand side recording CREDIT ENTRIES.

take-over. The acquisition by one company of sufficient shares in another company to give the purchaser control of that other company.

take-over bid. An offer by one company to acquire all, or a controlling holding, of the voting shares of another company. In the UK, take-over bids are regulated by company law, investor protection law, stock exchange regulations and the CITY CODE ON TAKE-OVERS AND MERGERS.

tally. An accounting device used by the English Exchequer until the early 19th century. The tally was a stick of wood in which transactions were represented by notches, the tally being split in order to give both parties evidence of the transaction. Most English tallies were deliberately destroyed in 1834 in a conflagration which also burnt down the Houses of Parliament. Some of the tallies that survived may be seen in the Museum of the Public Record Office in London.

tangible assets. Assets other than INTANGI-BLE ASSETS or INVESTMENTS. In the UK, the BALANCE SHEET FORMATS require the separate disclosure of fixed tangible assets.

taxable income. For an individual in the UK, EARNED INCOME plus INVESTMENT INCOME less expenses and allowances; for a company, income as adjusted for items not allowed for tax purposes, for revenues not taxed and for deductions (e.g. CAPITAL ALLOW-ANCES) not in the company's accounts.

tax allowances. Deductions from total income making part of that income tax-free regardless of the taxpayer's pattern of expenditure or source of income. The part remaining is the taxable income. Allowances granted vary over time but in the UK are or have been given in respect of marriage, children, age, blindness, dependent relatives, housekeepers, son's or daughter's services, etc.

tax avoidance and evasion. Respectively, manipulation within the law to reduce liability for tax and manipulation outside the law to reduce liability. The main causes of avoidance and evasion (the borderline between which is sometimes difficult to draw exactly) are high taxes, imprecise laws, insufficient penalties and lack of equity in the tax system.

tax base. The base on which a tax is levied, e.g., a stock of wealth, a flow of income, an expenditure.

tax code. (1) A means of summarizing the amount of allowances and deductions due to a taxpayer, so as to determine his taxable income. (2) The whole body of tax law, especially in countries where the law is codified rather than existing in statutes and decided cases.

tax credit. (1) Under the UK IMPUTATION SYSTEM of corporation tax, credits, linked to the basic rate of income tax, that accompany the payment of a dividend by a company to its shareholders. The latter are taxed on the dividend grossed up at the basic rate but can set the credits against their liability to income tax. A company receiving dividends (known as FRANKED INVESTMENT INCOME) from other UK resident companies cannot itself benefit from tax credits but can pass on the credit to its shareholders. Similar tax credits exist in other countries which have adopted the imputation system. (2) A synonym for NEGATIVE INCOME TAX.

taxes. Compulsory levies made by public authorities for which nothing is received directly in return. They are used in part to

169

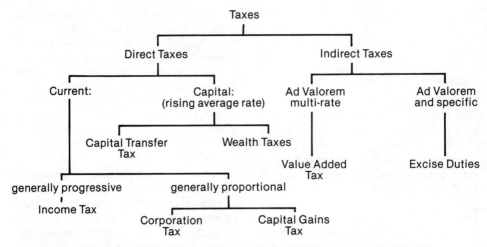

Source: S. James & C. Nobes, *The Economics of Taxation* (Deddington: Philip Allan, 2nd ed. 1983), p.18.

Taxes provide PUBLIC GOODS. Taxes may be classified in a number of ways, for example as in the diagram above.

tax expenditure. A fiscal advantage conferred by the reduction of a tax liability rather than by direct cash subsidy. A UK example is the tax deductibility of mortgage interest payments.

tax haven. A place which offers a combination of low taxes, stability and encouragement of free enterprise.

tax return. A statement to the fiscal authorities of a taxpayer's sources and totals of income and expenses during a given period.

technical analysis. Synonym for CHARTISM.

technical insolvency. An inability to meet debts as they fall due even though total assets exceed total liabilities.

teeming and lading. The misappropriation of cash remittances received from customers by using amounts from later remittances to fill the gap left by the earlier misappropriation. It can be avoided by not allowing a cashier both to handle remittances received and to make entries in the accounts of individual customers. The US term for this practice is lapping.

temporal method. *See* FOREIGN CURRENCY TRANSLATION.

temporal principle. *See* FOREIGN CURRENCY TRANSLATION.

10-K. *See* FORM 10-K.

10-Q. *See* FORM 10-Q.

terminal value. The amount to which an initial principal P invested at the beginning of period 1 at a compound interest rate of i per period will accumulate to after n periods, i.e. $P(1+i)^n$. This value can become very large indeed. For example, it has been pointed out that if the Red Indian who sold Manhattan for $24 in 1626 had invested it at 6% p.a. compounded semiannually it would have accumulated to $9,500 million by 1959.

terotechnology. The management of fixed tangible assets throughout their life cycle.

testator (testatrix). A person who, before his or her death, has made and left a valid will.

test deck. In an audit context, a set of simulated transactions that the auditor can put through a computer system in order to see whether they are processed accurately.

theory of games. *See* GAME THEORY.

time card. A document recording the time spent by an employee on particular jobs or processes, used both as a means of charging direct labour to jobs and of fixing responsibility for performance.

time series. A series of observations of the values of a variable at different points in time.

times interest earned. The number of times that a company's interest charges are covered by its earnings before interest and tax (EBIT).

time value of money. An expression of the fact that, if the rate of interest is positive, money in hand now is worth more than money to be received at a date in future. To calculate the time value of money it is necessary to use COMPOUND INTEREST techniques.

timing differences. Differences, capable of being reversed in future periods, between profits as computed for taxation purposes and profits as stated in financial statements. They result from the inclusion of items of income and expenditure in taxation computations in periods different from those in which they are included in financial statements. They may be contrasted with PERMANENT DIFFERENCES. The vagaries of tax legislation may sometimes make it difficult to distinguish a timing difference from a permanent difference or may change one into the other.

Timing differences arise in principle under the following four circumstances: tax deduction now, expense later; revenue now, taxable income later; taxable income now, revenue later; and expense now, tax deduction later. In the UK, timing differences arise as a result of the use for some items of CASH ACCOUNTING for tax purposes and ACCRUAL ACCOUNTING in financial statements. These normally reverse in the next accounting period. They also arise from CAPITAL ALLOWANCES that differ from the depreciation charges in financial statements; revaluation surpluses on fixed assets for which a taxation charge does not arise until the gain is realized on disposal; and surpluses on disposals of fixed assets which are subject to ROLLOVER RELIEF.

top-slicing. In public sector accounting, the deduction from any funding allocation, as a first charge, of funds needed by the funding body for its own operations, or for any reserves or priority schemes it supports, prior to the distribution of all remaining funds to lower tiers by criteria it may determine.

trade credit. Short-term sources of funds resulting from credit granted by the suppliers of goods or services purchased.

trade creditors. In the UK, CREDITORS arising out of trading transactions. The US term is trade accounts payable.

trade debtors. In the UK, DEBTORS arising out of trading transactions. The US term is trade accounts receivable.

trade discount. In the UK, a discount off the list price of a good. Trade discounts are not usually recorded in the accounts. *See also* CASH DISCOUNT.

trade mark. A distinctive identification, protected by law, of a manufactured product or service. Trade marks are INTANGIBLE ASSETS and in the UK company law permits their capitalization and subsequent amortization if they are acquired for valuable consideration or are created by the company itself. In the USA, the costs of trade marks may either be written off as incurred (the normal practice) or capitalized and then amortized.

trading account. An account showing an enterprise's sales, cost of sales and gross profit. In published accounts and financial statements it is often treated as a sub-section of the PROFIT AND LOSS ACCOUNT.

trading on the equity. Using fixed interest sources of capital to boost the rate of return on the EQUITY. The expression is American rather than British.

transaction. In an accounting context, an EVENT giving rise to a change affecting the operations or financial status of an accounting entity. Transactions may be external (e.g., the purchase of a machine on credit from a supplier) or internal (e.g., the subsequent depreciation of the machinery). All transactions can be expressed in terms of DEBIT ENTRIES and CREDIT ENTRIES, as can also events such as changes in general and specific prices, although these are not usually regarded as transactions.

transfer payment (income). In the context of NATIONAL ACCOUNTING, a payment (receipt) which does not form part of any exchange of goods or services (e.g., grants by local authorities to university students).

transfer prices. Prices charged for goods or services transferred by one PROFIT CENTRE (which may be a division or a subsidiary) of an enterprise or group of enterprises to another profit centre. Setting transfer prices poses many problems, especially when the price has to cross national boundaries. It is generally agreed that an ideal transfer price should not only lead to reported divisional profits that are a reasonable measure of the performance of the division but also motivate divisional managers to make decisions that are optimal, both from their point of view and from that of the enterprise as a whole (*see* GOAL CONGRUENCE). Transfer prices should also ideally not be destructive of divisional autonomy, i.e., they should be set with the minimum amount of central intervention and inter-divisional disagreement. In practice, most transfer prices are not able to live up to all these ideals.

Transfer prices can be market-based or cost-based. Market-based prices are used where possible since this gives no advantages to either the buying or selling profit centre, compared with trading with the outside world. It may be possible to estimate or construct a fair market price even when one does not exist. Cost-based prices may be based on actual or standard costs and on marginal cost (= variable cost if marginal cost is constant over the relevant range) or full cost. Standard costs are to be preferred to actual since they avoid the passing on of inefficiencies.

In terms of the conventional economic analysis of marginal costs and revenues, marginal costs are to be preferred to full costs, but they are unlikely to motivate divisional managers and are seldom used in practice. Full costs, on the other hand, mean that the supplying division's fixed costs become the buying division's variable costs, which may lead to decisions in the interest of the division which are not in the interest of the enterprise as a whole. Especially for cost-based transfer prices, prices may be fixed by negotiation, with some form of central arbitration mechanism.

Dual pricing is sometimes used, i.e., the buying division is debited with, say, variable cost but the selling division is credited with an estimate of what the market price would be if one existed. This may motivate the managers of both divisions but is not always optimal for the organization as a whole.

Transfer prices in multinational firms are heavily influenced by political, taxation and currency considerations. National governments are concerned that transfer prices are not used as a means of avoiding taxation or exchange control regulations. The sensitivity of transnational transfer prices means that little is known about practice. On the other hand, many multinationals are keen to argue that prices are set at 'arm's length'. This may not, however, be optimal for motivation.

Any inter-divisional or INTER-COMPANY PROFITS arising from the use of transfer prices need to be eliminated from financial statements drawn up from the point of view of the company or group of companies as a whole.

transition probability. The conditional PROBABILITY of moving from one STATE OF NATURE to another. Transition probability matrices are used in MARKOV ANALYSIS.

transportation method. A form of LINEAR

PROGRAMMING used for solving distribution and assignment problems.

treasurership. The provision to an enterprise of some or all of the following functions: capital-raising, investor relations, short-term financing, banking, custody of assets, the granting of credit, the collection of debts, investment policy, insurance. Contrast CONTROLLERSHIP.

treasury stock. In the USA, stock or shares issued by a company but later reacquired with the intention of reissue. Such shares are not entitled to dividends or votes. They may be accounted for by either the par-value method (i.e., treated as if they had been redeemed or retired) or the cost method (i.e., a special account is opened which is normally shown as a deduction from shareholders' equity but sometimes as an asset).

For the approximate UK equivalent see OWN SHARES.

trend analysis. Using movements in past figures to predict future figures, e.g. by the technique of MOVING AVERAGES.

trial balance. A statement listing the debit and credit ledger balances produced by a double entry recording system at a particular date. The totals of the debit and credit columns should agree but may not do so if errors have been made. Lack of agreement is more common when accounts are kept manually. Some sorts of errors, however, are not revealed by a trial balance and are perhaps more likely under non-manual systems. They include errors of principle, where an item has been posted to the wrong class of account (e.g., a debit in an expense account instead of in an asset account); errors of original entry (e.g., a mistake of amount in a sales or purchases journal carried through to the ledgers); errors of omission (e.g., sales or purchases omitted from the journals and thus not posted to the ledgers); errors of commission (e.g., a transaction entered in an incorrect account of the wrong class, as when, say, the wrong debtor's account is debited); and compensat-

ing errors (i.e., two or more errors which cancel each other out).

true and fair view. The overriding external financial reporting standard for UK companies and, through implementation of the FOURTH DIRECTIVE, companies throughout the European Economic Community. The requirement to give a true and fair view overrides the detailed requirements of UK company law relating to the form and content of financial statements, the notes thereto and accounting principles. If the statements and notes do not in themselves give a true and fair view, additional information must be provided. In special circumstances, the express requirements of the law must be departed from if this is necessary in order to give a true and fair view. Particulars of the departure, the reasons for it and its effect must be given in the notes. The law requires not that *the* true and fair view be shown but that *a* true and fair view be shown. It is thus possible for more than one set of financial statements to show simultaneously a true and fair view of a company's state of affairs and operations. Accounting standards in the UK are methods of accounting approved by the accountancy bodies for application to all financial accounts intended to give a true and fair view of financial position or profit and loss.

What constitutes a true and fair view is defined neither by statute nor by case law in the UK or in any other member state of the EEC. Differences in interpretation between member states may well occur. Some UK writers argue that a true and fair view is a philosophical concept with a social dimension and that this prevents it from being defined conclusively and completely by a set of prescriptive rules and means that professional judgment must be required to interpret it. Others, working so to speak from the bottom up rather than from the top down, have argued that a true and fair view involves adhering to GENERALLY ACCEPTED ACCOUNTING PRINCIPLES (also not clearly defined in the UK). It has also been argued that considerations of COST EFFECTIVENESS can be taken into account and that, for example, historical cost accounting may give a true and fair view for a small or medium company whereas additional current cost information may be necessary for a large company.

The concept of a true and fair view has been used by the Accounting Standards Committee to amend, in effect, the detailed requirements of company law. SSAP 19 requires that investment properties, unlike other fixed assets, should not be depreciated; SSAP 9 in effect prohibits the LAST IN FIRST OUT (LIFO) method of inventory valuation which the law expressly permits.

In 1983 the Accounting Standards Committee obtained a legal opinion that stated that a true and fair view is an 'abstraction or philosophical concept expressed in simple English', compared it with other such legal concepts as 'reasonable care'; and stated that the meaning of the concept can remain the same whilst the content given to it can change.

Trueblood report. The report *Objectives of Financial Statements* published by the American Institute of Certified Public Accountants in 1973. The report was prepared by a committee chaired by Robert M. Trueblood (1916-1974), a distinguished practitioner. The Report stated that the basic objective of financial statements is to provide information useful for making economic decisions; that financial statements should primarily serve those who have limited authority, ability or resources to obtain information; and called for the disclosure of cash flows, current values and forecasts where appropriate. STATEMENT OF FINANCIAL ACCOUNTING CONCEPTS No. 1 of the FASB owes much to the Trueblood report.

trust accounts. Accounts the main objects of which are to demonstrate that the trust funds, including the income thereof, have been applied in accordance with the provisions of the trust instrument and to convey to the trustees, beneficiaries and other interested parties information about the transactions and the current state of affairs of the trust. Income and capital transactions are segregated, often by the use of separate columns in the accounting records. The periodical accounts usually consist of a balance sheet of the whole of the trust estate, a capital account, an income account, and such supplementary schedules and subsidiary accounts as are appropriate.

trustee in bankruptcy. A person appointed to take charge of a bankrupt debtor's property pending its disposition. In England and Wales he must keep a record book, a cash book in prescribed form and, if the business of the debtor is being carried on, a trading account.

trustee investments. In the UK, investments authorized by law as suitable for the investment of trust funds. There are three ranges of such investments: 'narrower', 'wider', and 'special'.

turnover. In the UK, a synonym for sales and the word used for sales in the PROFIT AND LOSS ACCOUNT FORMATS.

Type I error. The error of rejecting the NULL HYPOTHESIS when it is true.

Type II error. The error of accepting the NULL HYPOTHESIS when it is false.

U

uncertainty. A situation in which nothing is known about the likely probabilities of future events. It can thus be distinguished from RISK where probabilities can be estimated. This distinction, made by F. Knight in *Risk, Uncertainty and Profit* (1921), is blurred if SUBJECTIVE PROBABILITIES are used to transform an uncertain situation into a risky one.

uncontrollable costs. Costs that cannot be influenced by a given manager within a given time period. In the very long run there are few costs that cannot be controlled by someone.

underabsorbed overhead. A debit balance resulting from the use of PREDETERMINED OVERHEAD RATES. Less overhead is charged to production than is actually incurred. In practice underabsorbed overhead is usually written off to cost of goods sold rather than prorated over cost of goods sold, finished goods and work in progress.

underwriting commission. A commission paid by a company to any person or persons (usually an ISSUING HOUSE or other financial institution) who guarantees, for the sake of a commission, to take up any shares or debentures offered by the company to the public for which the latter do not subscribe. In the UK, an underwriting commission must be authorized by the Articles of Association and may be paid in cash or in shares or debentures. Underwriting commission may not be capitalized as an asset. It can, however, be written off against any balance on the SHARE PREMIUM ACCOUNT.

undistributable reserves. In UK company law, the sum of the SHARE PREMIUM ACCOUNT; the CAPITAL REDEMPTION RESERVE; the amount by which the company's accumulated, unrealized profits, so far as not previously capitalized (except by transfer to a capital redemption reserve), exceed its accumulated, unrealized losses, so far as not previously written off in a reduction of capital; and any other reserves that a company is prohibited from distributing.

uniformity. A situation in which accounting conventions and financial statements are the same for all accounting entities. Uniformity can be more or less rigid depending on the degree to which different accounting treatments are allowed for what are, or are claimed to be, different circumstances. Uniformity is a feature of continental European accounting rather than ANGLO-SAXON ACCOUNTING, but the DIRECTIVES of the EEC have increased the amount of uniformity in UK accounting.

Union Européenne des Experts Comptables Economiques et Financiers (UEC). A regional accountancy group founded in 1951 with a membership of 21 professional accountancy bodies in 17 European countries. There is a permanent secretariat in Munich. The UEC has pursued an active publication policy including a multi-lingual Lexicon, a journal (discontinued in 1980) and statements on auditing and ethical matters.

unissued share capital. In the UK, the difference between the nominal amount of the AUTHORIZED SHARE CAPITAL and the ISSUED SHARE CAPITAL.

unitary tax. A tax based on a proportion of a business enterprise's worldwide income rather than its income derived in the territory of the fiscal authority. Unitary taxes may be seen in part as an attempt to prevent multinational companies from determining, by means of transfer prices, etc., which territories their profits will be taxed in.

unit cost. In the context of INVENTORY VALUATION, the cost of purchasing or manufacturing identifiable units of inventory (stock).

unit of account. The monetary unit (e.g., pounds sterling, US dollars) in which

ACCOUNTING RECORDS are kept and in which FINANCIAL STATEMENTS are drawn up. International organizations tend to use either the monetary unit of the country of their head office or a dominant currency such as US dollars. There are examples of companies with a legal residence in one country (e.g., Canada) publishing financial statements in the monetary unit of the country (e.g., UK) where most of their operations are carried on.

unit tax. A tax based on the weight or size of the TAX BASE. An example would be a tax of £1 per bottle of whisky. Also known as a specific tax, it can be contrasted with an AD VALOREM TAX.

unit trust. In the UK, an undertaking formed to invest in securities (mainly ordinary shares) under the terms of the trust deed. Unlike an INVESTMENT TRUST it is not a company and is open-ended.

unlimited company. In the UK, a company not having any limit on the liability of its shareholders. An unlimited company is exempt from filing its accounts with the Registrar of Companies.

usage variance. *See* EFFICIENCY VARIANCE.

user needs. The needs of the presumed users of published financial statements. The dominant users in the UK and USA are presumed to be equity investors; in most of continental Europe loan creditors (especially banks) and governments (as tax collectors) are equally if not more important. *The Corporate Report* issued by the UK Accounting Standards (Steering) Committee in 1975 identified the three users above plus employees, analyst-advisers, business contacts and the public. The needs of employees are increasingly taken into account in the UK by the issue of separate EMPLOYEE REPORTS.

utility function. A function stating on what an individual's (e.g., a decision-maker's) utility is dependent. The shape of the utility function depends upon the decision-maker's attitude to RISK. *See* RISK AVERSION.

V

value added statement. A financial statement disclosing for a period how much value has been added (wealth created) by the operations of an enterprise and how that value has been distributed among employees, government, providers of capital and for reinvestment in the business. Gross value added is equal to sales less bought-in goods and services; net value added is equal to gross value added less depreciation. Value added statements are more common in the UK (where they were popularized and encouraged by THE CORPORATE REPORT, 1975) and Continental Europe than in North America. The only entities that cannot in principle prepare a value added statement are those that do not sell their output of goods and services on a market.

The advantages claimed for the publication of a value added statement include the following:

(1) Unlike a profit and loss account (of which technically it is merely a rearrangement) it reflects the view that employees and government as well as shareholders and creditors have a stake in companies and all form part of a 'team';
(2) the dissemination of value added information is likely to improve the attitudes of employees towards their employing company;
(3) it makes easier the introduction of productivity incentive schemes for employees;
(4) many useful ratios (e.g., value added to payroll) can be derived from it;
(5) it gives a better measure of the size and importance of companies;
(6) value added rather than profit accords with the way in which the national income is measured by economists.

On the other hand it has been argued that:
(1) the assumption of a 'team' of employees, capital providers and government is invalid: their interests often conflict; also, a major supplier may be more committed to a company than a bank providing an overdraft; (2) readers of annual reports will be confused if told, for example, that value added is rising whereas profits are falling (which could happen if the value added is 'over-distributed' to the employees); (3) management may incorrectly adopt maximization of value added as a goal which could lead to subsidizing employees to make output that can only be sold for less than it costs to make; (4) unlike the profit and loss account, there is no equivalent position statement.

There are a number of disputed areas in the construction of value added statements:

(1) whether value added should be reported gross or net of depreciation (in favour of the latter it is argued that the wealth of a company would be maintained if 100% of net value added were distributed but not if 100% of gross value added were; that, assuming accrual accounting, depreciation is just as much an expense as other bought-in goods and services; that net value added avoids double counting when one enterprise sells a fixed asset to another; and gross value added absurdly treats depreciation as part of the 'team' to which value added is distributed);
(2) what taxes should be included under the heading of value added distributed to government. For example, should both direct and indirect taxes be included? Should taxes collected (e.g., PAYE deductions) be included? Should social security contributions be included?

There are no laws or accounting standards in the UK or the USA relating to value added statements.

value added tax (VAT). A multi-stage indirect tax. It is the most important indirect tax in the UK and most EEC countries but has not been adopted in the USA. In principle the tax is borne by the final consumer, as shown by the following example which assumes a gross retail price of £23, VAT rate of 15% and a manufacturer who extracts

	VAT paid on inputs	Net price	VAT charged	Gross price	VAT paid to government
Goods leaving manufacturer	0.00	10.00	1.50	11.50	1.50
Goods leaving wholesaler	1.50	15.00	2.25	17.25	0.75
Goods leaving retailer	2.25	20.00	3.00	23.00	0.75
					£3.00

Value added tax

his own raw materials and pays no VAT for any purposes.

The effective incidence of VAT will rest partly on suppliers if demand for their goods falls. Not all goods in the UK bear VAT: some are exempt (i.e., no VAT is charged on outputs and no VAT can be reclaimed on inputs); some are zero-rated (i.e., no VAT is charged on outputs but VAT can be reclaimed on inputs). There is a lower turnover limit (£18,000 in 1983-84) below which traders need not register for VAT purposes. Such traders can escape some compliance costs, and do not charge VAT on outputs, but cannot reclaim VAT on outputs. The administrative and compliance costs of VAT in the UK are high but could be reduced if VAT were assessed on quarterly accounts rather than on invoices. It is standard accounting practice (SSAP 5) in the UK to show turnover in financial statements net of VAT.

value for money (VFM) audit. An examination of the way in which resources are allocated and utilized. Such an audit is concerned with the interrelated concepts of economy (acquiring resources of an appropriate quality for the minimum cost); efficiency (maximizing the amount of output per unit of input); and effectiveness (taking account of the relationship between output and the objectives of an organization). VFM audits are more common in the public than in the private sector, since the profit criterion is lacking in the former.

value to the business. A method of ASSET VALUATION based on the concept that the measure of the value of an asset depends on the loss suffered from being deprived of it. It is also known as value to the owner, value to the firm and deprival value. It is the preferred method of the UK SANDILANDS REPORT and of SSAP 16.

The value to the business of an asset is one of current REPLACEMENT COST (RC), NET REALIZABLE VALUE (NRV) and NET PRESENT VALUE (NPV) depending on circumstances. The general rule is that value to the business is the lower of RC and RECOVERABLE AMOUNT, the latter being defined as the greater of NRV and NPV. It is argued that an asset can never be worth more to a business than its RC, because if the business were deprived of it, it could acquire a duplicate at RC. On the other hand, some assets are not worth replacing and are worth either their NRV (e.g., a fashion good in a sale) or their NPV (e.g., a highly specialized fixed asset: a NON-VENDIBLE DURABLE). The interrelationships between RC, NRV and NPV can be shown as in the following table:

Case	Interrelationship			Value to the business
1	PV	> RC	> NRV	RC
2	PV	> NRV	> RC	RC
3	NRV	> PV	> RC	RC
4	NRV	> RC	> PV	RC
5	RC	> NRV	> PV	NRV
6	RC	> PV	> NRV	PV

The value to the business concept is an attractive one but it can be criticized on a number of grounds: assets in a balance sheet may be valued in up to three different ways and the financial statements are thus perhaps lacking in ADDITIVITY; one of these ways can be NPV which is highly subjective (although it can be counterargued that an NPV is only used when it is bounded above by an RC and below by an NRV); it assumes that managers have already decided whether to use or exchange an asset; and, finally, it implicitly assumes that the sum of the value to the business of individual assets less liabilities is equal to the value of the business as a whole (i.e., there is an aggregation problem).

value to the firm. Synonym for VALUE TO THE BUSINESS.

value to the owner. Synonym for VALUE TO THE BUSINESS.

van den Tempel Report (1974). A report on the harmonization of corporation tax within the EEC. It recommended the classical system but the EC Commission later favoured the IMPUTATION SYSTEM, which has been adopted by all member states except the Netherlands, Luxembourg and Greece.

variable. A term in an expression or equation that can take different numerical values. Variables can be classified as discrete or continuous and as dependent or independent.

variable cost. A cost which, unlike a FIXED COST, varies, or is assumed to vary, with some measure of capacity (e.g. direct labour hours). Accountants usually assume that variable costs are constant (and thus equal to MARGINAL COST) over a RELEVANT RANGE of production.

variable costing. A method of costing (usually referred to in the UK as marginal costing and in the USA by the equally misleading name of direct costing) in which fixed FACTORY OVERHEAD is treated as a PERIOD COST and not as a PRODUCT COST, i.e., it is written off in the period incurred and not carried forward as part of the cost of stocks (inventories) to the extent that goods manufactured during the period remain un-

sold. Variable costing is not acceptable in the UK and the USA for external reporting or taxation purposes, where ABSORPTION COSTING is prescribed. It is possible, however, to use variable costing internally and to make year-end adjustments for external reporting purposes. It may be combined with actual costs or standard costs.

All material, labour and variable overhead variances are identical under both variable costing and absorption costing, but there is no fixed factory overhead volume variance under variable costing. If stocks increase during a period, variable costing will report less income than absorption costing; if stocks decrease, variable costing will report more income than absorption costing. This arises because absorption costing treats that part of fixed factory overhead relating to unsold stocks as income whereas variable costing does not. Under variable costing, income is a function of sales only, whereas under absorption costing it is a function of both sales and production.

variable cost ratio. The total VARIABLE COSTS divided by the total sales.

variables sampling. In an audit context, sampling plans based on quantitative characteristics (monetary amounts) rather than qualitative characteristics. Contrast ATTRIBUTES SAMPLING.

variance (accounting). A deviation of actual results from expected, budgeted or standard results. Variances are usually labelled favourable or unfavourable but should be regarded as attention directors rather than as answers.

See also EFFICIENCY VARIANCE, JOINT VARIANCE, LABOUR VARIANCES, MATERIALS VARIANCES, OVERHEAD VARIANCES, PRICE VARIANCE.

variance (statistics). The square of the STANDARD DEVIATION.

vector. A MATRIX comprising only one row or one column.

verification. An audit procedure (one of the

SUBSTANTIVE TESTS) the aim of which is to ascertain by the use of appropriate AUDIT EVIDENCE that assets and liabilities are properly recorded in a balance sheet so far as existence, ownership and valuation are concerned.

vertical equity. A tax principle supporting the different tax treatment of people in different circumstances.

virement. The use of savings on one subhead of public expenditure to meet overspending on another. The French word, in an accounting context, literally means transfer.

volume variances. Variances that arise from deviations from expected, budgeted or standard sales or production volume. A production volume variance arises under ABSORPTION COSTING if the normal level of activity assumed in the calculation of the predetermined fixed factory overhead rate differs from the actual level of activity (measured in, for example, direct labour hours). Production volume variances do not arise under VARIABLE COSTING or in relation to variable overhead. A sales volume variance represents the difference between an amount in a FLEXIBLE BUDGET and the corresponding amount in a static budget, unit prices being held constant. In a multiproduct company, the variance can be further analyzed for each product into sales quantity and sales mix variances. The former is a measure of the actual volume less the static budget volume in units multiplied by the budgeted average contribution margin

per unit. The latter measures the impact of the deviation from the budgeted average contribution margin associated with a change in the quantity of a particular product.

voluntary winding up. In the UK, a WINDING UP in which a company and its creditors are left to settle their affairs without coming to the court.

votes on account. In the UK, monies granted by Parliament to carry on public services from 1 April of the next financial year until the passing of the Appropriation Act, which authorizes the issue of the amount required for the full year.

vouching. An audit procedure (one of the SUBSTANTIVE TESTS) the aim of which is to ensure that the underlying records accurately reflect the nature of the transactions entered into. It invoives the examination of documentary evidence to establish the monetary amounts at which transactions are recorded and that the transactions are properly authorized.

voyage account. A profit and loss account not for a period of time but for a particular voyage of a ship. In the shipping industry, an account is opened for each voyage, debited with all expenditure, other than depreciation, ascribed to the voyage, and credited with freight and passage moneys earned. An accruals basis is not used for voyages still 'open' (in progress) at the end of an accounting period.

W

walk-through test. An auditing procedure in which the processing of typical transactions is followed through all the stages in a client's accounting system. The main purpose of the test is to enable the auditor to become familiar with the system.

waste. Material lost in a manufacturing process through evaporation, shrinkage or being left as a residue.

wasting asset. A non-renewable resource such as a copper mine. Extraction or removal results in the physical consumption of the natural resource. A wasting asset may be contrasted with a renewable resource such as a forest where replacement occurs through growth. Wasting assets are said to be subject to DEPLETION rather than DEPRECIATION. Their economic life depends upon the speed with which their reserves are extracted. *See also* OIL AND GAS ACCOUNTING.

wealth maximization. The assumption that the objective of a firm (company) is to maximize the wealth of its owners (shareholders). This assumption is fundamental to modern finance theory. Wealth is interpreted to mean the market price of a company's shares.

wealth tax. In general any tax on wealth (*see* DEATH DUTIES, ESTATE DUTY, CAPITAL TRANSFER TAX); in particular an annual levy on wealth as found in several continental European countries but not in the UK. It can be argued that an annual wealth tax is necessary in order to bring about HORIZONTAL EQUITY among taxpayers and that it would be more efficient than, say, capital transfer tax in redistributing wealth. The most important problems of implementation are which assets, if any, to exempt and how to value such assets as pension rights.

In the UK a green paper on a wealth tax was issued in 1974 and in 1975 examined by a select committee, which failed to reach agreement.

weighted average cost. In the context of INVENTORY VALUATION, the calculation of the cost of inventories (stocks and work in progress) by applying to the units on hand an average price computed by dividing the total cost of units by the total number of such units. This average price may be arrived at by means of a continuous calculation, a periodic calculation or a moving periodic calculation. In times of rising prices, the weighted average cost method normally results in a higher cost of goods sold figure (and therefore a lower profit figure) than the FIRST IN FIRST OUT (FIFO) method but in a lower cost of goods sold than the LAST IN FIRST OUT (LIFO) method. In the balance sheet, weighted average cost normally gives a lower figure than FIFO but a higher figure than LIFO.

Wheat Commission. A committee appointed by the American Institute of Certified Public Accountants in 1972 to consider the establishment of accounting principles. Its recommendations led to the establishment of the FINANCIAL ACCOUNTING STANDARDS BOARD in 1973.

will. A legal declaration of a person's wishes and intentions with reference to the disposal of his or her property after death.

windfall gains and losses. Gains and losses arising from actual or prospective receipts which are different from those originally expected and from changes in the net present value of such receipts arising from discount rates different from those originally expected.

winding up. In the UK, the process of liquidation of a company. The winding up may be by the court, voluntary, or subject to the supervision of the court.

winding up by the court. In the UK, a non-voluntary liquidation of a company. A company is usually wound up by the court because it is unable to pay its debts. Other grounds, much less common, are: the company has passed a special resolution to that effect; as a new public company, it has not obtained permission to commence business, and over a year has passed since its registration; as an old public company, it has failed, within the time limit, to re-register as a new public company; it has not commenced business within one year of incorporation or has suspended its business for a whole year; the number of shareholders is below the legal minimum of two; the court is of the opinion that it is just and equitable that the company should be wound up.

window dressing. Transactions the substance of which is primarily to alter the appearance of a company's financial statements and the financial ratios derived therefrom. Window dressing may be thought to include both the lawful, but misleading, arrangement of affairs over a year-end to make things look different from the way they usually are, and also the fraudulent falsification of accounts to make things look better than they really are.

withholding tax. Deductions made from interest, dividends and other periodic payments made to non-residents of the country in which the payment is made.

working capital. The short term assets and liabilities of a business, i.e. CURRENT ASSETS less CURRENT LIABILITIES. In a STATEMENT OF SOURCE AND APPLICATION OF FUNDS (US: STATE-MENT OF CHANGES IN FINANCIAL POSITION) working capital is often defined implicitly as current assets less current liabilities other than those for taxation and proposed dividends. On the management of working capital see CASH MANAGEMENT, CREDIT MANAGEMENT, INVENTORY CONTROL.

working papers. Files established by an auditor during the course of an audit. They typically contain: information of continuing importance to the audit; audit planning information; an assessment of the client's accounting and internal control systems; details of audit work carried out and con-

clusions reached; evidence that the work of the audit staff has been properly reviewed; records of relevant balances and other financial information; and a summary of significant points and how they have been dealt with. Audit working papers are prepared for a number of reasons. They enable the partner in charge of an audit to be satisfied that work delegated has been properly performed; they provide, for future reference, details of problems encountered, evidence of work performed and of conclusions drawn; and they encourage a methodical approach to audit work.

work in progress control account. An account recording in total the direct materials, direct labour and factory overhead charged in detail to individual jobs and recorded in a SUBSIDIARY LEDGER. As jobs are completed, transfers are made to a finished goods control account.

work in progress/work in process. Goods in intermediate stages of production. *See* LONG-TERM CONTRACT WORK IN PROGRESS, INVENTORY VALUATION.

work measurement. The process of quantifying relationships between inputs and outputs by analyzing a work task. It is applied mainly to manufacturing activities but can also be applied to some non-manufacturing activities.

worksheet. A sheet of calculations in columnar form, used, for example, as an aid to the construction of a consolidated balance sheet or a funds statement. *See also* SPREADSHEET.

writing-down allowance. In the UK, annual CAPITAL ALLOWANCES on plant and machinery and industrial buildings.

written-down value. In the UK, the net amount after depreciation of a fixed asset in the books of an enterprise. Alternatively, the value of the asset for tax purposes after deduction of CAPITAL ALLOWANCES. Written-down values are not designed to be equal to NET REALIZABLE VALUES and seldom are.

Y

Yellow Book. In the UK, the popular name of the publication *Admission of Securities to Listing* of The Stock Exchange, so called because of the colour of its cover.

yield. A rate of return relating cash invested to cash received (or expected to be received).

yield gap. The difference between the DIVI-DEND YIELD on EQUITIES and that on long-term fixed interest government securities. Because of risk, the yield on equities might be expected to be the higher of two but inflation and expectations of growth have led to a reverse yield gap in the UK since August 1959.

yield to maturity. A REDEMPTION YIELD.

Z

zero base budgeting (ZBB). An approach to the formulation of budgets in which managers have to justify their activities as though those activities were being started for the first time. Analysis and justification is thus shifted away from increments to existing activities and towards a systematic consideration of how objectives should be accomplished. This, it is claimed, is the advantage of ZBB over INCREMENTAL BUDGETS. Such an approach is more useful in the area of DISCRETIONARY COSTS than ENGINEERED COSTS, i.e., it is more applicable to non-manufacturing organizations.

It is argued in favour of ZBB that it leads to a sharper definition of goals and priorities, a better understanding of inputs and outputs, and a more efficient and effective allocation of resources. On the other hand, ZBB is very time-consuming and if it is regarded by managers as a threat it may fail through lack of their support.

zero sum game. A game in which the sum of the rewards to the players total to zero, i.e. if there are two players one player's gain is the other player's loss. *See* GAME THEORY, NON-ZERO SUM GAME.

Z-score. A measure of the SOLVENCY of a company, calculated from a linear equation, incorporating more than one FINANCIAL RATIO. The financial ratios used measure attributes such as profitability, working capital, financial risk and liquidity. Neither the ratios nor their weightings are constant over time or space. They are derived by the discriminant analysis of the published financial statements of companies that in the past have failed as against those that have not failed. Z-scores are thus in principle descriptive rather than predictive but they have been successfully used for prediction. Z-scores are measured on an ordinal scale (i.e., one can state that one company's Z-score is greater than another company's but not, say, that it is twice as great) but can be transformed to a ratio scale. This makes possible the calculation of industry-average Z-scores with which that of a particular company can be compared.